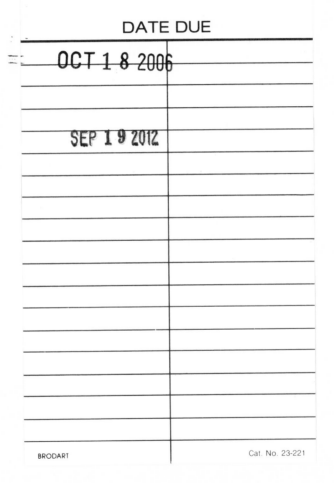

DATE DUE

OCT 1 8 2006

SEP 1 9 2012

BRODART   Cat. No. 23-221

Modern Critical Views

Chinua Achebe
Henry Adams
Aeschylus
S. Y. Agnon
Edward Albee
Raphael Alberti
Louisa May Alcott
A. R. Ammons
Sherwood Anderson
Aristophanes
Matthew Arnold
Antonin Artaud
John Ashbery
Margaret Atwood
W. H. Auden
Jane Austen
Isaac Babel
Sir Francis Bacon
James Baldwin
Honoré de Balzac
John Barth
Donald Barthelme
Charles Baudelaire
Simone de Beauvoir
Samuel Beckett
Saul Bellow
Thomas Berger
John Berryman
The Bible
Elizabeth Bishop
William Blake
Giovanni Boccaccio
Heinrich Böll
Jorge Luis Borges
Elizabeth Bowen
Bertolt Brecht
The Brontës
Charles Brockden Brown
Sterling Brown
Robert Browning
Martin Buber
John Bunyan
Anthony Burgess
Kenneth Burke
Robert Burns
William Burroughs
George Gordon, Lord
   Byron
Pedro Calderón de la Barca
Italo Calvino
Albert Camus
Canadian Poetry: Modern
   and Contemporary
Canadian Poetry through
   E. J. Pratt
Thomas Carlyle
Alejo Carpentier
Lewis Carroll
Willa Cather
Louis-Ferdinand Céline
Miguel de Cervantes

Geoffrey Chaucer
John Cheever
Anton Chekhov
Kate Chopin
Chrétien de Troyes
Agatha Christie
Samuel Taylor Coleridge
Colette
William Congreve & the
   Restoration Dramatists
Joseph Conrad
Contemporary Poets
James Fenimore Cooper
Pierre Corneille
Julio Cortázar
Hart Crane
Stephen Crane
e. e. cummings
Dante
Robertson Davies
Daniel Defoe
Philip K. Dick
Charles Dickens
James Dickey
Emily Dickinson
Denis Diderot
Isak Dinesen
E. L. Doctorow
John Donne & the
   Seventeenth-Century
   Metaphysical Poets
John Dos Passos
Fyodor Dostoevsky
Frederick Douglass
Theodore Dreiser
John Dryden
W. E. B. Du Bois
Lawrence Durrell
George Eliot
T. S. Eliot
Elizabethan Dramatists
Ralph Ellison
Ralph Waldo Emerson
Euripides
William Faulkner
Henry Fielding
F. Scott Fitzgerald
Gustave Flaubert
E. M. Forster
John Fowles
Sigmund Freud
Robert Frost
Northrop Frye
Carlos Fuentes
William Gaddis
Federico García Lorca
Gabriel García Márquez
André Gide
W. S. Gilbert
Allen Ginsberg
J. W. von Goethe

Nikolai Gogol
William Golding
Oliver Goldsmith
Mary Gordon
Günther Grass
Robert Graves
Graham Greene
Thomas Hardy
Nathaniel Hawthorne
William Hazlitt
H. D.
Seamus Heaney
Lillian Hellman
Ernest Hemingway
Hermann Hesse
Geoffrey Hill
Friedrich Hölderlin
Homer
A. D. Hope
Gerard Manley Hopkins
Horace
A. E. Housman
William Dean Howells
Langston Hughes
Ted Hughes
Victor Hugo
Zora Neale Hurston
Aldous Huxley
Henrik Ibsen
Eugène Ionesco
Washington Irving
Henry James
Dr. Samuel Johnson and
   James Boswell
Ben Jonson
James Joyce
Carl Gustav Jung
Franz Kafka
Yasonari Kawabata
John Keats
Søren Kierkegaard
Rudyard Kipling
Melanie Klein
Heinrich von Kleist
Philip Larkin
D. H. Lawrence
John le Carré
Ursula K. Le Guin
Giacomo Leopardi
Doris Lessing
Sinclair Lewis
Jack London
Robert Lowell
Malcolm Lowry
Carson McCullers
Norman Mailer
Bernard Malamud
Stéphane Mallarmé
Sir Thomas Malory
André Malraux
Thomas Mann

Modern Critical Views

Modern Critical Views

ZORA NEALE HURSTON

Edited and with an introduction by

Harold Bloom
Sterling Professor of the Humanities
Yale University

CHELSEA HOUSE PUBLISHERS
New York
Philadelphia

© 1986 by Chelsea House Publishers, a division
of Main Line Book Co.

Introduction copyright © 1986 by Harold Bloom

Printed and bound in the United States of America

10   9   8   7   6   5

∞ The paper used in this publication meets the
minimum requirements of the American National
Standard for Permanence of Paper for Printed Library
Materials, Z39.48-1984.

Library of Congress Cataloging-in-Publication Data
Main entry under title:
Zora Neale Hurston.
      (Modern critical views)
      Bibliography: p.
      Includes index.
      1. Hurston, Zora Neale—Criticism and interpretation
—Addresses, essays, lectures.   I. Bloom, Harold.
II. Series.
PS3515.U789Z96   1986   813'.52   85-30960
ISBN 0-87754-627-4

Contents

Editor's Note

This book gathers together what seems to me the most useful criticism so far available on the work of Zora Neale Hurston, arranged in the chronological order of its publication. I am grateful to Nancy Sales for her erudition and insight in helping to edit this volume.

The editor's introduction centers upon Hurston's best novel, *Their Eyes Were Watching God,* and particularly upon the heroic vitalism that constitutes the author's and the heroine's stance, experiential and rhetorical. Franz Boas, Hurston's great teacher in anthropology, appropriately begins the chronological sequence with his brief preface to her classic study, *Mules and Men.* With Nick Aaron Ford's account of a meeting with Hurston, we enter upon the immensely complex and controversial question of her position in relation to the fictive presentation of black life in America. An excerpt from Benjamin Brawley's *The Negro Genius* provides an early example of the rather conventional responses that initially greeted Hurston's genius.

Langston Hughes, poet and chronicler of the Harlem Renaissance, contributes an anecdote to the ever-burgeoning Hurston legend. The pioneering critical remarks upon *Their Eyes Were Watching God* by Robert Bone accurately urge us to apprehend the strength of Hurston's style. They are followed here by the novelist Fannie Hurst's vivid "personality sketch" of her one-time secretary, and by Larry Neal's brief tribute to Hurston's first novel, *Jonah's Gourd Vine.* With Roger Rosenblatt's eloquent overview of *Their Eyes Were Watching God,* we are given the useful insight that Janie and Tea Cake are closer to lovers in folklore than to lovers in the tradition of naturalistic fiction. Addison Gayle, analyzing both *Jonah's Gourd Vine* and *Their Eyes Were Watching God,* provides a more sociologically oriented reading than Rosenblatt's. Another interesting contrast is provided by Theresa R. Love's survey, which convincingly contextualizes itself in Hurston's own professional perspective as an anthropologist and folklorist.

Alice Walker, who takes Hurston as novelistic precursor, is represented in this book by three pieces, the first being a passionate defense of the ways in which Hurston became a cultural revolutionary merely by being herself. A biographical reading of *Their Eyes Were Watching God* by Robert E. Hemenway is supplemented here by his equally informative introduction to *Mules and Men*. Sherley Anne Williams, introducing *Their Eyes Were Watching God*, provides a fiercely feminist reading of Janie's burden and of her heroic effort to surmount that barrier to a more abundant existence. In both of the following pieces, Alice Walker again achieves an eloquent identification with Hurston's life and writings.

Mary Helen Washington, exploring Hurston's critical representation and misrepresentation, makes another high tribute to the seriousness of the novelist-anthropologist's creative exuberance. A more analytical account of that exuberance is provided by the critical sensibility of Michael G. Cooke, a distinguished scholar of Romantic and modern literature. Cooke rightly emphasizes how self-realization had to be problematic in Hurston's work, and how astonishing her achievement therefore is. Introducing *Moses, Man of the Mountain*, Blyden Jackson reminds us that: "Hurston was no social visionary," but wrote more in the spirit of Aristophanes and W. S. Gilbert. Finally, in the most advanced critical essay yet devoted to Hurston, Barbara Johnson subjects *Their Eyes Were Watching God* to a strict rhetorical analysis that aids us immensely in appreciating how extraordinary Hurston's linguistic art truly will continue to seem, the more deeply we ponder its resources.

Introduction

I

Extra-literary factors have entered into the process of even secular canonization from Hellenistic Alexandria into the High Modernist Era of Eliot and Pound, so that it need not much dismay us if contemporary work by women and by minority writers becomes esteemed on grounds other than aesthetic. When the High Modernist critic Hugh Kenner assures us of the permanent eminence of the novelist and polemicist Wyndham Lewis, we can be persuaded, unless of course we actually read books like *Tarr* and *Hitler*. Reading Lewis is a rather painful experience, and makes me skeptical of Kenner's canonical assertions. In the matter of Zora Neale Hurston, I have had a contrary experience, starting with skepticism when I first encountered essays by her admirers, let alone by her idolators. Reading *Their Eyes Were Watching God* dispels all skepticism. *Moses, Man of the Mountain* is an impressive book in its mode and ambitions, but a mixed achievement, unable to resolve problems of diction and of rhetorical stance. Essentially, Hurston is the author of one superb and moving novel, unique not in its kind but in its isolated excellence among other stories of the kind.

The wistful opening of *Their Eyes Were Watching God* pragmatically affirms greater repression in women as opposed to men, by which I mean "repression" only in Freud's sense: unconscious yet purposeful forgetting:

> Now, women forget all those things they don't want to remember, and remember everything they don't want to forget. The dream is the truth. Then they act and do things accordingly.

Hurston's Janie is now necessarily a paradigm for women, of whatever race, heroically attempting to assert their own individuality in contexts that continue to resent and fear any consciousness that is not male. In a larger perspective, should the contexts modify, the representation of Janie will

1

take its significant place in a long tradition of such representations in English and American fiction. This tradition extends from Samuel Richardson to Doris Lessing and other contemporaries, but only rarely has been able to visualize authentically strong women who begin with all the deprivations that circumstance assigns to Janie. It is a crucial aspect of Hurston's subtle sense of limits that the largest limitation is that imposed upon Janie by her grandmother, who loves her best, yet fears for her the most.

As a former slave, the grandmother, Nanny, is haunted by the compensatory dream of making first her daughter, and then her grandaughter, something other than "the mule of the world," customary fate of the black woman. The dream is both powerful enough, and sufficiently unitary, to have driven Janie's mother away, and to condemn Janie herself to a double disaster of marriages, before the tragic happiness of her third match completes as much of her story as Hurston desires to give us. As readers, we carry away with us what Janie never quite loses, the vivid pathos of her grandmother's superb and desperate displacement of hope:

> "And, Janie, maybe it wasn't much, but Ah done de best Ah kin by you. Ah raked and scraped and bought dis lil piece uh land so you wouldn't have to stay in de white folks' yard and tuck yo' head befo' other chillun at school. Dat was all right when you was little. But when you got big enough to understand things, Ah wanted you to look upon yo'self. Ah don't want yo' feathers always crumpled by folks throwin' up things in yo' face. And Ah can't die easy thinkin' maybe de menfolks white or black is makin' a spit cup outa you: Have some sympathy fuh me. Put me down easy, Janie, Ah'm a cracked plate."

II

Hurston's rhetorical strength, even in *Their Eyes Were Watching God*, is frequently too overt, and threatens an excess, when contrasted with the painful simplicity of her narrative line and the reductive tendency at work in all her characters except for Janie and Nanny. Yet the excess works, partly because Hurston is so considerable and knowing a mythologist. Hovering in *Their Eyes Were Watching God* is the Mosaic myth of deliverance, the pattern of revolution and exodus that Hurston reimagines as her prime trope of power:

> But there are other concepts of Moses abroad in the world. Asia and all the Near East are sown with legends of this character.

They are so numerous and so varied that some students have come to doubt if the Moses of the Christian concept is real. Then Africa has her mouth on Moses. All across the continent there are the legends of the greatness of Moses, but not because of his beard nor because he brought the laws down from Sinai. No, he is revered because he had the power to go up the mountain and to bring them down. Many men could climb mountains. Anyone could bring down laws that had been handed to them. But who can talk with God face to face? Who has the power to command God to go to a peak of a mountain and there demand of Him laws with which to govern a nation? What other man has ever commanded the wind and the hail? The light and darkness? That calls for power, and that is what Africa sees in Moses to worship. For he is worshipped as a god.

Power in Hurston is always *potentia,* the demand for life, for more life. Despite the differences in temperament, Hurston has affinities both with Dreiser and with Lawrence, heroic vitalists. Her art, like theirs, exalts an exuberance that is beauty, a difficult beauty because it participates in reality-testing. What is strongest in Janie is a persistence akin to Dreiser's Carrie and Lawrence's Ursula and Gudrun, a drive to survive in one's own fashion. Nietzsche's vitalistic injunction, that we must try to live as though it were morning, is the implicit basis of Hurston's true religion, which in its American formulation (Thoreau's), reminds us that only that day dawns to which we are alive. Something of Lawrence's incessant sense of the sun is paralleled by Hurston's trope of the solar trajectory, in a cosmos where: "They sat on the boarding house porch and saw the sun plunge into the same crack in the earth from which the night emerged" and where: "Every morning the world flung itself over and exposed the town to the sun."

Janie's perpetual sense of the possibilities of another day propels her from Nanny's vision of safety first to the catastrophe of Joe Starks and then to the love of Tea Cake, her true husband. But to live in a way that starts with the sun is to become pragmatically doom-eager, since mere life is deprecated in contrast to the possibility of glory, of life more abundant, rather than Nanny's dream of a refuge from exploitation. Hurston's most effective irony is that Janie's drive towards her own erotic potential should transcend her grandmother's categories, since the marriage with Tea Cake is also Janie's pragmatic liberation from bondage towards men. When he tells her, in all truth, that she has the keys to the kingdom, he frees her from living in her grandmother's way.

A more pungent irony drove Hurston herself to end Janie's idyll with Tea Cake's illness and the ferocity of his subsequent madness. The impulse of her own vitalism compels Janie to kill him in self-defense, thus ending necessarily life and love in the name of the possibility of more life again. The novel's conclusion is at once an elegy and a vision of achieved peace, an intense realization that indeed we are all asleep in the outer life:

> The day of the gun, and the bloody body, and the courthouse came and commenced to sing a sobbing sigh out of every corner in the room; out of each and every chair and thing. Commenced to sing, commenced to sob and sigh, singing and sobbing. Then Tea Cake came prancing around her where she was and the song of the sigh flew out of the window and lit in the top of the pine trees. Tea Cake, with the sun for a shawl. Of course he wasn't dead. He could never be dead until she herself had finished feeling and thinking. The kiss of his memory made pictures of love and light against the wall. Here was peace. She pulled in her horizon like a great fish-net. Pulled it from around the waist of the world and draped it over her shoulder. So much of life in its meshes! She called in her soul to come and see.

III

Hurston herself was refreshingly free of all the ideologies that currently obscure the reception of her best book. Her sense of power has nothing in common with politics of any persuasion, with contemporary modes of feminism, or even with those questers who search for a black aesthetic. As a vitalist, she was of the line of the Wife of Bath and Sir John Falstaff and Mynheer Peeperkorn. Like them, she was outrageous, heroically larger than life, witty in herself and the cause of wit in others. She belongs now to literary legend, which is as it should be. Her famous remark in response to Carl Van Vechten's photographs is truly the epigraph to her life and work: "I love myself when I am laughing. And then again when I am looking mean and impressive." Walt Whitman would have delighted in that as in her assertion: "When I set my hat at a certain angle and saunter down Seventh Avenue . . . the cosmic Zora emerges. . . . How *can* any deny themselves the pleasure of my company? It's beyond me." With Whitman, Hurston herself is now an image of American literary vitality, and a part also of the American mythology of exodus, of the power to choose the party of Eros, of more life.

FRANZ BOAS

Preface to
Mules and Men

Ever since the time of Uncle Remus, Negro folk-lore has exerted a strong attraction upon the imagination of the American public. Negro tales, songs and sayings without end, as well as descriptions of Negro magic and voodoo, have appeared; but in all of them the intimate setting in the social life of the Negro has been given very inadequately.

It is the great merit of Miss Hurston's work that she entered into the homely life of the southern Negro as one of them and was fully accepted as such by the companions of her childhood. Thus she has been able to penetrate through that affected demeanor by which the Negro excludes the White observer effectively from participating in his true inner life. Miss Hurston has been equally successful in gaining the confidence of the voodoo doctors and she gives us much that throws a new light upon the much discussed voodoo beliefs and practices. Added to all this is the charm of a loveable personality and of a revealing style which makes Miss Hurston's work an unusual contribution to our knowledge of the true inner life of the Negro.

To the student of cultural history the material presented is valuable not only by giving the Negro's reaction to every day events, to his emotional life, his humor and passions, but it throws into relief also the peculiar amalgamation of African and European tradition which is so important for understanding historically the character of American Negro life, with its strong African background in the West Indies, the importance of which diminishes with increasing distance from the south.

From *Mules and Men*. © 1935 by Zora Neale Hurston, renewed 1963 by John C. Hurston and Joel Hurston. Indiana University Press, 1978. Originally entitled "Preface."

NICK AARON FORD

A *Study in Race Relations*—A *Meeting with Zora Neale Hurston*

Can a leopard change his spots? Any school boy can give a satisfactory answer to such a hackneyed question. But the puzzle worded in a different manner may serve to ensnare a few who consider themselves wise in the ways of the world.

Is a Negro always a Negro? Here you have a question which requires the tact of an Abraham Lincoln, the courage of a Theodore Roosevelt, and the wisdom of a Solomon to answer satisfactorily to all concerned. To the white man it is as preposterous as the first, but to many Negroes it is freighted with the eternal issues of life and death.

A few months ago a friend and I were motoring leisurely through Central Florida. As we neared an insignificant crossroad, we noticed a narrow signboard pointing toward the west with the name "Longwood" written upon it. Ordinarily such a sign would have made no impression upon our consciousness, but it so happened that we had just finished discussing a novel written by a certain Zora Neale Hurston who lived in that vicinity.

What of it? you say. There are hundreds of novelists in America; they are more common than millionaires. Yes, but this one is a Negro—a rare species of novelist! There are scarcely two dozens of them now living in America.

"Shall we turn in?" asked my friend, who was at the wheel.

"Of course," I counselled. "It will be my second opportunity of seeing a live one." (I had met Langston Hughes several years before.)

When we reached the little village we were informed that Miss Hurston

From *The Contemporary Negro Novel: A Study in Race Relations.* © 1936 by Edward K. Meador. McGrath Publishing Company, 1936. Originally entitled "Postscript."

lived a few miles out on the banks of Longwood's only lake. Although we accepted the information without comment, we were rather dubious of finding a Negro woman occupying a cottage in an exclusive neighborhood on the banks of a lake in the state of Florida. But we did. She was not at home when we arrived, so we inquired from the next door neighbor (white) whether or not a Miss Hurston lived in the little cottage in whose yard our Ford was timidly standing with the engine still purring.

It was a kindly, gray-haired, red-faced man who ejaculated shrilly, "Yes, she lives right there! And by God, she is a mighty fine girl!"

We were not quite prepared for the final observation of our temporary host; for when he began with "By God!," we thought it was the prelude to "Get the h—l out of my yard." Although we are professors at a respectable Negro college, we knew that such an insult even to men of our training and sensibilities could be easily given in certain sections of our state on similar provocation.

After making a cursory examination of Miss Hurston's premises, we started back to the highway, disappointed in our failure to meet the author of *Jonah's Gourd Vine*. We had gone but a short distance when we caught sight of a brown Chevrolet coupe coming toward us. My friend's intuition prompted him to believe that it was the much-talked-of novelist. And so it was. She pulled on the side of the road and stopped, as if she knew our mission.

After a brief introduction she talked as freely as if she had known us for years.

"Many Negroes criticise my book," she said, as the conversation drifted to literature, "because I did not make it a lecture on the race problem."

"Well, why didn't you?" I asked.

"Because," she replied simply, "I was writing a novel and not a treatise on sociology. There is where many Negro novelists make their mistakes. They confuse art with sociology."

"But," I said, "how can you write without being forever conscious of your race and the multitude of injustices which is heaped upon it in our present social order?"

She smiled a bit condescendingly. "You see," she began benignantly, "I have ceased to think in terms of race; I think only in terms of individuals. I am interested in you now, not as a *Negro* man but as a *man*. I am not interested in the *race* problem, but I am interested in the problems of *individuals,* white ones and black ones."

This statement unnerved me. I did not care to answer it, for it had started a trend of thought in my own mind which I dared not interrupt then. I looked at her to see if she could possibly pass for white. I saw that she could not. She is fair, but not fair enough to be mistaken in racial identity. I concluded then that it must have taken courage to reach such a stage in one's thinking. It must be a feat comparable to sainthood. I seldom live through a whole day without being reminded that I am a Negro. I do not seek the reminder; it is thrust upon me. I am reminded of it at filling stations, in stores, in hospitals, in banks, in post offices, in theaters, and even in churches. What is the significance of Miss Hurston's philosophy?

II

It is such a philosophy as this held by Miss Hurston that drives Negro novelists into an unpleasant dilemma. To be consistent they must put aside the cloak of racial sympathy and understanding, and pretend to view the race problem in the light of a cold logician or a jesting critic. I do not hold that such an achievement is an unworthy one in all cases. In Sinclair Lewis it proves to be his greatest asset. He appears at his best when he is pointing out the foibles and absurdities of American life—the foibles and absurdities that are characteristic of his own race. But far from being condemned by the people whom he ridicules, he enjoys the distinction of being the most appreciated novelist in his generation. Why then is this not the case with the Negro writer who sets out to reveal the secret faults of his race?

Herein lies the difference. For fifty years the Negro has been the joker in American literature. His idiosyncrasies have been exaggerated and distorted beyond their natural due. Certain phases of his social and religious life, which to him are sacred, have been seized upon by unsympathetic word jugglers and turned into sentimental comedy. He has been looked upon as the funmaker of the world rather than a thinker whose thoughts are frozen within him by the coldness of an unfriendly environment. Even his ignorance and lack of social caste, elements over which he has had absolutely no control, have been exploited by unscrupulous writers of an alien race to further degrade him in the eyes of his fellow men. Is it surprising, then, that he should look askance at any member of his own race who could be so unkind as to wound him where he is weakest, and to join hands with his enemies who delight in heaping abuse upon his already bowed head?

There are many who will say that as long as the Negro is as thin-skinned as the above would indicate, he will never come into his own. They will say that literature is life. It is life as lived in the lowly tenement and in the Park Avenue penthouse. But an artist is not obliged to portray all of life; he may select any part of it he chooses. In fact, if he wants to be successful he must select only the striking points that stand out above the commonplace. If this is true, what objection can the Negro have to the representation of the life of his race at its worst? Does the white man object when thieves, prostitutes and fools of his race are exhibited before the gaze of mankind?

To be sure, the white man does not object. For him there is nothing to fear. His place in the vanguard of civilization is assured, and there is a current belief that he is superior to all other races within his domain. What harm then can a book of fiction do to a people thus secure? But to the Negro it can do much to reinforce the already prevalent doctrine of race inferiority. It can do much to convince many unfriendly fellow citizens that their vague and unsupported opinions concerning this stepchild of American civilization is absolutely true. If the Negro is to rise in the estimation of the world, he must be continuously presented in a more favorable light even in fiction. His ignorance and social backwardness must occupy a smaller place in public representation, and his virtues must be stressed. He must cease to be portrayed as the clown of the human family, and be represented in his normal activities as an ordinary American citizen. Such a portrayal would, of course, be less interesting to a certain section of the reading public, and writers of Negro literature might be in for some lean years. But is not the result likely to justify the sacrifice? White writers may balk at such a scheme, but Negro authors owe such loyalty to their people.

With the above facts in mind one can readily see why Miss Hurston's first novel, *Jonah's Gourd Vine,* was received with small enthusiasm from certain quarters of the Negro race. With a grasp of her material that has seldom been equaled by a writer of her race, she had every opportunity of creating a masterpiece of the age. But she failed. She failed not from lack of skill but from lack of vision. The hero, John Buddy, who rose from an outcast bastard of an Alabama tenant farm to a man of wealth and influence, could have been another Ben Hur, bursting the unjust shackles that had bound him to a rotten social order and winning the applause even of his enemies. But unfortunately, his rise to religious prominence and financial ease is but a millstone about his neck. He is held back by some unseen cord which seems to be tethered to his racial heritage. Life crushes him almost to death, but he comes out of the mills with no greater insight into the deep mysteries which surround him. Such a phenomenon, although not intended by Miss Hurston as a type of all Negro manhood, is seized upon by thoughtless readers of other races as a happy confirmation of what they already faintly believe: namely, that the Negro is incapable of profiting by experience or of understanding the deeper mysteries of life.

BENJAMIN BRAWLEY

One of the New Realists

Zora Neale Hurston, born in Eatonville, Florida, went for her preparatory school training to Morgan College in Baltimore, later studied at Howard, and in 1927 received a degree at Columbia. Since then she has lived mainly in New York. Her story "Spunk" took a prize in the *Opportunity* contest in 1925, and by that time her work was appearing in other periodicals also. In 1932 some of her folk sketches were presented for a brief run at the John Golden Theatre, and more recently she has been connected with the Federal Theatre Project.

Miss Hurston early began to go back to her old home to collect the tales heard in childhood and to inveigle people into telling her "big old lies." She would get together a group of men in a railroad or turpentine camp or in a phosphate mining village, talk informally until they were no longer self-conscious, and then see which could outdo the other with his yarn. Similarly she studied voodooism in New Orleans. With such a background she produced the novel, *Jonah's Gourd Vine* (1934). This is largely concerned with John Buddy Pearson, the offspring of a white tenant farmer and a Negro woman who leaves the sordid home of his stepfather to make his way in the world. Capable and magnetic, he prospers and rises in social position, eventually becoming moderator of a Baptist association; but he is far too amorous and at the end of a long lane meets his fate. The story is not well integrated, and any merit the book possesses is largely in such a detached episode as Pearson's sermon on the creation. The author struck her true vein with *Mules and Men* (1935), the first part of which brings together

---

From *The Negro Genius*. © 1937 by Dodd, Mead and Company. Originally entitled "The New Realists."

a number of folk tales, the latter portion describing voodoo practices in the South. There are animal tales, stories of race relations, and spontaneous and original creations, in all of which may be seen the lively imagination of the Negro. Like some others who have dealt in folk-lore, Miss Hurston has not escaped criticism at the hands of those who frowned upon her broad humor and the lowly nature of her material. Her interest, however, is not in solving problems, the chief concern being with individuals. As for the untutored Negro, she presents him without apology, a character as good as other characters but different. Taking a bright story wherever it may be found, she passes it on, leaving to others the duty and the pleasure of philosophizing.

LANGSTON HUGHES

A Perfect Book of Entertainment in Herself

Wallace Thurman laughed a long bitter laugh. He was a strange kind of fellow, who liked to drink gin, but *didn't* like to drink gin; who liked being a Negro, but felt it a great handicap; who adored bohemianism, but thought it wrong to be a bohemian. He liked to waste a lot of time, but he always felt guilty wasting time. He loathed crowds, yet he hated to be alone. He almost always felt bad, yet he didn't write poetry.

Once I told him if I could feel as bad as he did *all* the time, I would surely produce wonderful books. But he said you had to know how to *write,* as well as how to feel bad. I said I didn't have to know how to feel bad, because, every so often, the blues just naturally overtook me, like a blind beggar with an old guitar:

> *You don't know,*
> *You don't know my mind—*
> *When you see me laughin',*
> *I'm laughin' to keep from cryin'.*

About the future of Negro literature Thurman was very pessimistic. He thought the Negro vogue had made us all too conscious of ourselves, had flattered and spoiled us, and had provided too many easy opportunities for some of us to drink gin and more gin, on which he thought we would always be drunk. With his bitter sense of humor, he called the Harlem literati, the "niggerati."

From *The Big Sea.* © 1940 by Langston Hughes, copyright renewed © 1968 by Arna Bontemps and George Houston Bass. Hill and Wang, 1963 (originally published 1940). Originally entitled "Harlem Literati."

Of this "niggerati," Zora Neale Hurston was certainly the most amusing. Only to reach a wider audience, need she ever write books—because she is a perfect book of entertainment in herself. In her youth she was always getting scholarships and things from wealthy white people, some of whom simply paid her just to sit around and represent the Negro race for them, she did it in such a racy fashion. She was full of side-splitting anecdotes, humorous tales, and tragicomic stories, remembered out of her life in the South as a daughter of a travelling minister of God. She could make you laugh one minute and cry the next. To many of her white friends, no doubt, she was a perfect "darkie," in the nice meaning they give the term—that is a naïve, childlike, sweet, humorous, and highly colored Negro.

But Miss Hurston was clever, too—a student who didn't let college give her a broad *a* and who had great scorn for all pretensions, academic or otherwise. That is why she was such a fine folk lore collector, able to go among the people and never act as if she had been to school at all. Almost nobody else could stop the average Harlemite on Lenox Avenue and measure his head with a strange-looking, anthropological device and not get bawled out for the attempt, except Zora, who used to stop anyone whose head looked interesting, and measure it.

When Miss Hurston graduated from Barnard she took an apartment in West 66th Street near the park, in that row of Negro houses there. She moved in with no furniture at all and no money, but in a few days friends had given her everything, from decorative silver birds, perched atop the linen cabinet, down to a footstool. And on Saturday night, to christen the place, she had a *hand*-chicken dinner, since she had forgotten to say she needed forks.

She seemed to know almost everybody in New York. She had been a secretary to Fannie Hurst, and had met dozens of celebrities whose friendship she retained. Yet she was always having terrific ups-and-downs about money. She tells this story on herself, about needing a nickel to go downtown one day and wondering where on earth she would get it. As she approached the subway, she was stopped by a blind beggar holding out his cup.

"Please help the blind! Help the blind! A nickel for the blind!"

"I need money worse than you today," said Miss Hurston, taking five cents out of his cup. "Lend me this! Next time, I'll give it back." And she went on downtown.

ROBERT BONE

Ships at a Distance: The Meaning
of Their Eyes Were Watching God

Zora Neale Hurston was born and raised in an all-Negro town in Florida—
an experience with "separate-but-equal" politics which deeply affected her
outlook on racial issues, as well as her approach to the Negro novel. Her
father was a tenant farmer and jackleg preacher whose colorful sermons were
an important influence on Miss Hurston's style. Her mother urged her to
"jump at the sun," and at the first opportunity she left home, employed as
a maid in a traveling Gilbert and Sullivan company. An ambitious reader
in secondary school, she set her sights on college, achieving this aim largely
through her own efforts. She attended Morgan State College in Baltimore,
Howard University, and Columbia University, where she studied anthropology under Franz Boas.

At Howard she joined the Stylus, an undergraduate literary society
sponsored by Alain Locke. Drawn at once into the vortex of the Negro
Renaissance, she published several stories in *Opportunity,* and collaborated
with Langston Hughes and Wallace Thurman on the editorial board of *Fire!!*
In the early 1930's a prize story called "The Gilded Six-Bits" appeared in
Story magazine, leading to an invitation from Lippincott's to do a novel.
The result was *Jonah's Gourd Vine* (1934). Her second and more important
novel, *Their Eyes Were Watching God,* appeared in 1937, while a third novel,
Seraph on the Suwanee, was published in 1948. In addition to her short stories
and novels, Miss Hurston has written three books of folklore, an autobiog-
raphy, a one-act play, one or two librettos, and several magazine articles.

Jonah's Gourd Vine has style without structure, a rich verbal texture

From *The Negro Novel in America.* © 1958 by Yale University Press, revised edition © 1965
by Yale University. Originally entitled "Aspects of the Racial Past."

without dramatic form, "atmosphere" without real characterization. It is
the story of John Buddy, a field hand turned preacher whose congregation
accepts him as "a man amongst men," but is unprepared to find him also
a man amongst women. A great preacher (the author introduces a ten-page
sermon to prove it), John Buddy is no less a lover. An erratic tension arises
between folk artist and philanderer, but it is not carried forward to a suitable
denouement. In its emphasis on atmosphere and local color, in its exploitation of the exotic, and especially of exotic language, and in its occasional
hint of primitivism, *Jonah's Gourd Vine* expresses a sensibility molded pre-
dominantly by the Negro Renaissance.

The style of the novel is impressive enough. Zora Neale Hurston, whom
Langston Hughes has described as a rare *raconteuse,* draws freely on the verbal
ingenuity of the folk. Her vivid, metaphorical style is based primarily on
the Negro preacher's graphic ability to present abstractions to his flock.
Take the opening sentence of the novel: "God was grumbling his thunder
and playing the zig-zag lightning through his fingers"; or such an image as
"the cloud-muddied moonlight"; or the small-town flavor of "Time is long
by the courthouse clock." The danger is that these folk sayings may become
the main point of the novel. Overdone, they destroy rather than support
authentic characterization. In *Jonah's Gourd Vine* they are too nonfunctional,
too anthropological, and in the end merely exotic. Miss Hurston has not
yet mastered the form of the novel, but her style holds promise of more
substantial accomplishment to come.

The genesis of a work of art may be of no moment to literary criticism
but it is sometimes crucial in literary history. It may, for example, account
for the rare occasion when an author outclasses himself. *Their Eyes Were
Watching God* (1937) is a case in point. The novel was written in Haiti in
just seven weeks, under the emotional pressure of a recent love affair. "The
plot was far from the circumstances," Miss Hurston writes in her autobiography, "but I tried to embalm all the tenderness of my passion for him in
Their Eyes Were Watching God." Ordinarily the prognosis for such a novel
would be dismal enough. One might expect immediacy and intensity, but
not distance, or control, or universality. Yet oddly, or perhaps not so oddly,
it is Miss Hurston's best novel, and possibly the best novel of the period,
excepting *Native Son.*

The opening paragraph of *Their Eyes Were Watching God* encompasses
the whole of the novel's meaning: "Ships at a distance have every man's wish
on board. For some they come in with the tide. For others they sail forever
on the horizon, never out of sight, never landing, until the Watcher turns
his eyes away in resignation, his dreams mocked to death by Time. That is

the life of man." For women, the author continues, the dream is the sole reality. "So the beginning of this was a woman, and she had come back from burying the dead."

Janie has been gone for almost two years as the action of the novel commences. The townspeople know only that she left home in the company of a lover much younger than herself, and that she departed in fine clothes but has returned in overalls. Heads nod; tongues wag; and the consensus is that she has played the fool. Toward the gossiping women who, from the safety of a small-town porch "pass nations through their mouths," Janie feels only contempt and irritation: "If God don't think no mo' 'bout 'em than Ah do, they's a lost ball in de high grass." To Pheoby, her kissing-friend, she tells the story of her love for Tea Cake, which together with its antecedents comprises the main body of the novel.

Janie's dream begins during her adolescence, when she is stirred by strange wonderings as she watches a pear tree blossom. No sooner is her dream born, however, than it is desecrated by her grandmother. Nanny, who has witnessed her share of the sexual exploitation of Negro women, declares firmly: "[Neither] de menfolks white or black is makin' a spit cup outa you." Seeking to protect Janie from the vicissitudes of adolescent love, she puts her up on the auction block of marriage. To Nanny, being married is being like white folks: "You got yo' lawful husband same as Mis' Washburn or anybody else." Against her better judgment, therefore, Janie acquiesces in an early marriage with Logan Killicks, a hard-working farmer considerably older than herself.

"There are years that ask questions and years that answer: Did marriage compel love like the sun the day?" Janie soon realizes her mistake. She aspires to more than sixty acres and an organ in the parlor, and refuses to barter her fulfillment as a woman in exchange for property rights: "Ah ain't takin' dat ole land tuh heart neither. Ah could throw ten acres of it over de fence every day and never look back to see where it fell." Affairs reach a crisis with the appearance of Jody Starks, a younger man who offers Janie a fresh start in a neighboring county. "Janie pulled back a long time because he did not represent sun-up and pollen and blooming trees, but he spoke for far horizon." Her first dream dead, she runs off with Jody to the all-Negro town of Eatonville.

Janie's second dream scarcely fares better than the first. Although her husband becomes "a big voice," a property owner, and eventually mayor of the town, Janie remains restless, unfulfilled. Asked by Jody how she likes being "Mrs. Mayor," she replies: "It keeps us in some way we ain't natural wid one 'nother. Youse always off talkin' and fixin' things, and Ah feels lak

Ah'm jus' markin' time." A widening rift develops in the marriage as a fundamental clash of values becomes apparent. Janie can no more reconcile herself to Jody's store than to Logan Killicks' sixty acres: "The store itself was a pleasant place if only she didn't have to sell things." On one occasion, when the townsfolk playfully take off from work for the mock funeral of a dead mule, Jody remarks, "Ah wish mah people would git mo' business in 'em and not spend so much time on foolishness." Janie's reply is caustic: "Everybody can't be lak you, Jody. Somebody is bound tuh want tuh laugh and play."

By this time, the wider meaning of the novel has begun to emerge. A dramatic tension has arisen between the sound business instincts of Janie's two husbands and her own striving toward a full life, which is later to take on flesh in the person of Tea Cake. At first glance, what seems to be taking shape in the dramatic structure of the novel is the familiar cultural dualism of the Negro Renaissance. Although this Renaissance pattern is definitely present, Miss Hurston pitches her theme in a higher key. Janie rejects the Nanny-Killicks-Jody way of life because of its cramped quarters and narrow gauge: "Nanny belonged to that other kind that loved to deal in scraps." It is Janie's urge to touch the horizon which causes her to repudiate respectability.

Meanwhile, Janie's second marriage moves toward a culmination in Jody's illness and death. For many years their relationship has been purely perfunctory: "The spirit of the marriage left the bedroom and took to living in the parlor." Only on his deathbed does Janie confront her husband with the bitter knowledge of an inner life which she has been unable to share with him: "You done lived wid me for twenty years and you don't half know me atall." Taking stock after Jody's death, Janie senses in this repressed phase of her life an unconscious preparation for her great adventure: "She was saving up feelings for some man she had never seen."

If the first half of the novel deals with the prose of Janie's life, the latter half deals with its poetry. Not long after Jody's death, Tea Cake walks into her life. First off, he laughs; next he teaches her how to play checkers. One afternoon he urges her to close up shop and come with him to a baseball game. The next night, after midnight, he invites her on a fishing expedition. Their relationship is full of play, of impulsiveness, of informality, and of imagination. Easy-going, careless of money, living for the moment, Tea Cake is an incarnation of the folk culture. After a whirlwind courtship, he persuades Janie to leave Eatonville and to try his way.

On a deeper level, Tea Cake represents intensity and experience. As Janie puts it in summing up her two years with him: "Ah been a delegate to de big 'ssociation of life." Their new life begins with a trip to Jacksonville, "and to a lot of things she wanted to see and know." In the big city, Tea Cake deserts Janie for several days, while she suffers the torments and anxieties of a middle-aged lover. Upon his return she learns that he had won a large sum in a crap game and had immediately given a barbecue for his friends, in order to find out how it feels to be rich. When she protests at being left out, he asks with amusement, "So you aims tuh partake wid everything, hunh?" From that moment, their life together becomes an unlimited partnership.

From Jacksonville, Janie and Tea Cake move "down on the muck" of the Florida Everglades for the bean-picking season. Janie goes to work in the fields in order to be with Tea Cake during the long working day. They share the hard work and the hard play of the folk, laughing together at the "dickty" Negroes who think that "us oughta class off." In this milieu of primitive Bahaman dances, of "blues made and used right on the spot," and of "romping and playing . . . behind the boss's back," Janie at last finds happiness. In true Renaissance spirit, it is the folk culture, through Tea Cake, which provides the means of her spiritual fulfillment.

One night, "the palm and banana trees began that long-distance talk with rain." As the winds over Lake Okechobee mount to hurricane force, the novel moves to a swift climax. Janie and Tea Cake find themselves swept along with a crowd of refugees, amid awesome scenes of destruction and sudden death. In the midst of their nightmarish flight, Tea Cake is bitten by a dog and unknowingly contracts rabies. Some weeks later, suffering horribly, he loses his senses and attacks Janie when she refuses him a drink of water. In the ensuing melee, Janie is compelled to shoot Tea Cake to protect her own life. "It was the meanest moment of eternity." Not merely that her lover dies, but that she herself is the instrument—this is the price which Janie pays for her brief months of happiness. Her trial and acquittal seem unreal to her; without Tea Cake she can only return to Eatonville to "live by comparisons."

As the reader tries to assimilate Janie's experience and assess its central meaning, he cannot avoid returning to a key passage which foreshadows the climax of the novel: "All gods dispense suffering without reason. Otherwise they would not be worshipped. Through indiscriminate suffering men know fear, and fear is the most divine emotion. It is the stones for altars and the beginning of wisdom. Half gods are worshipped in wine and flowers. Real gods require blood." Through Tea Cake's death, Janie experiences the divine emotion, for her highest dream—to return to the opening paragraph of the novel—has been "mocked to death by Time." Like all men, she can only watch in resignation, with an overpowering sense of her own helplessness.

Yet if mankind's highest dreams are ultimately unattainable, it is still better to live on the far horizon than to grub around on shore. Janie does not regret her life with Tea Cake, or the price which is exacted in the end: "We been tuhgether round two years. If you kin see de light at daybreak, you don't keer if you die at dusk. It's so many people never seen de light at all. Ah wuz fumblin' round and God opened de door." As the novel closes, the scene returns to Janie and her friend in Eatonville. Pheoby's reaction to the story she has heard is a clinching statement of the theme of the novel: "Ah done growed ten feet higher from jus' listenin' tuh you, Janie. Ah ain't satisfied with mahself no mo'."

FANNIE HURST

A Personality Sketch

The late Zora Hurston first swung into my orbit when she was a new graduate of Barnard College. About a decade later she was to swing out of the orbit of so many of us into a mysterious limbo of sustained silence. It required nothing short of her recent death at fifty-five to reveal her whereabouts.

She walked into my study one day by telephone appointment, carelessly, a big-boned, good-boned young woman, handsome and light yellow, with no show of desire for the position of secretary for which she was applying. Her dialect was as deep as the deep south, her voice and laughter the kind I used to hear on the levees of St. Louis when I was growing up in that city. As Zora expressed it, we "took a shine" to one another and I engaged her on the spot as my live-in secretary.

What a quaint gesture that proved to be! Her shorthand was short on legibility, her typing hit-or-miss, mostly the latter, her filing, a game of find-the-thimble. Her mind ran ahead of my thoughts and she would interject with an impatient suggestion or clarification of what I wanted to say. If dictation bored her she would interrupt, stretch wide her arms and yawn: "Let's get out the car, I'll drive you up to the Harlem bad-lands or down to the wharves where men go down to the sea in ships."

Her lust for life and food went hand in hand. She nibbled constantly between meals and consumed dinner off the stove and out of the refrigerator before the meal was served. "Sorry I ate all the casaba melon for tonight's

From *The Yale University Library Gazette* 35, no. 1 (July 1960). © 1960 by Brandeis University and Washington University. Originally entitled "Zora Hurston: A Personality Sketch."

dessert, I was hungry for so many years of my life, I get going nowadays and can't stop."

This was before her first book. Up to this time she had mentioned only vaguely her writing intention and ambitions.

One day after reading the manuscript a strange young man had submitted for my opinion, I dictated a letter to him. When Zora gave it to me to sign, she pointed out that she had added a final paragraph of her own, something to this effect: "I, the secretary, have also read your manuscript. I think better of it than Miss Hurst. Atta-Big-Boy!"

Rebuke bounced off of her. "Get rough with me if you want results. I've been so kicked around most of my life that your kind of scolding is duck soup to me." But after more and more of the same her gay unpredictability got out of hand. "Zora," I exploded one morning after she yawningly announced she was not in the mood to take dictation but felt like driving into the countryside, "consider yourself fired. You are my idea of the world's worst secretary. As a matter of fact, I think I should be your secretary. But you are welcome to live on here until you are settled elsewhere." In the end she remained on for about a year, still in my employ, but now in the capacity of chauffeur. She drove with a sure relaxed skill on the frequent trips north, east, south, and west that we took together.

Uninhibited as a child, she had a subconscious fashion of talking to herself as she drove, expressing thoughts easily audible that ranged from gross vulgarities to florescence, from brash humor to bright flights of fancy and unsuspected erudition. A member of her own race, happening to cross in front of the car, was invariably the occasion for remarks provocative and revealing: "My, what a fine tail my cat's got. But you're not so light as you think. You are yellow, yellow." Next a line from Wordsworth or Millay might come tumbling from her memory.

She once remarked to herself: "I want to put Carl [Van Vechten] in a book. The way he is. The way nobody but me, knows." Then in song: "No one but God and me knows what is in my heart"; then spirituals for one mile, bawdy songs for the next.

An effervescent companion of no great profundities but dancing perceptions, she possessed humor, sense of humor, and what a fund of folklore! Although she seemed to have very little indignation for the imposed status of her race, she knew her people. Probably this insensibility was due to the fact that her awakening powers and subsequent recognition tended to act as a soporific to her early sufferings and neglect.

On one occasion we motored to Eaton[ville], Florida, her birthplace, the first incorporated Negro town in the United States. There we visited her deserted home, a dilapidated two-room shack that indicated what must have been deep squalor, even when its clapboards had been new. "Everybody in this town had the same chance to work themselves out of it that I did," she observed. "But not your talents," I countered. "Then let them use elbow grease for what they are fitted to do. I used it when I had to. I scrubbed and dish-washed. The world will treat you right if you are all right."

It was a vulnerable philosophy at variance with much of her splendor, for splendor she had. It irradiated her work and her personality, or perhaps that is putting the cart before the horse. It is probably because of her vividness, both vulgar and exquisite, that in her girlhood she had never known the pangs of discrimination, which can be even fiercer than those of poverty.

But regardless of race, Zora had the gift of walking into hearts.

Again she once said of her favorite, Carl Van Vechten: "If Carl was a people instead of a person, I could then say, these are my people." Considering her ragged and tattered childhood, this lack of identity with her race was surprising. But in spite of herself her rich heritage cropped out not only in her personality but more importantly in her writings.

Her book of folk tales, *Moses, Man of the Mountain,* was written out of race memory, if such a thing there be; her autobiography, *Dust Tracks on a Road,* was the result of experiences conditioned by race. But she herself was a gift both to her race and the human race. That she died in poverty and obscurity was because for a decade at least she had deliberately removed herself from the large group of us who felt puzzlement and still do. Where lurked her ultimate defeat, ending in retreat? Why and how?

Despite her bright accomplishments, her books, including *Tell My Horse* (the result of her explorations into Haiti), *Their Eyes Were Watching God, Dust Tracks on a Road,* are Negro Americana, to the smell of fried chitterlings, which by the way she loved.

Yet the inescapable conclusion persists that Zora remains a figure in bas relief, only partially emerging from her potential into the whole woman. She lived laughingly, raffishly, and at least in the years I knew her, with blazing zest for life. Daughter of a combined carpenter and self-ordained Baptist minister, she sang with the plangency and the tears of her people and then on with equal lustiness to hip-shuddering and finger-snapping jazz.

Illogically, indeed incredibly, irresponsibility was one of Zora's endearing qualities. Zora late, Zora sleeping through an appointment, Zora failing to meet an obligation, were actually part of a charm you dared not douse. One spring, after she was earning with her pen and living in her own little apartment, she importuned me to consent to visit and address one of her classes at Columbia University where she was majoring in anthropology under Dr. Franz Boas. I agreed, and on the appointed day arrived at the University only to find it closed for the Easter holidays and Zora off visiting friends up-state. She was casual about it all and, strangely and uncharacteristically, so was I.

And withal, that recurring and puzzling trait, lack of indignation. On our excursions, we repeatedly encountered the ogre of discrimination. At hotels, Zora was either assigned to servants' quarters or informed that they were full up. When I also refused accommodations, Zora's attitude was swift and adamant: "If you are going to take that stand, it will be impossible for us to travel together. This is the way it is and I can take care of myself as I have all my life. I will find my own lodging and be around with the car in the morning." And that was the way it was, although an ironic incident broke its continuity.

One hot August day returning from Vermont, we drove past a well-known Westchester County hotel. An idea struck me. Zora, in a red head-scarf and one of her bizarre frocks of many colors, looked hot and tired from a full day's driving. At my sudden request we stopped before the Inn. "Do me a favor, Zora. No questions please. Follow me." At the dining-room entrance I pushed ahead. A head-waiter appeared, his expression, when he saw Zora, as if a window shade had been drawn over his face. Before he could come through with the usual, "Sorry, everything reserved," I announced, "The Princess Zora and I wish a table." We were shown to the best in the room.

Following a good meal and some levity, Zora made a remark that revealed for an instant her mental innards: "Who would think," she soliloquized as we resumed driving, "that a good meal could be so bitter." Thus we must rest content with the memory of Zora, a woman half in shadow.

She lived carelessly, at least at the time I knew her, and her zest for life was cruelly at odds with her lonely death.

But death at best, is a lonely act.

But to life, to her people and to people, she left a bequest of good writing and the memory of an iridescent personality of many colors.

Her short shelf of writings deserves to endure. Undoubtedly her memory will in the minds and hearts of her friends. We rejoice that she passed this way so brightly but alas, too briefly.

LARRY NEAL

The Spirituality of Jonah's Gourd Vine

The central achievement of *Jonah's Gourd Vine* is Zora Neale Hurston's success in penetrating the "romantic" surface of rural, black Southern life. This achievement is notable despite her tendency to overwork her dialect; that is, to render it with such phonetic faithfulness that some of the real poetry embodied in black speech either is obscured or goes unexploited. She is at her best in her narrative, or when she allows her own voice to seep into the beautiful sermonistic passages in this novel. In these instances, she really illustrates the scope of her vision, and consequently challenges not only her Harlem contemporaries, but much of the literature of her time.

This is a remarkable first novel. It is somewhat autobiographical in nature; the central characters, John and Lucy Pearson, are loosely based on Zora's own father and mother. The town which is the setting for the novel is a composite of several towns in the vicinity of Eatonville, Florida, where Zora was born.

Assuming that intentions have *some* validity in a discussion of fiction, let us refer to the following remarks Miss Hurston made in a letter to James Weldon Johnson (April 16, 1934):

> Just a word about my novel. . . . I have tried to present a Negro
> preacher who is neither funny nor an imitation Puritan ram-rod
> in pants. Just the human being and poet that he must be to
> succeed in a Negro pulpit. I do not speak of those among us
> who have been tampered with and consequently have gone Pres-

From *Jonah's Gourd Vine* by Zora Neale Hurston. © 1971 by Larry Neal. Lippincott Company, 1971. Originally entitled "Introduction."

byterian or Episcopal. I mean the common run of us who love
magnificence, beauty, poetry and color so much that there can
never be too much of it. Who do not feel that the ridiculous has
been achieved when someone decorates a decoration. That is my
viewpoint. I see a preacher as a man outside of his pulpit and so
far as I am concerned he should be free to follow his bent as other
men. He becomes the voice of the spirit when he ascends the
rostrum.

There is a definite, culturally determined value system at work here.
But there is a tension within this value system. There are contending ideas
here concerning the nature of the spiritual life. And it is the resulting tension
that supplies the essential dynamic of *Jonah's Gourd Vine*. John Pearson,
Zora's preacher-protagonist, is a man doomed to agony because the essential
nature of his spiritual mission is constantly under assault by the world of
flesh. As a man of God, he must present to his community a demonstrable
set of ethics. As spiritual leader of the community, he must somehow embody
the community's highest sense of morality. But he is not merely a reaction
to the social demands of his group; or at least he will not allow himself to
be the model of virtue that we demand of him. And this is the reason that
Zora's character commands so much of our attention.

For, like all "saints," he is constantly being tempted by the enticements
of the flesh; that is to say, his Christian will toward *agape* is constantly being
challenged by Eros, the carnal impulse.

What makes all this so significant is that Miss Hurston is essentially
exposing us to two distinctly different *cultural* attitudes toward the concept
of spirituality. The one springs from a formerly enslaved communal society,
non-Christian in background, where there is really no clean-cut dichotomy
between the world of spirit and the world of flesh. The other attitude is
clearly more rigid, being a blend of Puritan concepts and the fire-and-
brimstone imagery of the white evangelical tradition. Zora's preacher and
his people were forced to accept Christianity, but it was impossible to accept
it without bringing to bear upon it their own ethos and social modality. In
accepting it, or at least in submitting to its main external tenets, they were
yet able to shape out of it unique forms of expression that reflected the most
retrievable, and hence the most important, aspects of the pre-Christian
cultural memory.

John Pearson, as Zora notes in her letter to Johnson, is a poet. That
is to say, one who manipulates words in order to convey to others the mystery
of that Unknowable force which we call God. And he is more; he is the

intelligence of the community, the bearer of its traditions and highest possibilities. But as Zora illustrates here, he is also human and, as such, beset with the burdens and temptations of human existence. As poet, his power rests in his projection of the Word. As bearer of the Word, he is both the Son of God and the Son of Man. His tragic dilemma is that he can be fully neither one nor the other; especially on the basis of some abstract morality. Even his community is aware of this dilemma. They bear witness to his love affairs, his moral failures, but they cling to him because he is the bearer of the Word, and hence the bearer of their holiness, their emotional history.

This is a novel which is exceedingly simple on the surface, and Zora may have intended to tell a simple story in the folk tradition. But she does more than that. And the theme, man's search for spiritual equilibrium, is large, mythic, and timeless. It achieves its own special power and, yes, universality by grounding itself honestly in the particular. It is not flawless. What is? But if one gives oneself to the strength of its emotional vision, the experience will be more than worthwhile.

ROGER ROSENBLATT

Their Eyes Were Watching God

Breaking a cyclical pattern in Zora Neale Hurston's *Their Eyes Were Watching God* is not conceived of in reaction to external white forces, as it always is in Wright, for example, but rather in opposition to various forms of repression which are more generally human, and sometimes self-manufactured. The love which the heroine, Janie, eventually achieves is her means of escape, both from the restrictive considerations of practicality and from the resultant deadness in herself. Her progress in the novel, which is opposite to the progress of almost every other black character in the literature, is toward personal freedom, yet unlike McKay's Jake in *Home to Harlem* or Bita in *Banana Bottom,* whose senses of personal freedom are inborn and ready-made, Janie earns that sense the hard way. She begins as a minor character in her own life story, and ends as a full-fledged heroine whose heroism consists largely of resilience.

Born in western Florida, raised by her grandmother, Janie leads a thoroughly uneventful life until the age of sixteen. One afternoon, Janie's grandmother sees "shiftless" Johnny Taylor "lacerating her Janie with a kiss." Fearful that Janie would be ruined, as Janie's mother was ruined, she pushes Janie into marriage with Logan Killicks, and his sixty acres, who looks to Janie "like some ole skullhead in de grave yard," but to Nanny means security. "Tain't Logan Killicks Ah wants you to have, baby, it's protection." Being a slave had made Nanny a realist about a number of things: "Honey, de white man is de ruler of everything as fur as Ah been able tuh find out. Maybe it's some place way off in de ocean where de black

From *Black Fiction.* © 1974 by the President and Fellows of Harvard College. Harvard University Press, 1974. Originally entitled "Eccentricities."

man is in power, but we don't know nothin' but what we see. So de white man throw down de load and tell de nigger man tuh pick it up. He pick it up because he have to, but he don't tote it. He hand it to his womenfolks."

Janie marries Logan, and for a long time attempts to love him. When she finally concludes that "marriage did not make love," her "first dream was dead, so she became a woman." One evening down the road comes Jody Starks, a quick-thinking, fast-talking, ambitious man, headed for a newly founded all black community, where he plans to make his fortune. Jody offers Janie a new start. Janie takes it and marries him, committing bigamy, but soon finds herself no better off than before. True to his ambition, Jody becomes mayor of the town, and the most powerful man in the area, but just as Logan had done, he begins to treat Janie like property. Finally, "something fell off the shelf inside [Janie]. Then she went inside there to see what it was. It was her image of Jody tumbled down and shattered."

Their marriage disintegrates. Jody becomes ill and dies. On the morning of his death Janie studies her reflection in the mirror:

> The young girl was gone, but a handsome woman had taken her place. She tore off the kerchief from her head and let down her plentiful hair. The weight, the length, the glory was there. She took careful stock of herself, then combed her hair and tied it back up again. Then she starched and ironed her face, forming it into just what people wanted to see, and opened up the window and cried, "Come heah people! Jody is dead. Mah husband is gone from me."

From that point on she performs as the respectable town widow, until her third man, Tea Cake, comes into her life. Tea Cake is a completely free spirit; each of Janie's men has successively been freer than the one before. With Tea Cake Janie finds love for the first time. Their happiness ends only when Tea Cake contracts rabies after rescuing Janie and himself from a flood. Tea Cake is driven mad by the disease and when, in delirium, he goes after Janie with a gun, she shoots and kills him in self-defense. Acquitted at her trial, Janie returns to the town where she and Tea Cake had started out, observing finally that Tea Cake "wasn't dead. He could never be dead until she herself had finished feeling and thinking. The kiss of his memory made pictures of love and light against the wall. Here was peace. She pulled in her horizon like a great fish-net. Pulled it from around the waist of the world and draped it over her shoulder. So much of life in its meshes! She called in her soul to come and see."

The images of the sea which express a certain serenity at the end of *Their Eyes Were Watching God* are used to express longing, specifically Janie's, in the first lines of the book: "Ships at a distance have every man's wish on board. For some they come in with the tide. For others they sail forever on the horizon, never out of sight, never landing until the Watcher turns his eyes away in resignation, his dreams mocked to death by Time." The Watcher in this instance is Janie, whose progress from states of longing to serenity in the novel seems largely accidental. Janie thinks of God as all-powerful, but disinterested, and credits the events, good and bad, of her life to an unchanging masterplan—"[God] made nature, and nature made everything else." As Tea Cake is dying, Janie ponders, "Somewhere up there beyond blue ether's bosom sat He. Was He noticing what was going on around here? He must because He knew everything. Did He *mean* to do this thing to Tea Cake and her?"

If it is impossible for Janie to deviate from her divine pattern, there are enough human patterns in the story available for breaking. The most binding is the prescription of her grandmother: to marry safely and well. Logan represents a sound marriage because he owns land and is therefore respectable. Jody initially appears to be a more romantic figure than Logan, but at heart is simply another, more eloquent, man of property. At a town ceremony where Jody presides over the setting up of a street lamp—"and when Ah touch de match tuh dat lamp-wick let de light penetrate inside of yuh"—a local woman bursts forth into a spiritual:

> We'll walk in de light, de beautiful light
> Come where the dew drops of mercy shine bright
> Shine all around us by day and by night
> Jesus, the light of the world.

The idea, with all of its usual ramifications, is that the dark needs the light. Jody may be the leader of an all-black community, but his vision for the town, and of himself, is white, and this is the vision which Janie must shake.

Neither Jody nor Logan is depicted as being evil. What they offer is a variety of death: passionless lives lacking any sense of creativity. Silas in "Long Black Song" (*Uncle Tom's Children*) is the same kind of man. Like Logan particularly, he has worked his whole life in order to own his own house. Wright put it that "he had worked hard and saved his money and bought a farm so he could grow his own crops like white men." But one day a white man, a college student, comes to his house when Silas is away, trying to sell his wife, Sarah, a combination clock and gramaphone. The white man seduces Sarah, and when Silas revenges himself, the house that he sought so long is burned to the ground with him inside of it.

The fact that Sarah allows herself to be seduced is not a sign of her promiscuity or boredom, but simply an effort at feeling human. When Silas discovers his wife's treachery, his outcry is self-condemning: "Fer ten years Ah slaved mah life out t git mah farm free." For ten years and probably more, that is, he had falsified his life, trying to be successful on standard (white) terms. Even at the end, resolving to murder his white pursuers, he decides, "Ahm gonna be hard like they is!" Sarah's marriage to him had been a lie, just as Janie's marriage to Logan and Jody were lies. For both women their marriages represented decisions to restrict themselves in the name of a kind of security which was white in color, and therefore unattainable.

The conflict which Janie represents, between freedom or passion and restraint or reserve, has a special quality in black fiction. The characters who deal with this conflict often seem to be carrying on the fight at a number of different levels. Gabriel Grimes's decision to become a man of God constitutes a denial or reversal of his true nature, but it also suggests an option which is significant in terms of black history. The condition of slavery was the ultimate restriction in which freedom to be oneself is out of the question. When Gabriel decides to bind his life to the straight and narrow, therefore, his decision is reactionary. As if unable to cope with his freedom, which is regarded by others as disgraceful, and by himself as perilous, he takes on the life of a slave to the church, for which he must work day and night for no pay, with no rest, and with no personal liberty in sight.

In the same way, Hager disapproves of Jimboy's singing and Harriet's dancing in implicit nostalgia for the time of her own slavery. Not that Hager would prefer slavery as an alternative to freedom, but that compared to total wildness, it seemed preferable because it was knowable. The conflict between freedom and restraint as it affects a single character is often a reflection of a particular historical situation in which freedom has been unknown for so many generations that a man would be fearful of trying it. Belonging to a people whose immediate past consisted of the freedom to serve others, it is no wonder that a character in black fiction may experience a special kind of anxiety as he contemplates being free.

As for Janie, the achievement of her freedom entails additional complications. Not only does Janie inherit the conception of the black in slavery, but of the woman in slavery as well. Remembering her grandmother's original admonition, she vents her exasperation upon Jody: "Sometimes God gits familiar wid us womenfolks too and talks His inside business. He told me how surprised He was 'bout y'all turning out so smart after Him makin' yuh different; and how surprised y'all is goin' tuh be if you ever find out you don't know half as much 'bout us as you think you do. It's so easy to make yo'self out God Almighty when you ain't got nothin' tuh strain against but women and chickens." Only Tea Cake understands the source of this outburst. Because he does understand it, it is through him that Janie discovers her pride.

This discovery, the discovery of Tea Cake himself, satisfies Janie's romanticism, which has been constant throughout the novel. Such satisfaction is a rarity in this literature, and Janie's ability to fall and stay in love, even if that love is cut short, is rarer than that. Ordinarily in black fiction, love turns out to be one-sided, not because the two people involved are not equally in love with each other, but because one of them is at the same time always trying to become successful in the sense of Jody's "success" or trying in some way to deal with the white world. In *Cane* ("Theater") it is John's notion of white respectability alone which prevents him from loving Dorris, the dancer, just as it is Muriel's idea of middle class propriety which drives Dan to distraction in "Box-Seat." Florence (*Go Tell It on the Mountain*) is unable to love Frank for no other reason than that Frank is too black in color, and Rufus cannot love Leona in *Another Country* because Leona is white. In *If He Hollers Let Him Go,* Alice will only marry Bob if Bob settles down and goes to law school. In Williams' *The Man Who Cried I Am,* Lillian will only marry Max if he gives up his writing career to take a steady job. In fact, she dies aborting Max's child in order to prevent that marriage.

Their Eyes Were Watching God is structurally a simple story, yet nothing in Janie's accomplishment is simple or easy. Indeed, the enormous effort she must make in order to feel human only serves to demonstrate how strong the opposition to her humanity is. It is only when Janie and Tea Cake marry and avoid the white world entirely that they flourish. Yet we know that Janie's achievement with Tea Cake is an unreal achievement. The two of them may escape temporarily into a fantasy of independence, but like other lovers of folklore they are aware all along that there is a world outside waiting and able to destroy them. The tragedy, and the difference, is that they have been told that the world is theirs.

ADDISON GAYLE, JR.

The Outsider

By the time Zora Neale Hurston (1903–60) published *Jonah's Gourd Vine* (1934), her first novel, Wallace Thurman and Rudolph Fisher were dead, and the forces they had helped to set in motion during the Renaissance were already being undermined by the efforts of the Communist party. The influence of the party on black writers could be seen in the short stories of Richard Wright, some of the poetry of Hughes and McKay. The battle against these new imagists, the successors to the Van Vechtenites, however, lay still some years in the future. In neither of her three novels did Miss Hurston react to the growing attempt by the party to influence the direction of black literature. Like Jessie Fauset, she was well liked by her contemporaries, and her reputation as a folklorist equaled her reputation as a novelist. Of her three novels, *Jonah's Gourd Vine* and *Their Eyes Were Watching God* (1937) are more closely allied to the spirit of the Renaissance than to that of the writers of the coming period.

Deserting the urban setting, already overworked by Hughes, McKay, Cullen, Thurman, and Fisher among others, Miss Hurston chose in her novels to return to the southland—a region far different from that of Toomer's *Cane* in 1923. Remnants of the old feudal order remain—cotton farming, tenantry, and sharecropping. The modern world, however, intrudes through trains, automobiles, and new ideas concerning the race question. To read her novel is to be aware of the distance of her people from those of Fisher or his environment. Still, *Jonah's Gourd Vine* is a novel of change.

The hero, John Pearson, is a realist living in an environment haunted

From *The Way of the New World: The Black Novel in America.* © 1975 by Addison Gayle, Jr. Anchor Press, 1975.

still by the ghosts of Harris, Dixon, and Page. It is one in which the images
created long ago are still adhered to by Blacks and whites alike and the
dramatic tension of the novel is created by the attempt of the major characters
to break completely with the definitions of the past. Pearson, itinerant laborer
become preacher, son of a white man and a black woman, is incapable of
doing so. His wife, Lucy, however, succeeds in breaking free of the images
which circumscribe her as a Black and a woman and, in so doing, presents
a positive image of black women seen, heretofore, only in such novels as
The Quest of the Silver Fleece and *Banana Bottom.*

Shortly after publication of *Jonah's Gourd Vine,* Miss Hurston, in a letter
to James Weldon Johnson, talked about her major character, John Pearson.
She had, she told her colleague, tried to present a different kind of preacher
from those depicted in legend and myth, one who was neither comical nor
an imitation of white ministers, who was "the common run of us who love
magnificence, beauty, poetry, and color so much that there can never be
too much of it." She added that the preacher was, outside of his pulpit, a
man like other men, and thus "should be free to follow his bent as other
men." There can be no quarrel with Larry Neal's observation that in this
statement "a definite, culturally determined value system is at work." Yet
the question for the reader is whose value system has determined the actions
of John Pearson? The implications of Miss Hurston's statement and the
actions that unfold in the novel contradict each other; for to suggest that
the preacher, outside the pulpit, should be free "to follow his bent as other
men" means to condone the actions which lead Pearson along the road to
his tragic end—a tragedy manifested by his inability to move beyond the
terms which circumscribe him.

Like the tragic mulatto of old, Pearson is marked for tragedy. His
stepfather, Ned, utters this fatalistic appraisal: ". . . Dese white folks orta
know and dey say dese half-white niggers got de worst part uf bofe de white
and de black folks." It is not, however, mixed blood that leads to the tragedy
of John Pearson, and here Miss Hurston offers a definition of tragedy peculiar
to her black characters alone. Such a concept had never seriously been applied,
in its highest meaning, to Blacks. Never seen as men of distinction and
nobility—those worthy of a tragic occurrence and having, according to
American definition, no place lower than his actual state to fall—few writers
thought of the life of an individual Black as bordering upon the tragic.
Looking into black history and folklore, however, Miss Hurston is capable
of divining a difference between tragedy as defined by the Euro-Americans
and tragedy as it occurs in the lives of Blacks. Not being born to power,
black men, unlike the Hamlets or King Lears, must travel long, separate

roads to status and distinction before pride and ego combine to produce the hubristic act, leading to downfall and destruction.

John begins life as the adopted stepson of Ned Crittendon, whose wife brings the mulatto child into the marital union. The distinguishing marks of his early life are poverty and hard work, coupled with animosity between himself and his stepfather, an ex-slave, who takes out the resentment of forty years upon the mulatto. "John is de house-nigger. Ole Marsa always kep de yaller niggers in de house and give 'em uh job totin' silver dishes and goblets. . . . Us black niggers is . . . s'posed tuh ketch de wind and de weather." The hostility between the two causes the stepfather to "bind" John over to a onetime overseer to work his land. Amy, the mother, knowing the overseer's reputation for cruelty, shepherds her son to the plantation from which she had come, to Massa Alf Pearson (presumably John's father) in Notasulga, a nearby town: "Tell im whose boy you is and maybe he mought put yuh tuh work." In addition to putting John to work, the former slaveowner allows him to attend school. In the environment of Notasulga, the future John Pearson is born. He develops a new sense of pride and accomplishment, through learning, and an ability to perform the most difficult and hardest tasks. He meets his future wife, Lucy Potts, and, after a brief sojourn from the plantation, returns to marry her against the wishes of her parents. Yet, the character flaw, so necessary to John's tragic denouement, appears. What elements of the tragic personality might a black man in the southland of the nineteen thirties possess? Pride, arrogance, or excessive jealousy leading to self-destruction were not possible for most Blacks. And though excessive pride, coupled with indecision, had served [Nella] Larsen well in *Quicksand,* for her male character, Miss Hurston had something else in mind. To find a clue to her thinking is to return to the letter to James Weldon Johnson, to the passage: "I see a preacher as a man outside of his pulpit and so far as I am concerned he should be free to follow his bent as other men." Take into account the sexual promiscuity of Pearson, and the conclusion seems to be that the "bent of other men" concerns sex. Whether intended or not, it is this flaw in Pearson's character that eventually brings about his downfall.

Due to his sexual promiscuity—postmarital affairs with women on the plantation—John is forced to leave. He travels to Florida, where he begins life anew. For a while, the John of old returns, sober, and hard working, apparently cured of the disease of sexual promiscuity. He sends for his wife and children and, due to Lucy's strength and loyalty, moves from town carpenter to minister of the town church and on into the church hierarchy, becoming pastor of an even larger church, to town mayor, and moderator of the State Association of Ministers. The key to his meteoric rise is Lucy, whose contribution is noticed in the words of Pearson's opponent: ". . . If me and him wuz tuh swap wives Ah'd go past im so fast you'd think it de A.C.L. passing uh go'her." Yet the flaw in John's character again asserts itself. Lucy senses the return of John to the ways of old: "a little cold feeling impinged upon her antennae. There was another woman."

Lucy, because of her loyalty, courage, and perseverance, stands out as the dominant character in the novel. Not as artificially conceived as the women of the novels of Nella Larsen and Jessie Fauset, nor the frivolous caricatures of the novels of Chesnutt, Griggs, and Dunbar, Lucy is the black woman come to maturity in a new South and a new age. Fidelity and courage are her chief characteristics, her willingness to suffer for her man and her children, an important element in her makeup as a black woman. Viewing her during these troubling times, the reader is made aware that only some supernatural force, something which defies Lucy's ability to combat it, can make complete the tragic ending of John Pearson, can enable him to bring about his own destruction. Here the old South exists even amid evidence of change. At the point where Lucy has brought the sinner to the altar of redemption, when he has broken his ties with "the other woman," Hattie Johnson, Hattie turns to the remedies of old, engages the assistance of the conjure woman, An' Dangie, in the battle for John Pearson's affections. "Stan over de gate whar he sleeps and eat dese beans and drop de hulls 'round yo' feet. Ah'll do de rest."

Lucy, woman of the future, unable to wage successful warfare against the forces of the past and incapable of redirecting the energy of her husband, after a long illness, goes to her grave. Following immediately upon her death, the countdown begins for John Pearson. He marries Hattie Johnson. The once neat home of Lucy and the well-cared-for children fall into disarray. Through innuendo and character assassination, his enemies dispossess him of his positions: moderator of "The Association" and pastor of the church. He turns to carpentry, his old profession, and discovers that the townspeople will not allow him to work. Hattie, like Lucy, a victim of his sexual license, yet lacking the latter's loyalty and patience, deserts him. Finally, he is forced to leave the town of his rise and fall.

The novel might have ended here. Miss Hurston is intent, however, upon making even more pronounced the mortal flaw in Pearson's character. The former minister leaves the town and the past behind him and settles in another, not far distant from the former. Here he meets Sister Lovelace, an older version of Lucy, and begins his rise once again. Yet success in a new town and recognition as a businessman and devoted husband are all jeopardized by the former minister's obsession with sex. Having journeyed to the former town once again and betrayed Sister Lovelace, his new wife, it seems only natural that his final end, his tragic denouement involve the old and new South: "The ground-mist lifted on a Florida sunrise as John fled homeward. The car droned ho-o-ome and tortured the man. False pretender: Outside show to the world. Soon he would be in the shelter of Sally's presence. Faith and no questions asked. He had prayed for Lucy's return and God had answered with Sally. He drove on but half-seeing the railroad from looking inward . . . the engine struck the car squarely and hurled it about like a toy."

Despite structural and formal defects, *Jonah's Gourd Vine* is most important for its depiction of the character of the black woman. Lucy is far from being completely developed as a character. She does, however, contain elements seldom seen in fiction by men which feature black women. Moreover, Miss Hurston, in her portrayal of Lucy, has begun early to deal with the conflict between black men and women, which receives fuller explication in Chester Himes's *Lonely Crusade* and John Williams' *Sissie* later in the century. The conflict centers around two victims of the same oppressive society. Take John and Lucy as metaphors of black men and women. John, unlike his stepfather, the former slave, is set free in a world which denies him the normal route for the pursuit of manhood. According to Miss Hurston, therefore, he must prove his manhood by having sexual relationships with women other than his wife. He has discovered, in other words, that the black man's route to manhood lay in the exploitation of black women. For no other men in the Euro-American society is this true.

It is not too far wrong to suggest that despite Miss Hurston's fondness for John, in him she has substantiated the theses concerning the black man's overt sexuality; if not more sexually potent than other men, he is assuredly more promiscuous. Thus, John, the metaphor of black men, remains, for Miss Hurston, essentially a creature of appetite, insatiable even though offered such a delectable morsel as Lucy Pearson. Her loyalty, perseverance, and love border upon the messianic. What her husband lacks in courage, strength, and initiative, she more than compensates for. The conflicts, therefore, given such personalities can be resolved only when black men correct the defects in character. That this was the author's implicit commentary upon black men might be attributable to her distorted conception of them. The chances are, however, that she was less interested in John Pearson than in Lucy, less interested in the men of her novels than in the women, who receive more multidimensional treatment.

In *Jonah's Gourd Vine* and *Their Eyes Were Watching God,* she views them as modern women, patterned upon paradigms of the past, those of the courage and strength of Harriet Tubman and Sojourner Truth. Far from being the images of old, the willing copartners of white men in the castration of black men, her women are, instead, the foundations of a new order, the leavening rods of change, from whose loins will eventually come the new man. Past stereotypes aside, therefore, her women need only search for greater liberation, move even beyond the stoiclike devotion of a Lucy Pearson, move toward greater independence and freedom. Put another way, black liberation meant burying the old images and symbols that had circumscribed black women along with black men. What is needed, McKay had argued in Banjo, is "women that can understand us as human beings and not as wild oversexed savages." In the context of *Jonah's Gourd Vine* and *Their Eyes Were Watching God,* this meant that both sexes must move collectively outside of American history and definitions. The race, Miss Hurston might have amended Du Bois' statement, will be saved by its liberated black women.

Much of her second novel, *Their Eyes Were Watching God* (1937), centers around the theme of the liberated black woman. In *Jonah's Gourd Vine,* Lucy Pearson, though an improvement over women in previous black novels, is, nevertheless, still the picture of loyalty and devotion. She is a woman hovering always near rebellion and assertion of individuality, yet she lacks the determination or, perhaps, desire to break completely with past mores and folkways. Janie Starks, the central character of Miss Hurston's second novel, has no such problem. She is a more completely developed character, and like her male counterparts in the fiction of McKay and Fisher, capable of moving outside the definitions of both black and white imagists. The problem confronting Janie is presented by her grandmother, aged relic of the past: ". . . de white man is de ruler of everything as fur as ah been able tuh find out. Maybe its some place way off in de ocean where de black man is in power, but we dont know nothin but what we see. So de white man throw down de load and tell de nigger man tuh pick it up. He pick it up because he have to, but don't tote it. He hand it to his womenfolks. De nigger women is de mule uh de world. . . ." The tension set up between adhering to this designation and rebelling against it constitutes the major conflict of the novel.

In rebelling against the definition of black women and moving to assert her own individuality, Janie must travel the route of tradition. The ending of *Their Eyes Were Watching God,* therefore, is in the beginning, and the novel, which gains its immediacy through first-person narration, merges past and present through use of flashbacks. In the opening pages of the novel, Janie, the outsider, returns to tell her own story. She left the town

of Eatonville with Tea Cake, happy-go-lucky gambler and part-time worker
who, said the townspeople, was "too young for her." For them, such an act
constituted rebellion against old and accepted standards of conduct. For
Janie, however, rebellion has brought about a dignity and stature unknown
before, has transformed her from a dreamer to an activist, has enabled her
to participate in experiences unusual for women of her time.

Consider her background before Tea Cake. A beautiful octoroon, who,
aided by her grandmother and constant association with white children, is
made early to believe that she differs from other Blacks, that the image to
which she must aspire is one of ". . . sittin on porches lak de white madam.
Dats what she wanted for me—don't keer whut it cost. . . ." Thus to
become like "de white madam," Janie married men, modeled in the image
of the master of the big house. First there was Logan Killicks, who, master
of over sixty acres of land, offers security, status, and protection, but not
love. After her grandmother passes away, Janie evidences the first sign of
rebellion: "The familiar people and things had failed her. . . . She knew
now that marriage did not make love. Janie's first dream was dead, so she
became a woman."

Killicks, however, is only the first stop along the path to complete
rebellion. The next, the most important, is Joe Starks. Egotistical, avari-
cious, and ambitious, he is a wealthy businessman, mayor of the small town
of Eatonville, and a man who is close to the image of the master in the big
house: "Take for instance that new house of his. It had two stories with
porches, with bannisters and such things. The rest of the town looked like
servants quarters surrounding the 'big house.' . . . It made the village feel
funny talking to him—just like he was somebody else." Years with Joe
Starks, however, convince the octoroon that the image depicted in the
philosophy of her "Nanny" was one of stagnation and circumscription, one
which denied freedom. This realization, long before Starks's death, had
caused "her image" of him to come tumbling down, to shatter. And yet
". . . looking at it she saw that it never was the flesh and blood of her
dreams." Joe Starks's death does not fill her with remorse but, on the
contrary, brings a feeling of relief. It is not, she related, that I worry over
"Joe's death, I just loves this freedom."

Freedom is a man named Tea Cake. Like Janie, he is an outsider and
in the eyes of the townspeople a ne'er-do-well, who has no business becoming
familiar with "somebody lak Janie Starks." Janie, however, is somebody like
Tea Cake. His search for a life-style outside that prescribed by tradition is
as determined as hers. His commitment to a life of chance, to living by the
roll of the dice, to moving outside of conventional values, stirs the rebellious

spirit in Janie, enables her to move completely outside the prescriptions of past mores: "So us is goin off somewhere and start all over in Tea Cake's way. Dis ain't no business proposition, and no race after property and titles. Dis is uh love game. Ah done lived Granma's way, now ah means tuh live mine." For Janie, this means to live a life-style which runs the gamut from gambling dives to bean picking, traveling from one end of Florida to the other. The rewards are that she is able, finally, to obey the inner voice, to experience things she "wanted to see and know." Tea Cake is cast in the mold of such vagabonds as Ray and Banjo and, thus, is not only capable of accepting Janie's new-found freedom as a woman, but of encouraging it. Adventures with Tea Cake complete the liberation of Janie Starks. At this point, she is ready to return to Eatonville, to tell her tale, to become a symbol of rebellion for others. Thus, the separation of Janie and Tea Cake is required.

The two are separated when Tea Cake meets death at the hands of Janie. During a hurricane and a flight down river in a "two hundred miles an hour wind" when "the sea was walking the earth with a heavy heel," Tea Cake is attacked and bitten by a wild dog. A few weeks after the hurricane, evidences of rabies appear. In an accompanying maddened seizure he attacks Janie, who reluctantly shoots him. Freed by a judge and jury who label the shooting incident as self-defense, she returns home. The little girl who played with white children so often that she became confused about her identity, who accepted, in part, a definition of herself, handed down from tradition via her grandmother and reinforced by the actions of the two husbands she outlasted, finally broke free of the images offered by both whites and Blacks, moved to validate her own womanhood in new terms. Neither sexual object, nor shallow imitation woman of the big house, she emerged from the novel as modern black woman, as strange and alien to American thought as the new men of the literature of McKay and Fisher.

Their Eyes Were Watching God, a novel of intense power, evidences the strength and promise of African-American culture. Miss Hurston, like Fisher, Toomer, Hughes, and McKay, went to the proletariat to seek values, to create and recreate images and symbols that had been partially obliterated or distorted through years of white nationalist propaganda. Her characters were outsiders in America because they were the inheritors of a culture different from that of others. It is true that, unlike Bita Plant, they have no Banana Bottom to which to return, are incapable at this point in time of recognizing the existence of the god, Obeah. They remain, however, oblivious as well to the gods of the Euro-Americans and are thus nomads in a world where identity for black people is founded upon the theology of such modern-day saints as Vachel Lindsay and Carl Van Vechten.

Yet the novel functions as an antithesis to *Nigger Heaven.* For Miss Hurston's characters, sex, atavism, joy, and pleasure do not constitute the essence of a people who must continually wage warfare for their very existence. The Lasca Sartorises and the Scarlet Creepers are revealed not only as vicious stereotypes when measured against Tea Cake and Janie but as cruel figments of the white imagination, created in order to enslave men anew. In addition, the novel also repudiates the values and images bequeathed black literature in the works of Johnson and Fauset. Fidelity to Euro-American values, to prosperity and status, are equally as enslaving and debilitating: Irene Redfield, a symbol of the new slavery in much the same way that Lasca Sartoris is. Both sanction an identity based upon stereotypes of the past; neither, like Janie Starks, is capable of "hearing the murmur of underground voices." For Miss Hurston, therefore, the path to liberation is not to be found in either the surrealistic hell of *Nigger Heaven,* or in the sterile imitative heaven of *There Is Confusion.*

Janie Starks, however, is not the completion of the new paradigm, but only evidence of an important beginning. After returning to the town from which her search for freedom began, she remains an outsider and yet is not able to continue her rebellion beyond the immediate present. Like Tea Cake, she, too, is dead to the realities of the world in which she lives. For though the white world remains more symbol than actuality for her, it is in actuality that it is oppressive. Thus the questioning, restless spirit which led to rebellion against the tradition that circumscribes her, due to race and sex, must lead her to challenge the equally restrictive patterns that deny physical freedom. This was the task of writers more talented and more angry than Miss Hurston, and that Janie Starks does not measure up in this respect, detracts neither from her importance as a character nor from the importance of *Their Eyes Were Watching God.*

The novel, over-all, is a fitting document with which to begin a final discussion of the Harlem Renaissance. Coming six years before *Native Son,* it marks the end of a period in African-American literature, in which the black writer engages once again in the task of freeing the minds of men from the stultifying images created in the works of the descendants of Page, Harris, and Dixon. It suggests that before men can move outside of the traditions and mores which seek to enslave them anew, they must become outsiders in the true sense of the term. Salvation for black people can come, therefore, only when they have taken the existential plunge outside canons which affront man's sense of decency and justice: To be an outsider is to be removed from the paradigms of the past and to be one with men, from ancient times to the present day, whose history and culture have been distinguished by a hatred of injustice and oppression and who have fought, long and hard, against man's tyranny, physically or mentally, against man.

Thus the critical reporters who place the death of the Harlem Renaissance movement in 1929—the date of the stock market crash—were no more accurate than those who argue that it continues to the present day. More accurately, not only did Fisher, McKay, and Hurston carry on the spirit of the movement well into the thirties but of all the blows dealt against it none were powerful enough to inflict a death blow until the publication of *Native Son* in 1940. This is not to minimize the effects of the forces that sought to topple the movement, forces which ranged from the lack of clearly defined ideological perspectives, on the part of the writers themselves, to the stock market crash which brought on the depression. There was no single ideological premise adhered to explicitly by one writer or another, and the internecine warfare that raged between proponents of varying literary ideas has been recorded in such works as "The Negro Artist and the Racial Mountain," *A Long Way from Home,* and *Infants of the Spring.*

This lack of ideological agreement was coupled with the dependence of most of the writers upon white sponsorship, and though this support was not as widespread as often believed, it was important enough to preclude ideological unanimity. Along with dependence upon white sponsorship were too many interracial parties at which literary discussion of the kind designed to foster independent black creativity was hardly forthcoming. The stock market crash which heralded the collapse of the American economy, therefore, only pointed up the major weaknesses of the movement, the inability of the people involved for instance to establish publishing institutions of their own. Because they were in hock to white publishers, once the depression was under way and the vogue in things "Negro" had ended, contracts for new books by black authors were few. All of these were contributing factors to the demise of the movement; none, however, in and of itself was sufficient. For the final deathblow, one must turn to Richard Wright and *Native Son,* while proper credit must be given the Renaissance writers for helping to pave the way for the efforts of Wright and his followers.

Their interests in black culture, their attacks upon the imagists, though tacit and not co-ordinated or sustained from one work to another, and their insistence upon new directions for black writers created the atmosphere for *Uncle Tom's Children* and *Native Son* and made acceptable the existence of the outsider. The works of Wright and his followers are indebted to the cultural foundation established by these writers—one that sought a value system from within the black community. At the apex of this system is a fidelity to a black life-style as lived by the urban black poor, one that demanded literature capable of exploiting the problems and concerns of that vast majority of Blacks unable to approximate the Euro-American norm. Out of this life-style had come courage, endurance, and rebellion against things as they were, and it is these which become the salient characteristics of black characters in the fiction of 1940 and beyond. Moreover, the assault upon the new images created by the early twentieth-century propagandists had been launched, though not often so vigorous or calculated as one might have wished. Still, the characters of Hughes, McKay, Fisher, and Hurston, despite their limitations, were antithetical to those in the works of their white contemporaries.

In refusing to sanction negative images which depicted black folks, the Renaissance writers continued the efforts begun by such novelists as Sutton Griggs and, in so doing, added to the importance and stature of the movement. Even the conservatives—Johnson, Fauset, Braithwaite, and Brawley— refused to accept in total, either socially or literarily, the images of black people offered up by Van Vechten. As ridiculous to the modern sensibility as many of the characters in the novels of Johnson and Fauset may be, they are attempts by the authors to unveil new images before the American public. Thus, *The Autobiography, There is Confusion,* and *Passing,* despite the intentions of their authors, only served to reinforce the argument that the search for black identity must begin with those characterized by Langston Hughes as the black poor, who care not "if they are like white people or any one else."

Here, among the poor, was the stuff of real tragedy; here the everyday themes which lead to a realistic art; here, still operative, though in muted form, the old cultural value systems that sustained a people for centuries. In the everyday world of the black proletariat was tragedy, hope, and faith, the ingredients of life which had helped to create the great art of the spirituals. Hughes, undoubtedly went too far in romanticizing them, for here, too, as first Miss Larsen and then Thurman demonstrated, are universal characteristics of avarice, enmity, and greed. Yet, the essence of the black man's major conflict against America—man torn between hope and despair in a world which held out promise, while every one of its institutions shouted the obverse—was enunciated more clearly here than anywhere else. In the streets of Harlem and in the cane fields of Georgia, the American dream lay prostrated; yet those who walked the streets and toiled in the fields clung to life and hope, refused to believe that man was less than what their biblical prophets had told them he was, continued to believe that at some time the veil would be rent and the victims would go free.

The return to the concerns of the black proletariat, initiated by Marcus Garvey, meant the departure by the novelist from the characters and themes of old. Gone were the aristocratic men and women of the novels of Frank Webb, Charles Chesnutt, and Sutton Griggs, and though the half-white imitations of the conservatives are still to be found in the latter part of the period, they are overshadowed by the representations of the black poor. All of this demanded a new sensibility and it is this, though not fully developed, that was most operative among the radicals. For however romantic and fanciful, Garvey's insistence upon a return to the glory of Ghana, Songhay, and Ethiopia, and Toomer and Hurston's championing of those who lived in the first home away from home was to return to an existence buried now in the recesses of memory. It was to return to a state of supposed racial innocence which meant to return to the cultural artifacts of long ago. For there was, as Imamu Baraka, among others, was to point out in the later years, a culture that had sustained Blacks long before and after the holocaust, and it is this culture which the best of the Renaissance writers sought to explore. In so doing, they were successful in moving the novel away from the path of assimilationism, to prevent once again the ascendancy of literature designed to make the black man a white everyman.

THERESA R. LOVE

Zora Neale Hurston's America

No analysis of the character of America is complete without a study of the institutions, values, and folkways of the approximately twenty-two million Americans who are of African descent, and, perhaps, no one has more effectively panned the Afro-American ingredients from the cultural alloy that is America's than has Zora Neale Hurston—anthropologist, folklorist, writer, and philosopher.

Born in Eatonville, Florida, on January 7, 1901, this daughter of a Baptist minister was so adept at anthropology that she was awarded a Guggenheim Fellowship in 1928 through the benevolence of Dr. Franz Boas, the famous anthropologist. She used the award to collect materials dealing with the traditional beliefs, legends, sayings, and customs of blacks. The outcome was two collections of tales, four novels, an autobiography, a stage play, and a number of essays, a canon important for those interested in Afro-American culture. While the main purpose of this paper is to show Miss Hurston's treatment of the folk materials which she collected, through a study of some of her essays, short stories and novels, particularly *Jonah's Gourd Vine,* readers will be able to discern her hopes and aspirations for her people as they live and die in their own social milieu.

When she agreed to study the folkways of those of African descent, Miss Hurston became one of a long line of blacks interested in preserving their heritage. Even during their captivity, there were those who tried to mold their African heritage into some tangible form which would express to subsequent generations whence they came. One such person was Gustavus

From *Papers on Language and Literature* 12, no. 4 (Fall 1976). © 1976 by the Board of Trustees of Southern Illinois University.

Vassa, who, in his *Narrative,* contrasts the idealistic value system of his Ibo
tribesmen with the materialistic values of European and American slave
traders. This burning desire to record their heritage led hundreds of Afro-
Americans to forge narratives recounting the anguish and hardships of those
who were brought to this country on slave ships, the cruelty and harshness
of American slavery, and the slaves' yearnings to escape.

These later narratives about slavery differ from that of Vassa in several
ways. Vassa tells of proud men who achieved a somewhat utopian society
in which slaves were treated as members of the family they served, whereas
narratives about American slavery stress its dehumanizing influence. Vassa
describes a highly structured social system based on the ideals of love and
loyalty; the later narratives show a people who are outside the mainstream
of the social structure with which they were perforce associated and whose
values have often been distorted into hatred and treachery. Vassa tells of a
people who have evolved a religious system which is an outgrowth of their
own civilization. The writers of the later slave narratives show either that
they have been entirely despoiled of the religion of their fathers, or that
they have concocted a mixture of the African religion and of Christianity
and have christened it "voodoo." (Katherine Dunham, the famous dancer
and anthropologist, who is a high priestess in this African religion, and
others who are prominent therein have decided that the French *voudoun* should
be used instead of the now vulgarized *voodoo.* I follow the modern term.) In
short, the descendants of the slaves who came from Africa lost their cultural
roots during the approximately two hundred years of their enslavement.

The loss of identity continued after the Civil War. As time went on,
many blacks denied anything pertaining to blackness. They rejected their
dark coloring and kinky hair. They endeavored to make the old Negro
spirituals sound like European anthems. They said that black writers should
not write about "low types" (meaning blacks of the lower social classes);
they warned that Paul Laurence Dunbar's use of black dialect did more harm
than good, since it did not present blacks in a "proper light." An understanding of what slavery and time did to Afro-Americans is important to
an understanding of Zora Neale Hurston, for these are the kinds of negative
attitudes which she abhorred.

It is impossible to say when one attitudinal climate ends and another
begins; however, it is generally concluded among historians that the race
riots at the time of, and following, World War I were a signal that a new
breed of blacks had arrived. They differed from their progenitors, loudly
proclaiming that they were proud of their color. Some disavowed any part
of America and said that they, like their leader, Marcus Garvey, wanted to

"return" to Africa. Others felt that they were too far removed from their original homeland to voice any claims to it; instead, they let it be known that they were Americans and that, as such, they were not going to be denied their place as contributors to its culture. They were also tired of being lynched, or butchered "like hogs," in the words of Claude McKay; therefore, they would not run, but like men they would "face the murderous, cowardly pack . . . dying but fighting back!" Millions, despairing of the results of racial tension in the South, moved to such northern cities as Chicago and New York.

A number of black writers migrated to New York about the same time—Claude McKay, Langston Hughes, and Zora Neale Hurston among them. These talented poets, novelists, dramatists, and essayists formed the nucleus of that literary movement which is commonly called the "Harlem Renaissance." Literary historians are apt to say that these representatives of "The New Negro" gathered in Harlem by accident, but Miss Hurston denies this. In her autobiography, *Dust Tracks on a Road,* she reports that they were invited there by Charles Spurgeon Johnson, who was just beginning *Opportunity,* the official organ of the Urban League. A sociologist, Johnson also encouraged Alain Locke and James Weldon Johnson to study black ancestral arts and culture and their relevance to the new consciousness.

The influence of Locke and Johnson on the younger writers cannot be overestimated. In his *New Negro,* the former enunciated the philosophy of the new blacks. James Weldon Johnson was one of the first to see the value of preserving black folklore. As early as 1912, he had already traveled throughout the South, collecting folk songs which he incorporated in his novel, *An Autobiography of an Ex-Colored Man.* Some believed that it was the duty of black artists to picture their race in the "best" possible light, thereby implying that only middle-class blacks were worthy of being depicted in art. In his novel Johnson shows his acceptance of the lower social classes— which in Europe would be called "the folk"—as a source for literary materials by pointing out that they constitute an opportunity unknown, in depicting the life, the ambitions, the struggles, and the passions of those of their race. In an effort to do just that, Johnson created what must surely be one of the most colorful characters in his novel, "Singing Johnson," the one-eyed lead singer at "big meetings," with his ability to "improvise at the moment lines to fit the occasion."

Credit must also be given to W. E. B. Du Bois for encouraging the Harlem Renaissance "literati," as Langston Hughes flippantly calls them, to seek out folk materials as a means of increasing racial awareness. Warning that there is an inherent danger in seeing oneself through the eyes of others,

Du Bois urged Afro-American writers to remember that "in art and literature, we should try to loose the tremendous emotional wealth of the Negro
and the dramatic strength of his problem through writing, the stage, pag-
eant, and other forms of art. We should resurrect forgotten ancient Negro
art and history, and we should set the black man before the world as both
a creative artist and a strong subject for artistic treatment." This belief of
Dr. Du Bois's is reflected in Langston Hughes's statement that one of the
aims of *Fire!!* [the literary magazine] was "to burn up a lot of the old dead
conventional Negro white ideas of the past, 'épater le bourgeois.' "

Miss Hurston took such pronouncements seriously. Her goal was not
merely to collect folklore but to show the beauty and wealth of genuine
Negro material. In doing so, she placed herself on the side of those who
saw nothing self-defeating in writing about the black masses, who, she felt,
are more imaginative than their middle-class counterparts. Consequently,
few of the latter are included in her works. Often, her characters work and
live in sawmill camps. Some are sharecroppers. Some work on railroads.
Most are uneducated and provincial. A statement from her short story, "John
Redding Goes to Sea," sums up their way of life: "No one of their community
had ever been farther than Jacksonville. Few, indeed, had ever been there.
Their own gardens, general store, and occasional trips to the county seat—
seven miles away—sufficed for all their needs. Life was simple indeed with
these folk." To the anthropologist, their economic and cultural isolation
made them the proper source for folk materials in their purest form.

While most of Miss Hurston's subjects are Floridians, many are West
Indians, for her interest in folklore led her to the Caribbean Islands, where
she again concentrated on the legends, superstitions, music, and dances of
the folk. She was especially intrigued by the blacks in the Bahamas, whom
she regarded as more prolific and better composers of music than their
American counterparts. And then there is Jelly, of "Story in Harlem Slang,"
the New York "pimp" who has his own variety of "racial prejudice," which
he describes to a friend in these words: "Man, I don't deal in no coal. Know
what I tell 'em? If they's white, they's right! If they's yellow, they's mellow!
If they's brown, they can stick around. But if they come black, they better
get way back!"

This passage suggests another important aspect of Zora Hurston's work.
Her decision to write about the ways of the folk necessitated her use of their
dialect as a means of achieving verisimilitude. Of course, the careful student
of a writer must always remember that the writer's rendition of a dialect
may or may not be authentic. Many writers are merely following a literary
tradition—that of attributing certain speech patterns to a given social or
ethnic group for artistic reasons. Inasmuch as most of Miss Hurston's char-

acters are represented as being speakers of Black Dialect, and inasmuch as she herself abandons her use of the General Dialect when she pictures herself as a researcher among those who speak the variant dialect, it would appear to be relevant to determine whether or not she is merely using a literary convention or is being scientific in her work as an anthropologist.

The following excerpt from *Mules and Men* reveals her use of the speech patterns of many blacks:

God was sittin' down by de sea makin' sea fishes. He made de whale and throwed dat in and it swum off. He made a shark and throwed it in and then he made mullets and cats and trouts and all swum on off.

De Devil was standin' behind him lookin' over his shoulder.

Way after while, God made a turtle and throwed it in de water and it swum on off. Devil says, "Ah, kin made one of those things."

God said: "Devil, Ah know you can't make none, but if you think kin make one go 'head and make it and Ah'll blow de breath of life into it for you."

You see, God was sittin' down by de sea, makin' de fish outa sea mud. But de Devil went on up de hill so God couldn't watch his workin', and made his outa high land dirt. God waited nearly all day befo' de Devil come back wid his turtle.

As soon as God seen it, He said, "Devil, dat ain't no turtle you done made."

Devil flew hot right off. "Dat ain't no turtle? Who say dat ain't no turtle? Sho it's a turtle."

God shook his head, says, "Dat sho ain't no turtle, but Ah'll blow de breath of life into it like Ah promised." . . .

So God blowed de breath of life into what de Devil had done made, and throwed him into de water. He swum out. God throwed him in again. He come out. . . .

God says: "See, Ah told you dat wasn't no turtle."

"Yes, suh, *dat* is a turtle."

"Devil, don't you know dat all turtles loves de water? Don't you see whut you done made won't stay in there?"

Devil said, Ah don't keer, dat's a turtle. Ah keep a 'telling you."

God disputed him down dat it wasn't no turtle. Devil looked it over and scratched he head. Then he says, "Well, anyhow it will go for one." And that's why we have gophers!

Even a cursory glance at this myth will show that the anthropologist and writer has been quite faithful in recording the speech patterns of her subjects. There are phonological deviations from those of the General Dialect: the substitution of the *d* sound for the *th* sound and that of *k* for *c* (kin); morphological features: the double negative ("Ah know you *can't make none*"); the inflection of strong verbs as if they were weak ("throwed"); overinflection ("All turtles love*s* water"); and the variant use of pronouns ("and scratched *he* head"). Yet there are other patterns which linguists have attributed to Black Dialect and which do not appear in this passage at all: the omission of the *s* signal as an indication of the third person singular present tense ("he eat") and the use of the pronominal appositive ("the gopher he couldn't stop"). These omissions are interesting because they represent two of the most frequently recurring features of the variant dialect. As a result, it would seem that Miss Hurston's use of Black Dialect forms substantiates the theory that she is willing to sacrifice her interest in anthropology—which discipline would emphasize the need for photographic descriptive passages—for the sake of artistic expediency. Otherwise her works might now be facing the same fate as those of Joel Chandler Harris, whose Uncle Remus tales are seldom read because of the difficulty which the modern reader has with the heavy, nineteenth-century Black Dialect in which they are written.

A careful student of Zora Neale Hurston must also distinguish between her use of slang and her use of dialect. In the short story in which Jelly appears, "Story in Harlem Slang," there is Black Dialect, but there is also "black slang." For example, there are these terms: "trying to jump salty," "gum beatin'," "ziggaboo," "coal scuttle blond," "conk buster," and "gut bucket" (meaning, respectively, "getting angry," "aimless talking," "a black person," "a black woman with very dark skin," "cheap liquor or an intellectual black," "low dive, a type of music.") Interestingly enough, these terms almost never appear in her novels, in which she is discussing the inhabitants of Florida, or in her books of folklore, but they do appear in this story about two Harlem pimps, who would like to think that they are irresistible to women, especially since they depend on women for a livelihood. They would also like to think that they have become more urbane since they have come north. They are not the simple, naïve men who watch girls from the porch of Joe Clark's store, which is the setting of most of Miss Hurston's works. They are, in the common vernacular, "hip." The writer thus gives them an appropriate vocabulary and thereby shows how skillfully she can combine her learning and her artistic abilities.

Langston Hughes has said that it was Miss Hurston's ability to adapt to circumstances which was the keystone of her success as an anthropologist.

This was an accurate observation, for when she first went back to Florida with a bachelor's degree, a new way of talking, expensive clothing, and a new Chevrolet, she was shunned by her former friends. It was not until she returned to her original speech and spread the rumors that her clothes were given to her by a former boyfriend and that the car was the fruit of her dealings as a bootlegger that she won their confidence. Then, and only then, did they invite her to the Saturday night dances at the "jooks," and to their story-telling sessions, which might occur anywhere and at any time but which were usually held on the porch of Joe Clark's store.

These "lies," as the tales were called, were of several kinds. Some centered around the exploits of a folk hero, John or Jack. They do not deal with an individual personality but with many who bear that name. John, a slave figure, recurs in varying types of situations which allow him to display the wit and cunning that enable him to overcome his enemies. "Ole Massa" underestimates John's cunning because he is blinded by his seeming humility and obedience, affections which allow John to pit himself successfully against stronger opponents. However, if circumstances warrant, he is not above using trickery. For example, in one tale John's horse is slaughtered by an unfeeling master because of a rumor that his slave has been mistreating the master's horse. Affecting acceptance of this injustice, John, who is a fortune-teller, skins the horse, cures its hide, wraps it around a stick, and goes about telling people that the hide can tell fortunes. Playing on the superstitions of many who are willing to have their fortunes told, John becomes a rich man. The master, not knowing the secret of John's success, assumes that he can do likewise. Consequently, he kills his own horse, cures its hide, and goes about trying to sell it for five thousand dollars. Not surprisingly, people assume that he is crazy. As time goes on, his greed, coupled with his blindness to John's tricks, leads to his death and thereby completes John's revenge.

Mules and Men, the tales which Joe Wiley, Jim Allen, Larkins White, and their friends tell the anthropologist, deals with a variety of other subjects. Many of the tales are based on Biblical situations. An example is a tale about a woodpecker, whose natural instinct to peck wood is stronger than Noah's warning that if he does not abstain from doing so, he will drill a hole in the ark and cause it to sink. As a result, Noah, angered by the bird's disobedience, bloodies his head with a sledge hammer, and "dat's why a peckerwood got a red head today." The possum also incurs an unfortunate incident with Ham, Noah's son, who loves to play the banjo and the guitar. During the great flood, Ham runs out of strings for his instruments, and so he goes down into the hold of the ship, finds the possum, and shaves the hairs off its tail, and that is why the possum's tail is without hairs today. In another tale, God is sympathetic to the snake, whom he suffers to crawl on the ground to ornament it. When men start treading on the defenseless creature, however, God gives him poison to protect himself. He also gives him rings to rattle, as a warning that man is near. This is done so that man may avoid stepping on him. Only when man does not heed the warning, may the snake strike. This last tale is designed to emphasize the mercy and justice of God. Many of the tales are moral lessons. Among them are those that show that selfishness and greed are punished, while virtue is rewarded. An example is a tale of a cat who eats nine fish, which are all of the food that a starving family and its dog possess. Eventually all die of starvation, except the cat who dies because he has eaten too much. When they reach heaven, God is so angry with the cat's selfishness and greed that he has his angels throw him out. The cat falls for nine days, "and there ain't been no cats in Heben since." The cat still has those nine lives in his belly and that is why "you got to kill him nine times before he'll stay dead."

Big Sweet, one of the few female story-tellers in Miss Hurston's works, recounts the tale of a man whose only virtue is his love of birds, especially mockingbirds, whom he always befriends. Because he so often gets into fights and kills people, he is sent to Hell when he dies. The birds are distressed that their friend has come to such a sad end, and they decide to quench the fires of Hell by dropping sand on them. Of course, because of their small beaks, each bird can carry only one grain of sand at a time. As a result, their progress is slow. All tire except the mockingbirds, which still pitch their grains of sand into Hell every Friday. Their dedication to this task of freeing their friend is his reward for having been kind to their tribe when he was on earth, and thus his virtue is rewarded by the loyalty of his feathered friends.

Not all of the tales which Miss Hurston recounts in *Mules and Men* are based on Biblical situations, nor do all teach moral lessons. Some attempt to explain elemental matters; "Why the Waves Have Whitecaps" is one of the most moving and touching of these. This myth moreover, is important, for it reveals that a sympathetic bond exists between the huge bodies of water which carve Florida into a peninsula and the people who inhabit it. In the Hurston version Mrs. Wind and Mrs. Water try to outdo each other in bragging about their children. Each claims that hers are the more gifted. Eventually, Mrs. Water tires of Mrs. Wind's bragging and begins to hate Mrs. Wind's children so much that one day, when they come over to her house for a drink of water, she grabs them and drowns them all. The grief-stricken mother goes over the ocean calling them, and every time she does so, the white fringes of their caps rise, and that is why the sea waves have white caps, and so, "When you see a storm on de water, it's de wind and de water fightin' over dem children."

Many of the "lies" which Miss Hurston's friends told her show that they have the ability to laugh at themselves. One of these humorously explains why their race is black, and not yellow or red or brown or white like other races. In the beginning of time, God made people, but He did not finish them completely. For example, He left off hands, feet, ears, and the like. Then, on certain days, he would call all of the partially made bodies together to hand out a certain part. Finally, it was time to give out color. On the appointed day, all of the groups arrived but one. Consequently Gabriel and Raphael were sent to look for them and discovered a huge group of people asleep on the green grass under the "Tree of Life." When Raphael called, "They all jumped up, and they was so skeered they might miss sumpin', they begin to push and shove one 'nother, bumpin' aga'st all de angels and turnin' over footstools. They even had de th'one all pushed one sided. Amid clamor, God hollered, " 'Git back! Git back!' " Thinking that God was ordering them to get the color black, they all rushed forward and took it, and that is why the black man is black. Stories like these usually end in sayings like "My people! My people!" or "Aunt Hager's chillun!" terms which many blacks use as a sign of disapproval of the actions of some persons of their race.

Miss Hurston's interest in the heritage of blacks led her to the Caribbean Islands, and to Haiti in particular. There she became an initiate in the voudoun religion, and, as a result, was able to uncover many legends which are a part of it. These legends are recounted in her book, *Tell My Horse*. Some of them are about an extensive list of gods that are divided into two groups: the Rada or Arada, the "good" gods, who are said to have originated in Dahomey; and the Petrogods, who came to Haiti from the Congo or Guinea and are said to do evil work. Because he is so great and aloof from mankind, there are few legends about Damballa, the god of gods. It is known, however, that his symbol is the snake, his servant, and obviously a symbol of fertility and power. This mighty god must be worshiped by propitiating him with things which are considered beautiful or good— flowers, fruits, and sweets, for example. Temples dedicated to him must always face the East, but there must also be a door facing the West; the temples thus become symbols of his greatness, which encompasses the beginning and the end of being. Although Damballa, as the father of the gods, occupies the same position in the African religions as does Jupiter or Zeus in the Mediterranean pantheon, his behavior differs from Zeus's, for while

Damballa does practice polygamy, there are no legends about his extravagant seductions of women such as exist with regard to his Mediterranean counterpart. This is not to say that Damballa does not "ride a large number of horses." (A god is said to "ride a horse" when he possesses a person; the term in voudoun has a sexual connotation.) The point is that he is viewed with respect when he chooses to possess those who attract his attention. He is not the anthropomorphic king of the gods of Greek and Roman legends. He is a god who must be worshiped at a distance.

This awe is not inspired by Damballa's female counterpart, Erzulie, who is closer to the popular conception of the Greek and Roman goddesses than she is to the Hebraic conception of divinity. The ideal mistress of the love-bed, she claims all the men of Haiti as her husbands. While some men vow to serve her of their own accord, many are chosen by this beautiful mulatto, who demands that they be faithful. She is satisfied to share those who are already married when they vow to be hers, provided that they absent themselves from their mortal wives at certain times, but those who are unmarried when they become her husbands must remain single forever, since she is so jealous that she might retaliate by causing physical, mental, or economic suffering.

Not all of the legends of the African religions deal with the lives of gods or goddesses. Some deal with human beings such as the beautiful mulatto, Marie Leveau, the queen of "conjure," whose likeness hangs in the Cabildo, in New Orleans. Marie's grandmother and mother were great practitioners of voudoun, but she wanted no part of their calling, since she preferred to dance and make love. Be that as it may, Marie was not destined for such a carefree life, and so when a snake crawled into her bedroom and spoke to her, she went to study under the tutelage of Alexander, a famous prophet, or "two-headed man" as such persons are often called. (Persons who are gifted psychically are said to be "two-headed." Because they are visionaries, they are thought to have "twice as much sense" as other people.) The results are that she became a legend. Her remarkable works brought her fame and renown. The rich and the powerful, seeking help, came from all over America to her house on St. Anne Street. Even Queen Victoria sent her gifts and asked for help.

But Marie never gave up her love of dancing. On the first Friday night in each month, she gave a dance in Congo Square. She would not dance herself, but others would come from far and near, and they would beat the drum with the jaw bone of an ass, eat crab gumbo and rice, and dance. White people would come to see the spectacle, which they mistook for a voudoun dance, not realizing that voudoun dances are always private. The police also did not know the difference between Marie's dances and religious dances, and so, hearing so much about her works and her dances, they came to arrest her, for the practice of voudoun was prohibited by law in New Orleans. At first, they sent a single policeman, who started turning round and round when Marie stretched out her left hand. Someone led him away. Then the police sent two of their group, who started running and barking like dogs when a curse fell on them. Finally, the whole police force came. The sorceress, knowing that they were coming before they arrived, went to her altar and prayed. Consequently, when they reached her steps, they all went to sleep.

Even the deeply wrinkled waters of Lake Pontchatrain were subject to Marie's powers. Once, on the Eve of St. John's, she arose out of the lake with a candle in each hand, walked toward the shore, and then submerged herself again—all in view of hundreds of people. When the time of her death drew near, the rattlesnake which had come to announce her calling came again, and there, at the foot of her altar, he died. Three days later, Marie sat before her Great Altar, the sky grew steel gray, the lightning skipped across the earth, Lake Pontchatrain rose in great heave, and Marie died—or so Miss Hurston was told by Turner, a pupil of the famous two-headed woman.

The frequent religious and moral flavor of the myths and legends of black people might be taken as an indication that religion plays a strong part in their lives, and, certainly, the works of Zora Neale Hurston would seem to suggest that she thought so herself. Any discussion of her attitude toward the religious practices of blacks must, however, take into account the fact that she makes a distinction between those who practice true Christianity and those who are hypocrites.

The distinction is made clear when one studies the behavior of the men and women who throng the "jooks" on Saturday night, as contrasted to those whom she pictures as frequenting the churches on Sundays. (A "jook," a term invented by the Eastern press, is a place of entertainment, a bar; it rhymes with *book* or *hook*.) The former drink, swear, and carry switch blades, which they use at the drop of an epithet; yet they are the epitome of kindness and love. For example, Big Sweet in *Mules and Men* is pictured as preferring jooks to churches, but there is no one who is more loyal and true than she. In fact, it is she who helps Zora Neale escape the knife of the jealous Lucy, for when Big Sweet gave her word that "I aims to look out for you . . . do your fighting for you," she meant it, and nobody bothers Big Sweet, not even the Quarters Boss, for she is so tough that if God gives her a pistol, she will send him a man.

In Miss Hurston's fiction, few examples of such devout love can be found among those characters who profess to be Christians, for she depicts many of them as being full of greed and malice. The incident in *Mules and Men* dealing with the traveling preacher and his two women companions— one on his left side and one on his right—may serve as an illustration. One evening, when the sun had set behind the living quarters of the sawmill workers and when their children had finished playing "Shoo-round," and "Chick-mah-chick," the "stump beater," as the novelist calls him, and his two females come walking into the area. After the woman on his left has sung "Death Comes a Creepin'," he announces his text, "Behold de Rib!" His message is that since God made the first woman from a man's rib, He means for men and women to work side by side—not one before, nor one behind, just side by side. When he has delivered this profound message, the preacher takes up a collection and leaves. Miss Hurston's satirical tone suggests that he was called to preach by hard work in the sun, as one of the quarters-women puts it, rather than by God.

Again, the churchgoers in *Jonah's Gourd Vine* are additional examples of Miss Hurston's attack on the belief that all blacks are basically religious, for she draws a fine line between those who profess adherence to the principles of Christianity and those who practice them. Although Big Sweet does not belong to a church, she has a large measure of love for mankind. On the other hand, the deacons of Zion Hope, the Reverend John Pearson's church in *Jonah's Gourd Vine,* are conniving and treacherous. They are entirely without mercy as they gossip about their pastor's illicit relations with women. These middle-class churchgoers are as malicious as the spiteful Miriam and the other Israelites whom Moses leads to freedom in Miss Hurston's novel, *Moses, Man of the Mountain.* Thus the novelist shows that, while it is true that many blacks profess Christian leanings, they differ greatly in the quality of their religious practices.

Zora Neale Hurston is so well known as a folklorist that her work as a novelist and as an essayist is often overlooked. Yet it is necessary to go to her novels and to her essays to recognize that she is also a philosopher who believes that personal and social happiness depends upon the practice of the central Christian virtue, love. The treatment of the minister in *Jonah's Gourd Vine* is an example of the sorrow and hurt which result from one who is incapable of love. Any analysis of the motives and actions of John Pearson must take into account that he is none other than the novelist's father, John Hurston.

John Hurston, like John Pearson, was a mulatto whose basic weakness was the inability to control his sexual desire for women. Although John

Pearson is married to a lovable and faithful wife, Lucy, his weakness causes him to neglect her when she needs him—for example, when she is in the act of childbirth. His tragic flaw eventually leads him to bankruptcy, among other things. As a result, his family suffers embarrassment and physical hardship. On the surface it seems that Miss Hurston defines his behavior as a basic weakness of character, but a closer scrutiny shows that her indictment of him goes further. The clue lies in his treatment of Lucy on her deathbed. Lucy had asked that the pillows remain under her head and that neither the clock nor the mirrors in the bedroom be covered until after her death. (The belief is that pillows should be taken from under the head of the dying so that they may die easily. Clocks and mirrors should be covered so as to deprive spirits of the opportunity of imprinting their images thereon.) Yet, in spite of her pleading eyes and in spite of Zora's entreaties, her father allows the women gathered around Lucy's death-bed to remove the pillows, and to cover clock and mirrors. To Miss Hurston her father's disregard for her mother's dying wish was symbolic of his disregard of his wife throughout their entire marriage. In *Dust Tracks on a Road* Miss Hurston questions whether he ever loved her mother: "I was to agonize over that moment for years to come. In the midst of play, in wakeful moments after midnight, on the way home from parties, and even in the classroom during my lectures. My thoughts would escape occasionally from their confines and stare me down."

Perhaps it is not too speculative to assume that the novelist was trying to come to grips with her negative conscious and subconscious feelings against her father when she created the Rev. John Pearson, whose behavior parallels that of his prototype. The minister is driven from his church because of his behavior. He then goes to another town and marries a good woman, who is as rich in charity and humility as she is in material wealth—all of which she lavishes on him. Within a year, he has not only become wealthy but has been called to another church. Through the love of his new wife and through the understanding and cooperation of his church members, he might have overcome his inherent weakness had he not met a persistent *femme fatale*, whose advances he is powerless to overcome. And so, once again, John Pearson, like John Hurston, betrays a woman who loves him, as well as a spiritual flock that looks to him for guidance. In utter despair, he drives onto a railroad track and is killed by a train, an act symbolic of his destruction by the worm which has continued to nibble away at his honest desire to be a good preacher and a faithful husband and father. Thus Miss Hurston, while not absolving her father for his bringing unhappiness to others and to himself, pictures his fall as the result of his inability to love.

The belief that love is a necessary ingredient in personal and social happiness may be seen in other novels and stories written by Miss Hurston. In the short story "The Gilded Six-Bits" Joe continues to love Missy May, his wife, although she has been unfaithful to him, just as Janie, in *Their Eyes Were Watching God,* continues to love her husband, Tea Cake, even though he has stolen a rather large sum of money from her. Conversely, in *Seraph on the Suwanee,* Miss Hurston's only novel in which the main characters are white, Arvay, an uneducated woman, is incapable of returning the love of Jim Meserve because he comes from an antebellum Georgia family of wealth and status. Frustrated because he cannot convince her of his good intentions, he leaves her. Thus, whereas the marriages of the two black couples hold fast in the face of adversity because of their love for each other, that of the white couple disintegrates because of the lack of it.

In the novel, Arvay is symbolic of persons who harbor prejudices of one kind or another. Not only is she hindered from having a meaningful relationship with her husband because of his superior social and economic background, she is also unable to relate to Joe, the black man whose loyal service is a main cause of her husband's financial success. Eventually, Joe goes into business for himself and is therefore replaced by a Portuguese, whom she also hates because he is a foreigner. After her husband has left her, she soon discovers that she needs Joe's son, who helps her handle her business so efficiently that she is able to forget her racial prejudices and to accept him as a personal friend. Her acceptance of him leads to her regeneration and thus to her understanding and appreciation of her husband, for it is not until Arvay is able to love her fellow men, without consideration of social and racial differences, that she is able to experience personal love.

Finally, Zora Neale Hurston has a special message for her people. Acknowledging that they have suffered many injustices, she insists that they turn from bitterness to hope. In one of her essays, "High John De Conquer," she recounts the legend of the African spirit who was brought to America by African slaves. A good spirit, he was always near when they needed him. Thus, when mothers were bereft of their babies by greedy slave traders, when scalding salt was poured on their backs which were trenched by strong leather straps, and when neither they nor their parents nor their parents before them could remember the royal-blue African skies, they endured because John the Conqueror was always there to give them hope. Some of Miss Hurston's friends told her that he went back to Africa after emancipation, since his work was done. Others said that he fused himself into a root where he waits to help the downtrodden, the needy, and the lovelorn. All they have to do is to find his hiding place, carry it in their pockets, or bury it in their hair, and immediately he will begin working.

Zora Neale Hurston never believed that "High John De Conquer" has gone back to Africa. Nor did she believe that he resides in some kind of root. She believed that he lives in the hearts of black men and that all they have to do is to call upon him. He will then bring them hope. Soon thereafter, they will find that they have love, and laughter too. Then they will overcome, which is the sum of her hope and aspirations for her people.

ALICE WALKER

A Cautionary Tale and a Partisan View

I became aware of my need of Zora Neale Hurston's work some time before I knew her work existed. In late 1970 I was writing a story that required accurate material on voodoo practices among rural southern blacks of the thirties; there seemed none available I could trust. A number of white, racist anthropologists and folklorists of the period had, not surprisingly, disappointed and insulted me. They thought blacks inferior, peculiar, and comic, and for me this undermined—no, *destroyed*—the relevance of their books. Fortunately, it was then that I discovered *Mules and Men,* Zora's book on folklore, collecting, herself, and her small, all-black community of Eatonville, Florida. Because she immersed herself in her own culture even as she recorded its "big old lies," i.e., folktales, it was possible to see how she and it (even after she had attended Barnard College and become a respected writer and apprentice anthropologist) fit together. The authenticity of her material was verified by her familiarity with its context, and I was soothed by her assurance that she was exposing not simply an adequate culture, but a superior one. That black people can be on occasion peculiar and comic was knowledge she enjoyed. That they could be racially or culturally inferior to whites never seems to have crossed her mind.

The first time I heard Zora's *name,* I was auditing a black literature class taught by the great poet Margaret Walker, at Jackson State College in Jackson, Mississippi. The reason this fact later slipped my mind was that Zora's name and accomplishments came and went so fast. The class was studying the usual "giants" of black literature—Chesnutt, Toomer,

From *Zora Neale Hurston: A Literary Biography.* © 1977 by the Board of Trustees of the University of Illinois. University of Illinois Press, 1977. Originally entitled "Foreword: Zora Neale Hurston—A Cautionary Tale and a Partisan View."

Hughes, Wright, Ellison, and Baldwin—with the hope of reaching LeRoi Jones very soon. Jessie Fauset, Nella Larsen, Ann Petry, Paule Marshall (unequaled in intelligence, vision, craft by anyone of her generation, to put her contributions to our literature modestly), and Zora Neale Hurston were names appended, like verbal footnotes, to the illustrious all-male list that paralleled them. As far as I recall, none of their work was studied in the course. Much of it was out of print, in any case, and remains so. (Perhaps Gwendolyn Brooks and Margaret Walker herself were exceptions to this list; they were both poets of such obvious necessity it would be impossible to overlook them. And their work—due to the political and cultural nationalism of the sixties—was everywhere available.)

When I read *Mules and Men* I was delighted. Here was this perfect book! The "perfection" of it I immediately tested on my relatives, who are such typical black Americans they are useful for every sort of political, cultural, or economic survey. Very regular people from the South, rapidly forgetting their southern cultural inheritance in the suburbs and ghettos of Boston and New York, they sat around reading the book themselves, listening to me read the book, listening to each other read the book, and a kind of paradise was regained. For Zora's book gave them back all the stories they had forgotten or of which they had grown ashamed (told to us years ago by our parents and grandparents—not one of whom could *not* tell a story to make us weep, or laugh) and showed how marvelous, and, indeed, priceless, they are. *This is not exaggerated.* No matter how they read the stories Zora had collected, no matter how much distance they tried to maintain between themselves, as new sophisticates, and the lives their parents and grandparents lived, no matter how they tried to remain cool toward all Zora revealed, in the end they could not hold back the smiles, the laughter, the *joy* over who she was showing them to be: descendants of an inventive, joyous, courageous, and outrageous people: loving drama, appreciating wit, and, most of all, relishing the pleasure of each other's loquacious and *bodacious* company.

This was my first indication of the quality I feel is most characteristic of Zora's work: racial health—a sense of black people as complete, complex, *undiminished* human beings, a sense that is lacking in so much black writing and literature. (In my opinion, only Du Bois showed an equally consistent delight in the beauty and spirit of black people, which is interesting when one considers that the angle of his vision was completely the opposite of Zora's.) Zora's pride in black people was so pronounced in the ersatz black twenties that it made other blacks suspicious and perhaps uncomfortable; after all, *they* were still infatuated with things European—*everything* European. Zora was interested in Africa, Haiti, Jamaica—and, for a little racial diversity (Indians), Honduras. She also had a confidence in herself as an individual that few people (anyone?), black or white, understood. This was because Zora grew up in a community of black people who had enormous respect for themselves and for their ability to *govern* themselves. Her own father had written the Eatonville town laws. This community affirmed her right to exist, and loved her as an extension of itself. For how many other black Americans is this true? It certainly isn't true for any that I know. In her easy self-acceptance, Zora was more like an uncolonized African than she was like her contemporary American blacks, most of whom believed, at least during their formative years, that their blackness was something wrong with them.

On the contrary, Zora's early work shows she grew up *pitying* whites because the ones she saw lacked "light" and soul. It is impossible to imagine Zora envying anyone (except tongue-in-cheek), and, least of all, a white person for being white. Which is, after all, if one is black, a clear and present calamity of the mind.

Condemned to a deserted island for life, with an allotment of ten books to see me through, I would choose, unhesitatingly, two of Zora's: *Mules and Men,* because I would need to be able to pass on to younger generations the life of American blacks as legend and myth, and *Their Eyes Were Watching God,* because I would want to enjoy myself while identifying with the black heroine, Janie Crawford, as she acted out many roles in a variety of settings, and functioned (with spectacular results!) in romantic and sensual love. *There is no book more important to me than this one.*

Having committed myself to Zora's work, loving it, in fact, I became curious to see what others had written about her. This was, for the young, impressionable, barely begun writer I was, a mistake. After reading the misleading, deliberately belittling, inaccurate, and generally irresponsible attacks on her work and her life by almost everyone, I became for a time paralyzed with confusion and fear. For if a woman who had given so much of obvious value to all of us (and at such risks: to health, reputation, sanity) could be so casually pilloried and consigned to a sneering oblivion, what chance would someone else—for example, like myself—have? I was aware that I had much less *gumption* than Zora.

For a long time I sat looking at this fear, and at what caused it. *Zora was a woman who wrote and spoke her mind—as far as one could tell, practically always.* People who knew her and were unaccustomed to this characteristic in a woman—one who was, moreover, (*a*) sometimes in error, and (*b*) successful, for the most part, in her work—attacked her as meanly as they could. *Would I also be attacked if I wrote and spoke my mind? And if I dared open my mouth to speak, must I always be "correct"? And by whose standards?* Only those who have read the critics' opinions of Zora and her work will comprehend the power of these questions to riddle a young writer with self-doubt.

Eventually, however, I discovered that I repudiate and despise the kind of criticism that intimidates rather than instructs the young; and I dislike fear, especially in myself. I did then what fear rarely fails to force me to do: I fought back. I began to fight for Zora and her work, for what I knew was good and must not be lost to us.

Robert Hemenway was the first critic I read who seemed indignant that Zora's life ended in poverty and obscurity, that her last days were spent in a welfare home, and that her burial was paid for by "subscription"; though Zora herself—as he is careful to point out in this book—remained gallant and unbowed until the end. It was Hemenway's efforts to define Zora's legacy and his exploration of her life that led me, in 1973, to an overgrown Fort Pierce, Florida, graveyard in an attempt to locate and mark Zora's grave. Although by that time I considered her a native American genius, there was nothing grand or historic in my mind. It was, rather, a duty I accepted as naturally mine—as a black person, a woman, and a writer—because Zora was dead and I, for the time being, was alive.

Zora was funny, irreverent (she was the first to call the Harlem Renaissance literati the "niggerati"), good-looking, and sexy. She once sold hot dogs in a Washington park just to record accurately how the black people who bought them talked. She would go anywhere she had to go—Harlem, Jamaica, Haiti, Bermuda—to find out anything she simply *had* to know. She loved to give parties. Loved to dance. Would wrap her head in scarves as black women in Africa, Haiti, and everywhere else have done for centuries. On the other hand, she loved to wear hats, tilted over one eye, and pants and boots. (I have a photograph of her in pants, boots, and broad-brim hat that was given to me by her brother Everette. She has her foot up on the running board of a car—presumably hers, and bright red—and looks racy.) She would light up a fag—which wasn't done by ladies then (and thank our saints, as a young woman she was never a lady) on the street.

Her critics disliked even the "rags" on her head. (They seemed curiously incapable of telling the difference between an African-American queen and Aunt Jemima.) They disliked her apparent sensuality: the way she tended to marry or not marry men, but enjoyed them anyway, while never missing a beat in her work. They hinted slyly that Zora was gay, or at least bisexual—how else could they account for her drive?—though there is not a shred of evidence that this was true. The accusation becomes humorous—and, of course, at all times irrelevant—when one considers that what she *did* write about was some of the most healthily rendered heterosexual loving in our literature. In addition, she talked too much, got things from white folks (Guggenheims, Rosenwalds, and footstools) much too easily, was slovenly in her dress, and appeared maddeningly indifferent to other people's opinions of her. With her easy laughter and her southern drawl, her belief in doing cullud dancing *authentically,* Zora seemed—among these genteel "New Negroes" of the Harlem Renaissance—*black*. No wonder her presence was always a shock. Though almost everyone agreed she was a delight, not everyone agreed such audacious black delight was permissible, or indeed, quite the proper image for the race.

Zora was before her time—in intellectual circles—in the lifestyle she chose. By the sixties everyone understood that black women could wear beautiful cloths on their beautiful heads and care about the authenticity of things cullud *and* African. By the sixties it was no longer a crime to receive financial assistance, in the form of grants and fellowships, for one's work. (Interestingly, those writers who complained that Zora "got money from white folks" were often themselves totally supported, down to the food they ate—or, in Langston Hughes's case, *tried* to eat, after his white "godmother" discarded him—by white patrons.) By the sixties, nobody cared that marriage didn't last forever. No one expected it to. And I do believe that now, in the seventies, we do not expect (though we may wish and pray) every black person who speaks to *always* speak *correctly* (since this is impossible); or if we *do* expect it, we deserve all the silent leadership we are likely to get.

During the early and middle years of her career Zora was a cultural revolutionary simply because she was always herself. Her work, so vigorous among the rather pallid productions of many of her contemporaries, comes from the essence of black folklife. During her later years, for reasons revealed for the first time in this monumental work (as so much is!), she became frightened of the life she had always dared bravely before. Her work, too, became reactionary, static, shockingly misguided and timid. This is especially true of her last novel, *Seraph on the Suwanee,* which is not even about black people, which is no crime, but *is* about white people who are bores, which is.

A series of misfortunes battered Zora's spirit and her health. And she was broke.

Being broke made all the difference.

Without money of one's own in a capitalist society, there is no such thing as independence. This is one of the clearest lessons of Zora's life, and why I consider the telling of her life a "cautionary tale." We must learn from it what we can.

Without money; an illness, even a simple one, can undermine the will. Without money, getting into a hospital is problematic, and getting out without money to pay for the treatment is nearly impossible. Without money, one becomes dependent on other people who are likely to be—even in their kindness—erratic in their support and despotic in their expectations of return. Zora was forced to rely, like Tennessee Williams's Blanche, "on the kindness of strangers." Can anything be more dangerous, if the strangers are forever in control? Zora, who worked so hard, was never able to make a living from her work.

She did not complain about not having money. She was not the type. (Several months ago I received a long letter from one of Zora's nieces, a bright ten-year-old who explained to me that her aunt was so proud that the only way the family could guess she was ill or without funds was by realizing they had no idea where she was. Therefore, none of the family attended either Zora's sickbed or her funeral.) Those of us who have had "grants and fellowships from 'white folks' " know this aid is extended in precisely the way welfare is extended in Mississippi. One is asked, *curtly,* more often than not: How much do you need *just to survive?* Then one is— if fortunate—given a third of that. What is amazing is that Zora, who became an orphan at nine, a runaway at fourteen, a maid and manicurist (because of necessity and not from love of the work) before she was twenty, *with one dress,* managed to become Zora Neale Hurston, author and anthropologist, at all.

For me, the most unfortunate thing Zora ever wrote is her autobiography. After the first several chapters, it rings false. One begins to hear the voice of someone whose life required the assistance of too many transitory "friends." A Taoist proverb states that *to act sincerely with the insincere is dangerous* (a mistake blacks as a group have tended to make in America). And so we have Zora sincerely offering gratitude and kind words to people one knows she could not have respected. But this unctuousness, so out of character for Zora, is also a result of dependency, a sign of her powerlessness, her inability to pay back her debts with anything but words. They must have been bitter ones for her. In her dependency, it should be remembered, Zora was not alone. For it is quite true that America does not support or honor us as human beings, let alone as blacks, women, or artists. We have taken help where it was offered because we are committed to what we do and to the survival of our work. Zora was committed to the survival of her people's cultural heritage as well.

In my mind, Zora Neale Hurston, Billie Holiday, and Bessie Smith form a sort of unholy trinity. Zora belongs in the tradition of black women singers, rather than among the "literati," at least to me. There were the extreme highs and lows of her life, her undaunted pursuit of adventure, her passionate emotional and sexual experience, and her love of freedom. Like Billie and Bessie she followed her own road, believed in her own gods, pursued her own dreams, and refused to separate herself from "common" people. It would have been nice if the three of them had had one another to turn to in times of need. I close my eyes and imagine them: Bessie would be in charge of all the money; Zora would keep Billie's masochistic tendencies in check and prevent her from singing embarrassingly anything-for-a-man songs, thereby preventing Billie's heroin addiction; in return, Billie could be, along with Bessie, the family that Zora felt she never had.

We are a people. A people do not throw their geniuses away. If they do, it is our duty *as witnesses for the future* to collect them again for the sake of our children. If necessary, bone by bone.

ROBERT E. HEMENWAY

Crayon Enlargements of Life

Their Eyes Were Watching God is a love story. The impetus for the tale came from Zora's affair with a man of West Indian parentage whom she had first met in New York in 1931 and then found again during her short-lived attempt at graduate school. The relationship was stormy, perhaps doomed from the first. He could not abide her career, but she could not break away. Her collecting trip with Lomax and her Guggenheim Fellowship were both intended to sever the relationship, to "smother" her feelings; both times her return brought them back together. As she admitted, "The plot was far from the circumstances, but I tried to embalm all the tenderness of my passion for him in *Their Eyes Were Watching God*."

This affair is instructive because it illustrates how Hurston used personal experience for her fiction. *Their Eyes Were Watching God* is autobiographical only in the sense that she managed to capture the emotional essence of a love affair between an older woman and a younger man. The prototype for the man, Tea Cake, was not a laborer, but a college student of twenty-three who had been a member of the cast for *The Great Day*. Handsome, lithe, muscular, he owned a smile that brightened rooms. But he was not a gambler and vagabond like Tea Cake; in fact, he was studying to be a minister, and the two of them held long conversations about religious issues. His quick intelligence and considerable learning no doubt attracted her as much as anything else. What Zora took from this relationship was the quality of its emotion: its tenderness, its intensity, and perhaps its sense of ultimate impossibility. Sooner or later it had to end, and when she left for the West

---

From *Zora Neale Hurston: A Literary Biography*. © 1977 by the Board of Trustees of the University of Illinois. University of Illinois Press, 1977.

Indies, she did so with a stoic toughness. The man she was leaving remembers
that outwardly she was calm and that he was left hurt and confused, wondering if she was "crying on the inside." She gave him her answer in *Their
Eyes Were Watching God.*

Whatever its personal matrix, Hurston's novel is much more than an
outpouring of private feeling. It is both her most accomplished work of art
and the authentic, fictional representation of Eatonville she had been struggling for in *Jonah's Gourd Vine.* The novel culminates the fifteen-year effort
to celebrate her birthright, a celebration which came through the exploration
of a woman's consciousness, accompanied by an assertion of that woman's
right to selfhood. By the time she wrote *Their Eyes Were Watching God*—or
perhaps in the act of writing it, struggling to reconcile public career and
private emotion—Zora Neale Hurston discovered one of the flaws in her
early memories of the village: there had usually been only men telling lies
on the front porch of Joe Clarke's store.

Their Eyes Were Watching God is about Janie Crawford, raised by her
grandmother to "take a stand on high ground" and be spared the traditional
fate reserved for black women as beasts of burden: "Ah been prayin' fuh it
tuh be different wid you," Nanny tells her granddaughter. The search to
fulfill through Janie her "dream of what a woman oughta be and to do"
leads to Logan Killicks, owner of sixty acres, a house, and a mule. Older,
looking "like a skullhead in de grave yard," Killicks marries Janie shortly
before the grandmother's death. When the marriage proves loveless, Janie
searches for something or someone to represent "sun-up and pollen and
blooming trees." She finds Joe Starks, an assertive, self-confident striver on
his way to Eatonville, Florida, the town made "all outa colored folks," where
a man can be his own boss. Joe intends to become a "big voice," and shortly
after their arrival he buys 200 acres of land, sets up a store, secures a post
office, and campaigns for mayor. Jody is the kind of man who has "uh throne
in de seat of his pants," who "changes everything, but nothin' don't change
him." He expects his wife to act like a mayor's wife, keep her place, sub-
ordinate herself to her master. The spirit of Janie's second marriage leaves
the bedroom and takes "to living in the parlor," and she finally reacts to
Joe's constant disparagement by publicly questioning his manhood. He dies
a short time later, bitter over her revolt, shaken by the challenge to his
authority.

Now a woman of means, Janie is beset by status-conscious suitors; but
she rejects her class role and falls in love with Vergible "Tea Cake" Woods,
a free-spirited laborer much younger than she. Tea Cake is a "glance from
God"; he teaches her "de maiden language all over." To Tea Cake, Janie is
the "keys to de kingdom."

Without the hypocrisy and the role-playing that characterized her other marriages, this love is strong enough to make both parties open and giving. Tea Cake accepts Janie as an equal. She travels with him from job to job, even though her money would enable them to settle comfortably in Eatonville. They eventually end up working happily together in the bean fields of the "muck," the rich black land reclaimed from Lake Okeechobee in the Everglades. Their bliss is short lived, for during their escape from a hurricane Tea Cake saves Janie but is bitten by a rabid dog. He develops rabies, and his illness drives him mad; eventually he attempts to shoot Janie. Reacting in self-defense, she shoots back, killing him, and then is tried and acquitted by a white jury. Janie is left at the end with the memories of a transcendent love and a wise awareness of its relativity. Yet she knows that Tea Cake will "never be dead until she herself had finished feeling and thinking."

This ending seems poorly plotted, and the narration shifts awkwardly from first to third person. But on the whole the novel is remarkable, with a consistent richness of imagery. Most critical commentary has either ignored this element or treated it superficially; yet the novel's effect depends largely upon the organic metaphors used to represent Janie's emotional life. The imagery is introduced early, when the sixteen-year-old Janie is at the moment of sexual awakening. Using a symbol which will reappear often, Hurston identifies Janie with a blossoming pear tree. To the girl stretched on her back beneath the tree, the tree seems to represent the mystery of the springtime universe: "From barren brown stems to glistening leaf-buds; from the leaf-buds to snowy virginity of bloom it stirred her tremendously. How? Why?" As she lies there, "soaking in the alto chant of the visiting bees," the mystery is revealed: "The inaudible voice of it all came to her. She saw a dust bearing bee sink into the sanctum of a bloom; the thousand sister calyxes arch to meet the love embrace and the ecstatic shiver of the tree from root to tiniest branch creaming in every blossom and frothing with delight. So this was a marriage! She had been summoned to behold a revelation. Then Janie felt a pain remorseless sweet that left her limp and languid."

The orgasm described here comes to represent the organic union Janie searches for throughout her life: she wants "to be a pear tree—any tree in bloom." Yet events conspire to deny her a feeling of wholeness. Her hand-picked husband, Logan Killicks, is a "vision . . . desecrating the pear tree." Joe Starks does not "represent sun-up and pollen and blooming trees," but he does speak for a new life away from Killicks; Janie mistakenly thinks that perhaps he can become "a bee for her bloom." After Joe refuses to recognize Janie's autonomy, she discovers that she has "no more blossomy openings dusting pollen over her man, neither any glistening young fruit where the petals used to be." Tea Cake, however, embodies the organic union of completion: "He could be a bee to a blossom—a pear tree blossom in the spring. He seemed to be crushing scent out of the world with his footsteps." Tea Cake's only material legacy is a package of seeds he had meant to plant before his death. Janie vows to plant them for remembrance, commemorating the organic unity of their marriage with a living monument.

This organic imagery permeates the novel and suggests a resolution of time and space, man and nature, subject and object, life and death. In an episode borrowed from "Mule Bone," Hurston tells of a local mule, legendary for its meanness, that dies and is given a burial by the village. Dragging the mule to the swamp, the town makes a "great ceremony" of the interment with speeches and singing; one man even imitates John Pearson preaching a funeral sermon. They mock "everything human in death," then leave the mule to the buzzards. In a surrealistic scene, startling in a realistic novel, Hurston reports on the buzzards' conversation as the birds pick out the eyes "in the ceremonial way" and then go about their feast. Some commentators have criticized this scene for being an imposition of folklore on the narrative; but it is as natural for buzzards to speak as for bees to pollinate flowers, as for a human being to be a "natural man." When not a part of the organic process of birth, growth, and death, one is out of rhythm with the universe. This is represented in the novel by Janie's dissociation of sensibility before she grows to consciousness. She discovers that "she had an inside and an outside now and suddenly she knew how not to mix them." She can sit and watch "the shadow of herself going about tending store and prostrating herself before Jody," but all the time "she herself is sitting under a shady tree with the wind blowing through her hair." Jody denies Janie participation in the mule's burial, and the restriction illustrates how she is out of touch with the cadence of nature. She tells Joe that "in some way we ain't natural wid one 'nother." Later, with Tea Cake, Janie feels in tune with natural process, just as she did under the pear tree as a child.

One might argue that Janie's finding the one true bee for her blossom is hardly a satisfactory response from a liberated woman. But the action is symbolic, demonstrating Janie's ability to grow into an adult awareness of self, and it is not until the imagery of the pear tree fuses with the motif of the horizon that this symbolic action is completed. Janie's romantic "dreams" of the pear tree are tempered by growth and time. What was thought to be the truth at puberty is gradually transformed by experience. Her childhood had ended when a neighbor boy failed to fulfill her romantic dreams. Killicks initiated her further, showing that "marriage did not make love. Janie's first dream was dead. So she became a woman." Joe Starks took Killicks's place, but Joe was a false dream too, "just something she had grabbed up to drape her dreams over." It is not until Tea Cake that her dream—now toughened by knowledge—can become truth. The reason is that Tea Cake suggests the horizon—he is the "son of Evening Sun"—and the horizon motif illustrates the distance one must travel in order to distinguish between illusion and reality, dream and truth, role and self.

Hurston claims at the beginning of the novel that men and women dream differently. For men, "ships at a distance have every man's wish on board. For some they come in with the tide. For others they sail forever on the horizon, never out of sight, never landing until the Watcher turns his eyes in resignation, his dreams mocked to death by time." Women, however, believe that the horizon is close at hand, willing it so: "Now women forget all those things they don't want to remember and remember everything they don't want to forget. The dream is the truth. Then they act and do things accordingly."

This complicated opening passage begins to make sense midway into the book, when Janie comes to an awareness that her grandmother has pointed her in the wrong direction:

> She had been getting ready for her great journey to the horizons in search of *people;* it was important to all the world that she should find them and they find her. But she had been whipped like a cur dog, and run off down a back road after *things.* It was all according to the way you see things. Some people could look at a mud-puddle and see an ocean with ships. But Nanny belonged to that other kind that loved to deal in scraps. Here Nanny had taken the biggest thing God ever made, the horizon—for no matter how far a person can go the horizon is still way beyond you—and pinched it in to such a little bit of a thing that she could tie it about her granddaughter's neck tight enough to choke her.

This second passage parallels the first in imagery and diction, demonstrating Janie's growing self-confidence in her own judgments and her realistic appraisal of her failed dreams. Only when thus prepared can she accept Tea Cake as an equal, without illusion, discovering love because she is finally accepted for herself. Tea Cake is certainly not an ideal husband, but he does grant Janie the dignity of self. On the final pages of *Their Eyes Were Watching God* Janie tells her friend, Pheoby, "Ah done been tuh de horizon and back and now ah kin set heah in mah house and live by comparisons." She has experienced the reality rather than dreamed it—"you got

tuh *go* there tuh *know* there," she says—which means that the novel can end
with an imagistic resolution of the distance between here and there, self and
horizon. Escaping from a horizon that can be tied tight enough to choke,
Janie peacefully gathers in the world: "She pulled in her horizon like a great
fish-net. Pulled it from around the waist of the world and draped it over
her shoulder. So much of life in its meshes! She called in her soul to come
and see."

Janie's poetic self-realization is inseparable from Zora's concomitant
awareness of her cultural situation. The novel also celebrates the black woman's liberation from a legacy of degradation. Janie's grandmother had given
wrong directions because of her historical experience; she wants her granddaughter to marry Logan Killicks because of her own slave memories: "Ah
didn't want to be used for a work-ox and a brood sow. . . . It sho wasn't
mah will for things to happen lak they did." Janie's mother was also born
into slavery, the offspring of the master, and Nanny had hoped that Emancipation would bring her daughter freedom. But she is raped by her schoolteacher, and Janie is conceived in the violence. Her mother leaves home a
ruined woman, destroyed in spirit. Janie is left with Nanny, who sees the
child as another chance: "Ah wanted to preach a great sermon about colored
women sittin' on high, but they wasn't no pulpit for me. . . . Ah been
waitin a long time, Janie, but nothin' Ah been through ain't too much if
you just take a stance on high ground lak ah dreamed." Nanny "can't die
easy thinkin' maybe de men folks white or black is makin a spit cup outa
yuh." To her, Logan Killicks is "big protection" from this vision; when
Janie complains about the absence of love, her grandmother responds, "Dis
love! Dat's just whut's got us [black women] uh pullin and uh haulin' and
sweatin' and doin from can't see in de mornin' till can't see at night."

Janie has, therefore, both a historical and a personal memory to react
against in her search for autonomy. Much of the novel is concerned with
her struggle to understand the inadequacy of her grandmother's vision. Tea
Cake is not the means to self-understanding, only the partner of Janie's
liberation from an empty way of living; she tells Pheoby: "Ah done lived
Grandma's way, now ah means tuh live mine." Asked to explain, Janie says,

> She was borned in slavery time when folks, dat is black folks,
> didn't sit down anytime dey felt lak it. So sittin' on porches lak
> de white madam looked lak uh mighty fine thing tuh her. Dat's
> whut she wanted for me—don't keer whut it cost. Git upon uh
> high chair and sit dere. She didn't have time tuh think whut tuh
> do after you got up on de stool uh do nothin'. De object wuz

tuh git dere. So Ah got up on de high stool lak she told me, but Pheoby, Ah done nearly languished tuh death up dere. Ah felt like de world wuz cryin' extry and Ah ain't read de common news yet.

The vertical metaphor in this speech represents Hurston's entire system of thought, her social and racial philosophy. People erred because they wanted to be *above* others, an impulse which eventually led to denying the humanity of those below. Whites had institutionalized such thinking, and black people were vulnerable to the philosophy because being on high like white folks seemed to represent security and power. Janie's grandmother had believed that "de white man is de ruler of everything as fur as ah been able tuh find out." She thinks that freedom is symbolized by achieving the position on high. Zora Hurston had always known, just as Janie discovers, that there was no air to breathe up there. She had always identified with what she called "the poor Negro, the real one in the furrows and cane breaks." She bitterly criticized black leaders who ignored this figure while seeking "a few paltry dollars and some white person's tea table." She once wrote that in her opinion some black leaders wanted most to be able to return from a meeting and say, "No other Negro was present besides me." This sense of racial pride had contributed much to *Their Eyes Were Watching God:* "I am on fire about my people. I need not concern myself with the few individuals who have quit the race via the tea table."

Zora Neale Hurston had spent an entire career chronicling the cultural life of "the Negro farthest down," the beauty and wisdom of "the people"; she did not find racial liberation in the terms of white domination, or selfhood for the black woman in the arrogance of male supremacy. Black people became free not by emulating whites, but by building from the cultural institutions of the black community; women discovered an organic relationship with men only when there was consent between equals. This is the key to Janie's relationship with Tea Cake. In their very first meeting Janie apologizes for not being able to play checkers; no one has taught her how. She is surprised to discover that Tea Cake wants her to play, that he "thought it natural for her to play." When she resorts to role-playing in the competition, coyly asking him not to jump her exposed king, he jumps anyway, applying the rules of the game equally. In similar fashion they share the labor of the fields and the hardships of migrant life. While Jody would not let her take part in storytelling sessions, with Tea Cake it is perfectly natural for her to be a participant in oral tradition: "The men held big arguments here like they used to do on the store porch. Only here she could listen and laugh and even talk some herself if she wanted to. She got so she could tell big stories herself from listening to the rest."

It is important to note that Janie's participation comes after she has learned to recognize sexism, a necessary preliminary to her self-discovery. In the lying sessions on Joe's store porch, the philosophy of male dominance, often a part of black folklore, was everywhere present. Somebody had to think for "women and chillun and chickens and cows." Men saw one thing and understood ten, while women saw ten things and understood none. Janie eventually informs this male enclave that they will be surprised if they "ever find out yuh don't know half as much about us as you think you do." Her later life with Tea Cake, freely contracted for, without illusion (Tea Cake can be sexist, too), is a natural result of this developing consciousness.

Janie's verbal freedom might not seem such an important matter on the surface, but the reader should remember Hurston's conception of the store porch as a stage for the presentation of black folklore. The one time in the novel Janie takes over this male sanctuary, she is praised by the storytellers for being a "born orator. Us never knowed dat befo'. She put jus' de right words tuh our thoughts." However, Joe's sense of wifely propriety does not permit her repeat performances, and although "Janie loved the conversation and sometimes she thought up good stories," her husband forbids her to indulge. The storytellers are "trashy," because they lack his drive. As Janie later realized, "Jody classed me off."

When Hurston writes of Eatonville, the store porch is all-important. It is the center of the community, the totem representing black cultural tradition; it is where the values of the group are manifested in verbal behavior. The store porch, in Zora's language, is "the center of the world." To describe the porch's activities she often uses the phrase "crayon enlargements of life"— "When the people sat around on the porch and passed around the pictures of their thoughts for the others to look at and see, it was nice. The fact that the thought pictures were always crayon enlargements of life made it even nicer to listen to." It is on the store porch that the lying competition takes place, "a contest in hyperbole and carried out for no other reason." Borrowing from the verbal competition over Daisy in "Mule Bone," Hurston uses the store porch as the center of a courtship ritual which provides the town with amusement. Yet "they know it's not courtship. It's acting out courtship and everybody is in the play." The store porch is where "big picture talkers" use "a side of the world for a canvas" as they create a portrait of communal values.

The rhythms and natural imagery which structure the novel refer not only to liberation from sexual roles, but also to the self-fulfillment inherent in this sense of community. Janie's "blossoming" refers personally to her discovery of self and ultimately to her meaningful participation in black tradition. Janie discovers a way to make use of the traditions of slavery—her grandmother's memories—not by seeking to "class off" and attempt to "sit on high" as the white folks did, but by celebrating blackness. She asks the color-struck Mrs. Turner, "We'se uh mingled people and all of us got black kinfolks as well as yaller kinfolks. How come you so against black?" June Jordan calls *Their Eyes Were Watching God* the "most successful, convincing and exemplary novel of blacklove that we have. Period." She is speaking of Janie's growth into an awareness of the possibilities of love between black men and black women—both individually and collectively, as selves and as members of a racial community.

Their Eyes Were Watching God responds in subtle ways to the criticism Zora had received. Certainly not a protest novel in the tradition of Richard Wright, parts of the book do capture the "smouldering resentment" of the black South. After the hurricane's destruction, a natural disaster the races suffer together, the white authorities are quick to reimpose supremacy by conscripting black men to bury the victims in segregated graves. Janie's trial has an arrogance about it; her freedom depends on the sanction of twelve white men who simply cannot understand her relationship with Tea Cake. The trial, however, is not grafted to the book to demonstrate the inequity of southern justice. It serves, rather, to illustrate the depth of Janie's discovery of self; for not only is she faced with a white power-structure irrelevant to her feelings, she is also blamed for the killing by Tea Cake's friends. She is not supposed to have the right of self-defense; they murmur that "uh white man and uh nigger woman is de freest thing on earth. Dey do as dey please." This is literally true for Janie, but only because she has become a complete woman, no longer divided between an inner and an outer self, a woman at home with the natural cycles of birth and death, love and loss, knowledge and selfhood. Janie's growth is Hurston's subject. Although that growth is affected by the racism surrounding her, white oppression is not the dominant factor in Janie's development. Zora is saying once again that it is arrogant for whites to think that black lives are only defensive reactions to white actions.

This very complicated argument was misinterpreted by almost all the novel's reviewers. The white establishment failed to recognize that her subject was purposefully chosen; they liked the story, but usually for the wrong reasons. Hershel Brickell in the *New York Post* compared Hurston favorably to D. H. Lawrence in her depiction of sensory experience. The *Saturday Review* called the novel "a simple and unpretentious story, but there is nothing else quite like it." Richard Wright, a Communist party member at the time, reviewed it for *New Masses,* complaining bitterly about the minstrel image that he claimed she was perpetuating. He admitted that "her dialogue manages to catch the psychological movements of the Negro folk-mind in their pure simplicity"; but as a Marxist intellectual working for social change, he felt that was counter-revolutionary. As with Sterling Brown, the lack of bitterness offended Wright: "Her characters eat and laugh and cry and work and kill; they swing like a pendulum eternally in that safe and narrow orbit in which America likes to see the Negro live: between laughter and tears."

Wright's review had to hurt, and it no doubt fed Zora's lifelong suspicion of communism. But the review that infuriated came well after publication, in Alain Locke's January, 1938, *Opportunity* survey of the previous year's "literature by and about the Negro." Locke called the title magical and praised Zora's "cradle-gift" for storytelling. But he criticized the book because folklore was its "main point." Admittedly, it was "folklore fiction at its best"; but when was Hurston going to "come to grips with motive fiction and social document fiction"? Modern southern fiction had to get rid of condescension as well as oversimplification.

Zora's response was to write a malicious, angry portrait of Locke, which she insisted *Opportunity* publish and which they wisely refused. Openly libelous, the attack was unfair; the intensity of the invective was characteristic of the Hurston temper. She called the review "an example of rank dishonesty" and "a conscious fraud." She claimed that Locke "knows that he knows nothing about Negroes" and that he "pants to be a leader"; yet "up to now, Dr. Locke has not produced one single idea or suggestion of an idea that he can call his own." Her specific objection was to Locke's complaint that folklore intruded in the novel, detracting from the fiction, and she was enraged by his implication that the author condescended to her folk subjects. Zora claimed, in typical overstatement, that "there is not a folk tale in the entire book." She proposed, "I will send my toe-nails to debate him on what he knows about Negroes and Negro life, and I will come personally to debate him on what he knows about literature on the subject. This one who lives by quotations trying to criticize people who live by life." She felt that it was Locke, the Harvard Ph.D. and Oxford scholar, who condescended when he referred to the "pseudo-primitives" who were her folk characters.

All of this was directed at a man who had helped Zora often. It shows the frustration of an author whose novelistic talents were deprecated because her fiction dealt with intraracial folkloric situations rather than with interracial confrontations—it was not "social document fiction." The difference in these perspectives is not between protest and accommodation, as Wright implied, but between different conceptions of the folk community. The difference is illustrated on the first page of *Their Eyes Were Watching God*. Janie has returned to Eatonville to tell her story; it is sundown and people are sitting on their porches: "It was the time to hear things and talk. These sitters had been tongueless, earless, eyeless, conveniences all day long. Mules and other brutes had occupied their skins. But now the sun and the bossman were gone, so the skins felt powerful and human." Just as Janie's struggle is to move beyond Nanny's observation that a black woman is "the mule of the world" into an awareness of her own humanity, so is Hurston's subject men rather than mules. Zora wrote of black life after the warrior stances preserving self-dignity in a hostile environment have been set aside for community fellowship. Folklore transmission is a natural product of this sense of security, for it is on these front porches that one's image can be turned from a negative to a positive identification ("I'm like that old mule / Black and don't give a damn / You got to take me / Like I Am"). Locke denied the validity of Zora's fictional environment when he claimed that she imposed folklore on reality rather than represented reality itself. It was natural for her response to be excessive, for she perceived a threat to her entire fictional world. Her fiction represented the processes of folkloric trans-mission, emphasizing the ways of thinking and speaking which grew from the folk environment. But it was fiction, not folklore. Zora replied to Locke by asserting, "To his discomfort I must say that those lines came out of my own head." Like Janie reacting to Joe Starks, Zora Hurston was claiming her right to an autonomous imagination, both as a woman and as a member of the black American community. She was reacting in defense of a people who had been stereotyped as pseudoprimitive minstrels.

ROBERT E. HEMENWAY

That Which the Soul Lives By

In the spring of 1951 Zora Neale Hurston arrived in the coastal village of
Eau Gallie, Florida, carrying a few clothes and a portable typewriter. She
moved into a long-vacant, one-room house that rented for five dollars a week.
Weather-beaten and isolated, on a large lot, the frame shack was covered
by vines and surrounded by weeds. Five huge oaks loomed over it, cabbage
palms dotted the yard. She began transforming the place, making it livable;
she reported to a friend: "I have to do some pioneering, but I find that I
like it. I am the happiest I have been in the last ten years. . . . I am up
every morning at five o'clock chopping down weeds and planting flowers
and things. . . . It looked like a jungle three weeks ago, and it took a strong
heart and an eye on the future for me to move in when I arrived. The place
had run down so badly." She brought in electricity, cleaned and painted,
and began landscaping the grounds. Clearing out an artesian well, she then
constructed a fountain and arranged butterfly ginger around it. She planted
bright red and yellow poppies, scattering the seeds throughout the
grass.

It was not the first time Zora Hurston had lived in Eau Gallie, nor
the first time she had come to stay in this isolated, one-room shack. She
labored hard—"I still must remove tons of junk, old tin cans, and bottles
from the premises"—because she hoped to restore the property to its original
image in her memory. It was here, twenty-two years earlier, that she had
first begun to write *Mules and Men*. When she first stayed in the house, in

From *Mules and Men* (by Zora Neale Hurston). © 1978 by Robert Hemenway. Indiana
University Press, 1978. Originally entitled "Introduction."

the spring of 1929, it served as a way station for a very energetic folklore collector who needed to organize her field notes; she had been transcribing materials for eighteen months while criss-crossing the rural South, and she needed to assess the significance of what she had found. Surrounded by 95,000 words of folk-tale material, dozens of children's games, hundreds of folk songs, and a confusing compilation of hoodoo rituals, the youthful scholar quickly saw that her collections could alter the popular conception of the Southern black folk. Although she stayed for only three months and *Mules and Men* was not published until 1935, Eau Gallie was where the book really began. That single room and the grounds surrounding it held some of the best of an author's memories, and when she returned in 1951, Hurston looked beyond tin cans and weeds, willing herself a vision of another "pioneer," a vibrant young folklorist at the height of her powers. At the age of fifty, Zora Neale Hurston was searching for her past, seeking to reclaim the creative magic that had made her famous.

By the time she returned to Eau Gallie, the discoveries first made in the tiny house had helped to produce a distinguished career. Although she had not made much money, Hurston had earned considerable recognition. Author of four novels, two books of folklore, and an autobiography, she had been on the cover of *Saturday Review,* the subject of interviews on national radio, and a contributor to the *Saturday Evening Post.* The New York and Chicago daily papers had written features about her. She had produced a Broadway concert, written movies for Paramount Studios, and received an honorary Doctor of Letters from Morgan State College. She had spoken at major universities, and had swapped stories with Ernest Hemingway. In the words of one prominent folklorist, she was "probably the most informed person today on Western Negro folk-lore."

Such fame had been hard-won, earned with single-minded drive and intellect against great odds in a racist and sexist country. She wrote about rural Southern black people because it was the world she knew best. Born in 1901 in Eatonville, Florida, an all-black village in central Orange County, she had spent the first decade of her life listening to her father preach at the Macedonia Baptist Church and receiving her mother's encouragement to "jump at de sun." Mrs. Hurston wanted no one to "squinch" her daughter's spirit, "for fear that I would turn out to be a mealy-mouthed rag doll by the time I got grown." Most importantly, Zora hung around Joe Clarke's general store, post office, village center, and municipal gossip mill in order to listen to the folk tales and observe the human drama of Eatonville performing for itself:

Men sat around the store on boxes and benches and passed this
world and the next one through their mouths. The right and the
wrong, the who, when and why was passed on, and nobody
doubted the conclusions. . . . But what I really loved to hear
was the menfolks holding a "lying" session. That is, straining
against each other in telling folks tales. God, Devil, Brer Rabbit,
Brer Fox, Sis Cat, Brer Bear, Lion, Tiger, Buzzard, and all the
woodfolk walked and talked like natural men.

After her mother's death, when Hurston was nine, she left home to
become a maid in a traveling Gilbert and Sullivan troupe, eventually finishing
high school in Baltimore and enrolling at Howard University. With the
encouragement of Howard professors, she began a career as a creative writer,
and after two years in Washington she moved to New York; a scholarship
eventually enabled her to enter Barnard College, where she received her B.A.
in 1928.

New York was alive with "New Negroes" arriving to establish Harlem
as the artistic capital of black America, and Hurston quickly became a part
of the movement of the twenties called "The Harlem Renaissance." She was
widely known for her storytelling abilities; the gusto and flavor of her tales
became a local legend. Her friend Langston Hughes called her the "most
amusing" of all the Harlem Renaissance artists, "a perfect book of entertainment" who could "make you laugh one minute and cry the next." Arna
Bontemps admitted, "I don't know anybody else just like Zora Neale
Hurston."

Although she published a few short stories during this period, Hurston's
energies were chiefly spent on the study of black American folklore in the
anthropology departments of Barnard and Columbia. She became a student
of Franz Boas, the nation's most distinguished anthropologist, a formal,
Germanic gentleman whom she addressed as "Papa Franz." After graduation,
Hurston sought to collect folklore in the South and obtained a patron, Mrs.
R. Osgood Mason, who financed an extended field trip of two years, 1928–
30, in Florida, Alabama, Louisiana, and the West Indies.

The collecting was arduous but exciting, and Hurston approached it
with zest and courage. A tam-o'-shanter atop her head, a $1.98 mail-order
dress draping her big-boned frame, she roamed dusty roads in a Chevrolet
coupe, looking for storytellers, guitar players, church singers, and hoodoo
doctors. She carried her worldly goods in her suitcase and packed a pearl-
handled pistol in her purse. She searched for folklore in places few other

scholars would go. Once she was forced to steal a black cat with her bare hands, then kill it by tossing it into a boiling cauldron; after the flesh dropped away, she was told to pass the bones through her mouth until one tasted bitter, then carry the black cat bone with her forever. In New Orleans, in a hoodoo initiation, she participated in a ceremony requiring her to lie for sixty-nine hours, completely nude, on a conjurer's couch, navel touching a snakeskin. When she awoke on the seventieth hour, five men lifted her naked body and put her through a complicated ritual that ended with the painting of a lightning symbol down her back from the right shoulder to the left hip. Only then was she allowed to dress, and only after drinking wine mixed with the blood of all present was she accepted by the spirit. Hurston said of this period, "I could have been maimed or killed on most any day," an honest assessment of the extreme risks that she took to collect the lore. She was a true participant-observer, willing to subject herself to almost any danger to gather materials.

A sure-handed driver, she pushed the Chevrolet across Florida and Alabama, sometimes singing bawdy songs as she drove, stopping at share-croppers' shacks to ask directions to turpentine stills far back in the piney woods. When sawmill camp workers greeted her suspiciously, she charmed them with a story that she was a bootlegger's woman on the run, as much a fugitive from justice as they. She would sit for hours, listening to the elaborate tales they called "lies": "They certainly lied up a mess. The men would start telling stories, and one man would stop another and say, 'Wait a minute, let me put my dime in your dollar.' " Light brown, attractive, with sparkling eyes, high cheekbones, and a smile that lighted dark corners, she took care to make friends with the job's toughest woman, an alliance that she had learned could protect her from a jealous girlfriend angry over the time her man spent with the outsider.

Such experiences became a part of *Mules and Men.* . . . Although the collecting was largely completed by the time Hurston paused in Eau Gallie in 1929, the book had to await publication for six years, both because she had a difficult time shaping the book for popular consumption and because her publisher, Lippincott, did not become interested until after her first novel, the autobiographical *Jonah's Gourd Vine* (1934), was well received. (The *New York Times* reviewer called *Jonah's Gourd Vine* "the most vital and original novel about the American Negro that has yet been written by a member of the Negro race.")

Mules and Men, published in 1935, established Hurston's reputation as a folklorist and helped secure a Guggenheim fellowship to study magic practices in the West Indies from 1936 to 1938. While there, she wrote a

second novel, *Their Eyes Were Watching God,* one of the lesser-known mas-
terpieces of American literature. The story of a woman's quest for love and
freedom, it is considered the finest novel by a black American prior to
Richard Wright's *Native Son.* At the height of her fame in the late thirties
and early forties, she published her account of the West Indies in *Tell My
Horse* (1938), wrote another novel, *Moses, Man of the Mountain* (1939), and
completed an autobiography, *Dust Tracks on a Road* (1942). In the late forties
she searched for a lost city in Central America; while there she wrote her
final novel, a story of Florida whites, *Seraph on the Suwanee* (1948).

Something else happened in 1948 that deeply hurt her and sent her
into isolation for an extended period. She was falsely accused in New York
of impairing the morals of a minor. Although the charge was dismissed and
her innocence proven, the story reached the newspapers. She contemplated
suicide, and then tried to start life anew. The episode marked the beginning
of a bad time, and by 1950 she was broke, forced to hire out as a maid to
a wealthy Miami family. When her employer picked up a copy of the *Saturday
Evening Post* and discovered fiction written by her domestic help, the Miami
paper made it into a feature story. Although male writers laboring for
experience and expenses between books provoke relatively little comment,
Hurston's domestic labor was widely lamented, interpreted either as a publicity stunt or as evidence that she could not handle her affairs. Intensely
proud, fearful that the morals charge might surface again, she told the
reporters that her work was to gain experience for future writing about
domestics.

The *Post's* money and other journalism lifted her out of the hole, and
when she returned to Eau Gallie in 1951, she had savings of around $1,000,
enough to fix up her house and settle in. The recent rejection of a new novel
did not augur well for her career, however, and her creative powers had
clearly begun to fail. She spent five relatively peaceful years in the tiny house,
more time than she had ever spent in one place since leaving Eatonville forty
years earlier; she worked hard, but no book and only a little journalism saw
print. She had grown politically conservative, convinced of a Communist
menace. Given her conservatism, her reaction to the 1954 Supreme Court
desegregation decision was understandable; she objected to the ruling on the
grounds that it insulted black teachers and implied that Blacks could only
learn if they sat next to Whites.

In the spring of 1956 her landlord announced plans to sell the Eau
Gallie property, and she was left with no money and no place to go. In
May, Bethune Cookman College in Daytona Beach awarded her special
honors at their commencement; she accepted proudly in her Doctor of Letters

robes. Two weeks later she took a job at $1.88 per hour as a clerk in the technical library at Patrick Air Force Base in Cocoa, Florida. The job lasted only a year, the unemployment benefits only a few months after that. Her life ended in 1960 in Ft. Pierce, Florida; she was sick, forgotten, penniless, and a resident of the St. Lucie County Welfare Home. Her funeral was paid for by donations; her body was placed in an unmarked grave.

Hurston's last years were sad, but her appetite for experience and her accomplishments are what deserve to be remembered; she was violently opposed to all forms of pity. The solitary figure setting up her household in Eau Gallie demonstrated that Zora Neale Hurston, even in her declining years, sought help from no one; she struggled to reclaim creative energy through the sheer force of will.

Mules and Men is a collection of seventy folk-tale texts, a series of hoodoo rituals, a glossary of folk speech, an appendix of folk songs, conjure formulas, and root prescriptions, plus a personal account of Zora Neale Hurston's collecting experiences. Interspersed among all of this are proverbs, a folk sermon, rhymes, blues lyrics, and street cries. Some of the material had been collected before, and lurid hoodoo stories had appeared in popular magazines. But the book presented mostly new, authentic materials, and presented them in a different context than had previously existed.

Its publication was historically important, the first book of Afro-American folklore collected by a black American to be presented by a major publisher for a general reading audience. In the nineteenth century, black novelists William Wells Brown and Charles Chesnutt had reported on the folklore of slaves and ex-slaves. The establishment of an American Folklore Society chapter at Hampton Institute in 1893 led to the reporting of folklore in the Institute's journal, the *Southern Workman,* but it had only a limited circulation. Many popular periodicals had reported on black folklore during and after the Civil War, but the collectors were always white and often looked upon the material as quaint or exotic. The second issue of the *Journal of American Folklore* in 1888 called for the study of the "lore of Negroes in the Southern states of the Union," and the *Journal* printed many Afro-American materials, but the plantation context so prominent in the popular accounts was frequently present in these scholarly reports as well, and, again, the collectors were usually white. The twentieth century saw increasing interest in black folkways, but generally speaking, Afro-American folklore between 1850 and 1930 was almost always collected by whites and usually preselected to conform to either the collector's romantic notion of black people (humble, God-fearing, simple folk) or racist stereotype (inferior beings lost in a complex society).

For a variety of reasons black folklorists were few. When *Mules and*

Men appeared, only two other black scholars, J. Mason Brewer and Arthur Huff Fauset, had professional training similar to Hurston's. *Mules and Men* is a pioneering book, and Hurston thought of it as part of a mission; she wrote that she was "weighed down by the thought that practically nothing had been done in Negro folklore when the greatest cultural wealth of the continent was disappearing without the world ever realizing that it had ever been."

If there is a theme to the folk tales and hoodoo of *Mules and Men,* it is that the folklore of the black South is an expressive system of great social complexity and profound esthetic significance. *Mules and Men* was published at a time when racism and racist stereotypes were very evident. Minstrel shows were a popular form of American entertainment; the United States Senate could not agree that lynching was a crime; many newspapers still refused to capitalize the word Negro. At a time when the men on Joe Clarke's store porch were considered by whites to be lazy and ignorant, Hurston presented these storytellers as the tradition-bearers for an Afro-American world view. At a time when spirituals were accepted because they had become so harmonized that they were barely distinguishable from Bach chorales, when Paul Robeson and Roland Hayes were being praised for concert interpretations of the "sorrow songs," Hurston claimed, "Robeson sings Negro songs better than most, because, thank God, he lacks musical education. But we have a cathead man in Florida who can sing so that if you heard him you wouldn't want to hear Hayes or Robeson. He hasn't the voice of either one. It's the effect." At a time when hoodoo was considered a bizarre superstition, she compared it to Christianity:

> I am convinced that Christianity as practised is an attenuated form of nature worship. Let me explain. The essentials are a belief in the Trinity, baptism, sacrament. Baptism is nothing more than water worship as has been done in one form or the other down thru the ages. . . . I find fire worship in Christianity too. What was the original purpose of the altar in all churches? For sacred fire and sacrifices BY FIRE. . . . Symbols my opponents are going to say. But they cannot deny that both water and fire are purely material things and that they symbolize man's tendency to worship those things which benefit him to a great extent. . . . You know of course that the sacrament is a relic of cannibalism when men ate men not so much for food as to gain certain qualities the eaten man had. Sympathetic magic pure and simple. *They have a nerve to laugh at conjure.* (My italics.)

Mules and Men refutes the pathological view of uneducated rural black people. Hurston's method is presentational, and she does not impose folklore theory on the reader. She operates from the premise, however, that what she presents is "the greatest cultural wealth of the continent," and as a trained anthropologist she understood the word "culture." *Mules and Men* does not exactly ignore the brutal oppression of black people in the South, but it subordinates the economic and social deprivation to achieve a cultural perspective. Even in the face of an historically brutal experience, black people affirmed their humanity by creating an expressive communication system that fostered self-pride and taught techniques of transformation, adaptation, and survival. The tales of *Mules and Men* prove that human beings are not able to live without some sense of cultural cohesion and individual self-worth—no matter how hard their circumstances, no matter how much effort is directed toward denying them a sense of personal value. Why is the slave John, as Hurston claims, "the wish fulfillment hero of the race"? Sack Daddy, a sawmill worker from Polk County, answers: "John sho was a smart nigger now. He useter git de best of Ole Massa all de time."

Aware of the historical importance of her effort, Hurston paid considerable care to the choice of approach for *Mules and Men,* the communication context she would offer the reader. Her decision was to report from a black communal perspective. As the black poet June Jordan has stated, "white America lies outside the Hurston universe . . . you do not run up on the man/the enemy"; in Hurston's work black people put aside the "warrior postures" that enable them to deal with that enemy and adopt the "person postures" that enable them to relax and freely express themselves. Hurston reports on what happens on Clarke's store porch after the day's labors. The tale-tellers at Clarke's store understood the ancient black folk song:

> Got one mind for white folks to see,
> Nother for what I know is me;
> He don't know, he don't know my mind.

The verse affirms identity; the singer knows that there is a *me,* that this person is someone quite different from the stereotypical figure seen from the outside. Even though white possessiveness may seem to consume all, it cannot take possession of the private self.

Black identity receives expression in Afro-American folklore because folklore permits the presentation of emotions so deeply felt that they often cannot be openly articulated. Hurston understood this process in a way Joel Chandler Harris did not. The Uncle Remus tales are always told from within the plantation tradition; the context is always a serene, kindly old darky relating animal tales to pre-adolescents—the mask is never dropped. In *Mules and Men* the folklorist works in a different setting, encounters tale-tellers in a different frame of mind:

> They are most reluctant at times to reveal that which the soul lives by. And the Negro, in spite of his open-faced laughter, his seeming acquiescence, is particularly evasive. . . . The Negro offers a feather-bed resistance. . . . The theory behind our tactics: "The white man is always trying to know into somebody else's business. All right, I'll set something outside the door of my mind for him to play with and handle. He can read my writing but he sho' can't read my mind. I'll put this play toy in his hand, and he will seize it and go away. Then I'll say my say and sing my song.

The sayings and songs of *Mules and Men* document a culture. The tales here are *not* the quaint, childish entertainments of a primitive tribe. They are the complex cultural communications permitted an oppressed people, their school lessons, their heroic biographies, their psychic savings banks, their children's legacies. Black folk tales illustrate how an entire people adapted and survived in the new world experience, how they transformed what they found into a distinctive way of life; they describe the human behavior the group approves, indicate when the behavior is appropriate, and suggest strategies necessary for the preservation of the group in a hostile environment.

Consider, for example, the John-Massa tale told in Chapter Five. Newly transported to America as a slave, John is taught a language: the white man's house is called a "kingdom"; his fireplace is a "flame vaperator"; his bed is "his flowery bed of ease." When forced to communicate in this new vocabulary, John does so only up to a point, then breaks through the pretense of the artificial nomenclature and speaks directly.

Such a tale resonates with historical, cultural, and psychological significance. Although the tale is known in many cultures, it was adapted to the Afro-American experience. It recreates the unsuccessful attempt at cultural genocide the slaves overcame. There was an attempt to strip the African of his language, penalizing him, as Alex Haley has so recently shown, for the desire to preserve the linguistic fragments of Africa. The tale reminds us that whoever attempts to control language, the naming process, attempts to control our understanding of who we are, our definition of reality. What kind of person would call a fireplace a "flame vaperator"? A person given to pretentious labels, one who wished to measure self-worth by material objects, one unwilling to look upon reality (bricks and mortar) and call it by its correct name. A person, in other words, characteristic of the master-oppressor class, looking upon slavery and calling it beneficent. Such whites, thanks to the labor of slaves, sleep on a "flowery bed of ease," and psychic satisfaction arises from the opportunity to label it truthfully. The twist at the end of the tale, John's dropping of the pretense that he has accepted the artificial nomenclature, is the final triumphant irony of the tale. It objectifies the secret knowledge that John had held from the first. He had always known what the truth was, and his master had known that John knew. They were participating in an elaborate ritual of self-delusion. Black listeners did not have to look far to apply the tale's truths. White people might say "separate but equal," and black people might temporarily have to accept the label, but both knew that they were participating in a verbal hoax. Sooner or later the institution had to collapse from the weight of illusion language had been asked to serve.

Mules and Men is a storehouse of such revelations, a repository of coded cultural messages preserved and passed by word of mouth from generation to generation. When it was published, Carl Sandburg called it "a bold and beautiful book, many a page priceless and unforgettable." Alan Lomax calls *Mules and Men* "the most engaging, genuine, and skillfully written book in the field of folklore."

Any book purporting to present an interior view of black Americans is bound to create controversy, since no single book can capture the rich diversity of Afro-American culture. *Mules and Men,* although generally well received at the time of its publication, also has had its critics. There have been understandable complaints about its lack of cross-cultural analysis, comparative notes, and scholarly apparatus. There have been objections to the absence of social consciousness in Hurston's storytellers, the charge made that their lack of bitterness creates a false image of romantic pastoralism for the black South. It is worth mentioning, however, that the expectations of scholarly form were relatively unsophisticated in 1935, and that in any case Hurston knew very well she was not presenting her collections in the normal, scholarly fashion. She had done so once before, publishing hoodoo findings in the *Journal of American Folklore* for 1931, only to have "all the flaming glory," as she called it, end up "buried" on the "shelves of scientific societies." The hoodoo sections of *Mules and Men* are taken, with very little revision, from this earlier scholarly publication. In a letter to Boas in 1934, she admitted that "I have inserted the between-story conversation and business because when I offered it without it, every publisher said it was too monotonous. Now three houses want to publish it. So I hope the nonscientific matter that must be there for the sake of the average reader will not keep you from writing the introduction." Boas refused to go ahead until he had checked the entire manuscript for authenticity, then stressed in his preface the value of these conversations.

The between-story "business" is only unscientific in the sense that Hurston is apparently calling upon her collecting memories to provide continuity between tales. She told Boas, "It so happens that the conversations and incidents are true"; although she may be creatively rearranging them, they have seemed to modern scholars to simulate tale-telling situations, at least in a selectively edited form. That is, Hurston's invention seems to have been limited to condensation and arrangement; she did not invent any folklore for the book. Her informants may not have told quite so many tales while walking to the lake to fish, but the words are their own, not Zora Neale Hurston's.

Finally, ethnographic observations occur in these "between-story conversations." When challenged to tell a story, one man says, "Ah don't know it well enough to say it. Ah jus' know it well enough to know it." He clearly understands his role as a passive tradition-bearer, a self-correcting force who will insure that the active bearer—the tale-teller—will not violate too extensively the community's expectation of a given performance. While most folklore collections include objective discussions of the field techniques used to collect the data, Hurston shows rather than tells the same information. Folklorist Sandra Stahl has remarked on Hurston's temporary role-playing to gain the trust of her informants. This field methodology, which would be discussed operationally in conventional ethnography, is dramatized in *Mules and Men*.

The charge of romantic pastoralism is more complicated, and may best be summarized by Sterling Brown, poet, scholar, folklorist, one of the distinguished Afro-American artists of the twentieth century. Brown reviewed *Mules and Men* in 1936 and praised it for its simplicity, raciness, earthiness, and plausibility. However, he objected to the lack of political awareness among Hurston's storytellers. Brown had collected folklore in the South and saw people living "in a land shadowed by squalor, poverty, disease, violence, enforced ignorance, and exploitation." He concluded: "From the reviewer's own experiences he knows that harsher folk tales await the collector. These people brood upon their hardships, talk about them 'down by the big gate,' and some times even at the big house. They are not blind, and they are not being fooled; some have lost their politeness, and speak right out. *Mules and Men* should be more bitter; it would be nearer the total truth."

Such criticism is still relevant. The Eatonville of the 1930s, with such a high unemployment rate that Hurston felt compelled to solicit funds to help the town, is seldom in evidence. Yet Zora Neale Hurston was not blind to racial prejudice, or the economic hardship that her people bore. From the age of ten until twenty she knew the smell of poverty, with its "dead dreams dropping off the heart like leaves in a dry season and rotting around the feet."

Hurston's personal experience of poverty and her commitment to an integrated society were subordinated in *Mules and Men* so that she could address the negative image of the black folk publicly held by most Whites and by some Blacks. (Some of Hurston's strongest opposition came from middle-class black people who thought of the folk heritage as something which should be forgotten, a legacy of ignorance which could be used to justify racism.) The problem was that too many people confused material and ideological poverty. Because the men at Joe Clarke's were sometimes unemployed, often uneducated, occasionally hungry, it was assumed that no significant *ideas,* expressive *forms,* or cultural *creations* could emanate from the store porch. The black folk were placed in a kind of ideological strait jacket that interpreted their responses to the environment as either the product of social pathology, cultural deprivation, or an understandable, but simplistic desire to "protest."

Mules and Men creates a black communal perspective in order to emphasize the *independent* cultural creation of black people. Because Hurston was not a theorist, and *Mules and Men* was meant for the "average reader," her method was presentational. The folklore was expected to speak for itself. It said many things, but one of the most important was that Afro-American culture was not simply a *reactive* phenomenon. Black people's behaviors could not always be interpreted in the light of white oppression. What much of *Mules and Men* demonstrates, to paraphrase Ralph Ellison, is that black Americans are not the creation of the white man. As Ellison puts it, "Negro folklore, evolving within a larger culture which regarded it as inferior, was an especially courageous expression. It announced the Negro's willingness to trust his own experiences, his own sensibilities as to the definition of reality, rather than allow his masters to define these crucial matters for him."

Hurston once told Langston Hughes that he should make a Southern tour and read his poetry in sawmill camps and turpentine stills, on docks and levees: "There never has been a poet who has been acceptable to his Majesty, the man in the gutter before, and laugh if you will, but that man in the gutter is the god-maker, the creator of everything that lasts." Hurston identified with that figure, whom she called the "Negro farthest down"; *Mules and Men* was meant to affirm his place in the artistic universe. She was less interested in the economic system that made him poor than in the sensibility that enabled him to create a God. The book was written so that the folk's artistic works—anonymous in their authorship, dramatized in performance, transmitted orally—would not be forgotten. Hurston told a Chicago reporter, "It would be a tremendous loss to the Negro race and to America if we should lose the folklore and folk music, for the unlettered Negro has given the Negro's best contribution to America's culture."

In a sawmill camp, the jook was the dance hall and bar in which men and women danced, drank, and gambled. A "jook woman" was not noted for her spotless reputation, a "jook man" was prone to violence, good times, and rough talk. Zora Neale, with her Barnard degree, learned to be at home in such surroundings, because she knew the significance of what went on there. In 1934 she reported: "Musically speaking, the jook is the most important place in America. For in its smelly, shoddy confines has been born the secular music known as blues, and on blues has been founded jazz. The singing and playing in the true Negro style is called 'jooking.' "

Mules and Men was an attempt to present a "true Negro style," one which had been ignored and maligned by a racist society. It is not the whole story of Blacks in the South, or even a comprehensive anthology of all forms of Afro-American folklore. It remains today, however, as it was at the time of its publication, one of the most important collections of Afro-American folklore ever to be published.

It is a long way from a jook's noisy excitement to a quiet Barnard classroom, but it is not so far from a sawmill jook in Polk County, Florida, to a one-room house in Eau Gallie. The middle-aged woman in the tropical sunshine struggling to reclaim past glories has largely shared her fate with the artists who perform in *Mules and Men*. American society has tended to forget about them both, tale-teller and collector, while the tales live on. That fact is both an affirmation of the communicative art in Afro-American folklore and a commentary on the way black artists have been received in this country.

As for Zora Neale Hurston, she understood the whole process but did not spend a moment in regret. As she said, "I have been in sorrow's kitchen and licked all the pots."

SHERLEY ANNE WILLIAMS

Janie's Burden

I first encountered Zora Neale Hurston in an Afro-American literature course I took in graduate school. She was one of numerous authors surveyed in the two-semester course, which began with Lucy Terry in 1746 and ended with the Black Arts writers of the sixties. Hurston's works were studied as a sort of holdover from the Harlem Renaissance, that period that coincided, at least in part, with the Jazz Age and witnessed the first concerted out-pourings of formal artistic expression among Afro-Americans. The most important stylistic developments of the period were the attempt to use Afro-American folk culture as a basis for creating distinctive black contributions to serious or "high" culture, and the attempt to repudiate the false and degrading stereotypes promulgated in Anglo-American popular (and high) culture by exploring the individual consciousness hidden behind the enveloping Sambo mask. *Their Eyes Were Watching God* was published in 1937, almost ten years after the stock market crash of 1929, the date most often given as the end of the Harlem Renaissance. The book's rural southern settings, the use of dialect and folkloric materials, even its romantic theme represent much that was distinctive and significant about this period.

It would have been difficult for most of the students in that class to prove these statements. We "read at" Zora Neale in the same way we had read at most of the writers studied to that point (and quite a few that came after): in snatches. And although I'd never seen—much less read—an em-barrassing number of the works discussed in the course, I felt lucky to be there. Afro-American literature was still an exotic subject then, rarely taught

From *Their Eyes Were Watching God* (by Zora Neale Hurston). © 1978 by the Board of Trustees of the University of Illinois. University of Illinois Press, 1978. Originally entitled "Foreword."

on any regular basis. Most of the works of the writers we studied had been out of print for a long time, and students relied on lectures, anthology selections (when available), what samplings could be garnered in a Saturday spent in a rare-book collection or an evening in the reserve book reading room, and Robert Bone's *The Negro Novel in America* for our impressions of William Wells Brown, Frances Harper, William Attaway, Jessie Fauset, and Zora Neale Hurston. We were fortunate to be in Washington, D.C., with its several large university and public libraries and the Library of Congress. But library holdings really couldn't make up for those out-of-print books. The few personal or library copies of this or that were shared around, but there were about forty students in the class. By the time a person got the book, it had usually been discussed at least four weeks prior, and the owner needed it back to write a paper. So, like many students in the class, out of sheer frustration I ended by concentrating on contemporary authors (i.e., Wright, Ellison, Baldwin), whose works were more readily available.

It did, however, finally become my turn to read *Their Eyes Were Watching God,* and I became Zora Neale's for life. In the speech of her characters I heard my own country voice and saw in the heroine something of my own country self. And this last was most wonderful because it was most rare. Black women had been portrayed as characters in numerous novels by blacks and nonblacks. But these portraits were limited by the stereotypical images of, on the one hand, the ham-fisted matriarch, strong and loyal in the defense of the white family she serves (but unable to control or protect her own family without the guidance of some white person), and, on the other, the amoral, instinctual slut. Between these two stereotypes stood the tragic mulatto: too refined and sensitive to live under the repressive conditions endured by ordinary blacks and too colored to enter the white world.

Even the few idealized portraits of black women evoked these negative stereotypes. The idealizations were morally uplifting and politically laudable, but their literary importance rests upon just that: the correctness of their moral and political stance. Their value lies in their illuminations of the society's workings and their insights into the ways oppression is institutionalized. They provide, however, few insights into character or consciousness. And when we (to use Alice Walker's lovely phrase) go in search of our mother's gardens, it's not really to learn who trampled on them or how or even why—we usually know that already. Rather, it's to learn what our mothers planted there, what they thought as they sowed, and how they survived the blighting of so many fruits. Zora Hurston's life and work present us with insights into just these concerns.

The date of her birth, like many of the facts of her life, is a matter of uncertainty. Robert E. Hemenway, in a first and much-needed biography, *Zora Neale Hurston* (Urbana: University of Illinois Press, 1977), cites January 7, 1901, as the date that makes the most sense. Eatonville, Florida, the small, all-black town where Zora was born, is the setting for two of her four published novels, *Jonah's Gourd Vine* (1934) and *Their Eyes Were Watching God*. The gatherings on the front porch of the town's general store came to symbolize for Hurston the richness of Afro-American oral culture, and she struggled for much of her career to give literary renderings of that oral richness and to portray the complex individuality of its unlettered, "uncultured" *folk* creators. Hurston studied cultural anthropology under Franz Boas, first as a student at Barnard College and later at Columbia University. In 1927 she returned to the South, where she lived off and on for the rest of her life, collecting examples of and participating in the dynamic culture created in the saw mills, turpentine camps, and small-town jook joints and cafés. She had at her command a large store of stories, songs, incidents, idiomatic phrases, and metaphors; her ear for speech rhythms must have been remarkable. Most importantly, she had the literary intelligence and developed the literary skill to convey the power and beauty of this heard speech and lived experience on the printed page.

Hurston's evocations of the lifestyles of rural blacks have not been equaled; but to stress the ruralness of Hurston's settings or to characterize her diction solely in terms of exotic "dialect" spellings is to miss her deftness with language. In the speech of her characters, black voices—whether rural or urban, northern or southern—come alive. Her fidelity to diction, metaphor, and syntax—whether in direct quotations or in paraphrases of characters' thoughts—rings, even across forty years, with an aching familiarity that is a testament to Hurston's skill and to the durability of black speech. Yet Zora's personality and actions were so controversial that for a long time she was remembered more as a *character* of the Renaissance than as one of the most serious and gifted artists to emerge during this period. She was a notable tale-teller, mimic, and wit, confident to the point of brashness (some might even say beyond), who refused to conform to conventional notions of ladylike behavior and middle-class decorum. To one of her contemporaries, she was the first black nationalist; to another, a handkerchief-head Uncle Tom. Larry Neal, in his recent introduction to her autobiography, *Dust Tracks on a Road* (1942; reprinted, New York: J. B. Lippincott, 1971), calls her a "kind of Pearl Bailey of the literary world . . . a conservative in her political outlook with a remarkable understanding of a blues aesthetic and its accompanying sensibility." To Alice Walker and others of our generation,

Zora was a woman bent on discovering and defining herself, a woman who spoke and wrote her own mind.

Something of the questing quality that characterized Zora's own life informs the character of Janie—without, of course, the forcefulness of Hurston's own personality. In this and other instances, the character is more conventional than the author, for despite obvious idealizations, Janie operates in a "real" world. Her actions, responses, and motivations are consistent with that reality and the growing assertiveness of her own self-definitions. Where Janie yearns, Zora was probably driven; where Janie submits, Zora would undoubtedly have rebelled. Author and character objectify their definitions of self in totally different ways. Zora was evidently unable to satisfactorily define herself in a continuing relationship with a man, whereas such definition is the essence of Janie's romantic vision and its ultimate fulfillment provides the plot of the novel. But in their desire and eventual insistence that their men accord them treatment due equals, they are one.

Janie is raised by her grandmother, Nanny, an ex-slave who has suffered most of the abuses heaped upon black women in slavery: hard physical labor, poor rations, whippings, the threat of being separated from children and mate, coerced sexual relations with the master, and vindictive treatment at the hands of the mistress. Nanny doesn't fare much better in freedom; her daughter, whom she'd hoped to make into a schoolteacher as the fulfillment of her own frustrated dreams, is raped by a local schoolteacher. Janie is the result of this brutal coupling. After Janie's birth, the mother runs away, leaving Janie in Nanny's care. Nanny sees in the baby girl another chance to fulfill her own dreams "of whut a woman oughta be and to do." Nanny works for a white family, and Janie is raised (as the saying goes) in the white folks' yard, elevated above the common run of black people and separated from the sustenance that the community provides. She is six before she even realizes that she is black. The revelation doesn't devastate Janie. Rather, it stands as both a symbol of Nanny's unrealistic attempts to shield the girl from life and a metaphor for Janie's lack of self-knowledge.

Janie is just entering young womanhood when Nanny, frightened by the advent of that maturity, tries to school Janie about the lot of black women: "Honey, de white man is de ruler of everything as fur as Ah been able tuh find out. . . . de white man throw down de load and tell de nigger man tuh pick it up. He pick it up because he have to, but he don't tote it. He hand it to his womenfolks. De nigger woman is de mule uh de world so fur as Ah can see." The image of the black woman as the mule of the world becomes a metaphor for the roles that Janie repudiates in her quest for self-fulfillment and the belief against which the book implicitly argues.

Love, for the old ex-slave, is "de very prong all us black women gits hung on": that is, as Nanny goes on to explain, wanting a dressed-up dude who can't keep himself in shoe leather, much less provide for someone else; his women tote that burden for him. Love doesn't kill; it just makes a black woman sweat. Nanny dies believing that the only armor against this fate is money or the protection of good white people.

Janie holds onto her vision of a fulfilled and fulfilling love through two loveless marriages. Nanny arranges Janie's first marriage, to Logan Killicks, an older farmer whose sixty acres ought to provide Janie with the security Nanny has been able to achieve only through working for white families. Killicks, however, can't see any further than his plow, and Janie is stifled by his plodding nature. Realizing that Janie doesn't return his love, he tries to destroy her spirit by threatening to make her help with the back-breaking labor of the farm. Nanny's metaphor is almost actualized, but Janie rebels. She runs away with Joe Starks, an ambitious go-getter who pauses on his way to becoming "a big voice" in the world (mayor and postmaster, principal landowner and businessman in Eatonville) to marry Janie. Joe stops making "speeches with rhymes" to Janie almost as soon as the wedding ceremony is over. Instead of love talk, he buys her the best of everything.

Joe provides Janie with the "front porch" existence of Nanny's dreams, but in doing so, he isolates her from direct participation in any life except his own. His stranglehold on her life and definition of self is symbolized in his prohibition against her participation in the tale-tellings, mock flirtations, and other comic activities that center around or emanate from the porch of his general store. Despite his own pleasure in these sessions, he charges that the people who gather at them are "trashy," and Janie is Mrs. Mayor Starks. They don't even own their own houses, and a woman of Janie's respectability shouldn't want to pass the time of day with them. Thus, "when Lige or Sam or Walter or some of the other big picture talkers were using a side of the world for a canvas, Joe would hustle her off inside the store to sell something." The link between selling and Joe's attempt to isolate Janie from authentic membership in the community is striking and deliberate: Janie is Joe's personal possession, "de mayor's wife." It is an image that, as Hurston says of their marriage, is soon deserted by the spirit. But it is not only class that Joe uses as a means of browbeating Janie into submission. She is a woman; her place is in the home (or wherever he tells her to be, like the store, where he forces her to clerk because her many mistakes give him another opportunity to belittle her intelligence). Someone has to think for women, children, chickens, and cows. The instances of Joe's chauvinism are obvious and many. The metaphor of the mule is further reified in Joe's insistence that Janie tote his narrow, stultifying notions of what behavior is appropriate to her class and sex. Rooted at first only in the specificity of the Afro-American female experience, the metaphor has been transformed into one for the female condition; Janie's individual quest for fulfillment becomes any woman's tale.

Joe dies of a kidney ailment after some years of marriage. Janie, now a widow with property and still a very attractive woman, meets and marries Vergible "Tea Cake" Woods, an itinerant laborer and gambler much younger than herself. Tea Cake is love and laughter and talking in rhymes. However, he fulfills Janie's dreams because he requires only that she be herself. At home with himself, he has no need to dominate Janie or curb her self-expression in order to prove his masculinity. In contrast to the social status that her previous marriages gave her (and the book is filled with contrasts), Janie's place in her relationship with Tea Cake is on the muck, a booming farming area, picking beans at his side. Janie has come *down,* that paradoxical place in Afro-American literature that is both a physical bottom and the setting for the character's attainment of a penultimate self-knowledge (think of Ellison's Invisible Man in his basement room or the hero of Baraka's *The System of Dante's Hell* in the Bottoms). Down on the muck, Janie's horizons are expanded by the love and respect she shares with Tea Cake. She becomes a participant in the life that Nanny, Logan, Joe, and other friends and advisors would have her believe is beneath her. "The men held big arguments here like they used to do on the store porch. Only here, she could listen and laugh and even talk some herself if she wanted to. She got so she could tell big stories herself from listening to the rest." Janie comes at last into her own, at home with herself, her man, and her world. This unity is symbolized in a final play on the black-woman-as-mule image. Tea Cake asks and Janie consents to work in the fields with him, because neither wants to be parted from the other even during the working day. Their love for each other makes the stoop labor of bean picking seem almost play. The differences between the image and the reversal of that image are obvious: Tea Cake has asked, not commanded; his request stems from a desire to be with Janie, to share every aspect of his life with her, rather than from a desire to coerce her into some mindless submission. It isn't the white man's burden that Janie carries; it is the gift of her own love.

ALICE WALKER

On Refusing to Be Humbled by Second Place in a Contest You Did Not Design

A friend of mine called one day to tell me that she and another woman had been discussing Zora Neale Hurston and had decided they wouldn't have liked her. They wouldn't have liked the way—when her play *Color Struck!* won second prize in a literary contest at the beginning of her career—Hurston walked into a room full of her competitors, flung her scarf dramatically over her shoulder, and yelled "COLOR .. R.R STRUCK .. K.K!" at the top of her voice.

Apparently it isn't easy to like a person who is not humbled by second place.

Zora Neale Hurston was outrageous—it appears by nature. She was quite capable of saying, writing, or doing things *different* from what one might have wished. Because she recognized the contradictions and complexity of her own personality, Robert Hemenway, her biographer, writes that Hurston came to "delight" in the chaos she sometimes left behind.

Yet for all her contrariness, her "chaos," her ability to stir up dislike that is as strong today as it was fifty years ago, many of us love Zora Neale Hurston.

We do not love her for her lack of modesty (that tends to amuse us: an assertive black person during Hurston's time was considered an anomaly); we do not love her for her unpredictable and occasionally weird politics (they tend to confuse us); we do not, certainly, applaud many of the *mad* things she is alleged to have said and sometimes actually did say; we do not even claim never to dislike her. In reading through the thirty-odd-year span of

From *I Love Myself When I Am Laughing . . . And Then Again When I Am Looking Mean and Impressive: A Zora Neale Hurston Reader*. © 1979 by Alice Walker. The Feminist Press, 1979. Originally entitled "Dedication: On Refusing to Be Humbled by Second Place in a Contest You Did Not Design: A Tradition by Now."

her writing, most of us, I imagine, find her alternately winning and appalling, but rarely dull, which is worth a lot. We love Zora Neale Hurston
for her work, first, and then again (as she and all Eatonville would say), we
love her for herself. For the humor and courage with which she encountered
a life she infrequently designed, for her absolute uninterest in becoming
either white or bourgeois, and for her *devoted* appreciation of her own culture,
which is an inspiration to us all.

Reading *Their Eyes Were Watching God* for perhaps the eleventh time,
I am still amazed that Hurston wrote it in seven weeks; that it speaks to
me as no novel, past or present, has ever done; and that the language of the
characters, that "comical nigger 'dialect' " that has been laughed at, denied,
ignored, or "improved" so that white folks and educated black folks can
understand it, is simply beautiful. There is enough self-love in that one
book—love of community, culture, traditions—to restore a world. Or create
a new one.

I do not presume to judge or defend Zora Neale Hurston. I have nothing
of finality to say of Hurston the person. I believe any artist's true character
is seen in the work she or he does, or it is not seen. In Hurston's work,
what she was is revealed. . . .

Is *Mules and Men* racist? Or does it reflect the flawed but nonetheless
beautifully creative insights of an oppressed people's collective mythology?
Is "The Gilded Six-Bits" so sexist it makes us cringe to think Zora Neale
Hurston wrote it? Or does it make a true statement about deep love functioning in the only pattern that at the time of its action seemed correct?
Did Zora Neale Hurston never question "America" or the status-quo, as
some have accused, or was she questioning it profoundly when she wrote
phrases like "the arse-and-all of Democracy"? is Janie Crawford, the main
character in *Their Eyes Were Watching God,* light-skinned and silken-haired
because *Hurston* was a colorist, as a black male critic has claimed, or because
Hurston was not blind and therefore saw that black men (and black women)
have been, and are, colorist to an embarrassing degree?

Is Hurston the messenger who brings the bad news, or is she the bad
news herself? Is Hurston a reflection of ourselves? And if so, is that not,
perhaps, part of our "problem" with her?

I think we are better off if we think of Zora Neale Hurston as an artist,
period—rather than as the artist/politician most black writers have been
required to be. This frees us to appreciate the complexity and richness of
her work in the same way we can appreciate Billie Holiday's glorious phrasing
or Bessie Smith's perfect and raunchy lyrics, without the necessity of ridiculing the former's addiction to heroin or the latter's excessive love of gin.

Implicit in Hurston's determination to "make it" in a career was her need to express "the folk" and herself. Someone who knew her has said: "Zora would have been Zora even if she'd been an Eskimo." That is what it means to be yourself; it is surely what it means to be an artist.

It is instructive to consider the lives of Zora Hurston and Bessie Smith (whom no one, it seems, thought to ask what *she* thought of things like integration!) particularly in relation to the white "patrons of the Negro" they both knew. There is a wonderful story told of how Bessie Smith once attended a Carl Van Vechten party which that reigning patron of Negro Art threw in her honor. As she entered, never having seen Carl or Fania Van Vechten before (and dragging her full length, white ermine on the floor behind her, an ermine purchased with money from her bestselling records), Fania Van Vechten flung herself into Bessie's arms. Bessie knocked her flat, exclaiming over a glass of straight gin: 'I never *heard* of such shit!"

Bessie Smith knew shit when she saw it, and from Zora Hurston's work, we can assume she did too. Yet she never knocked anyone flat for having the audacity to patronize her, nor does she ever complain in print about the hypocrisy she must have borne. The difference between Hurston and Smith? One's work—singing, to which one could dance or make love— supported her. The other's work—writing down the unwritten doings and sayings of a culture nobody else seemed to give a damn about, except to wish it would more speedily conform to white, middle-class standards—did not.

Financial dependency is the thread that sewed a cloud over Hurston's life, from the time she left home to work as a maid at fourteen to the day of her death. It is ironic that *this* woman, who many claimed sold her soul to record the sources of authentic, black American folk art (whereas it is apparently cool to sell your soul for a university job, say, or a new car) and who was made of some of the universe's most naturally free stuff (one would be hard pressed to find a more nonmaterialistic person), was denied even a steady pittance, free from strings, that would have kept her secure enough to do her best work.

It has been pointed out that one of the reasons Zora Neale Hurston's work has suffered neglect is that her critics never considered her "sincere." Only after she died penniless, still laboring at her craft, still immersed in her work, still following *her* vision and *her* road, did it begin to seem to some that yes, perhaps this woman *was* a serious artist after all, since artists are known to live poor and die broke. But you're up against a hard game if you have to die to win it, and we must insist that dying in poverty is an unacceptable extreme.

We live in a society, as blacks, women, and artists, whose contests we do not design and with whose insistence on ranking us we are permanently at war. To know that second place, in such a society, has often required more work and innate genius than first, a longer, grimmer struggle over greater odds than first—and to be able to fling your scarf about dramatically while you demonstrate that you know—is to trust your own self-evaluation in the face of the Great White Western Commercial of white and male supremacy, which is virtually everything we see, outside and often inside our own homes. That Hurston held her own, literally, against the flood of whiteness and maleness that diluted so much other black art of the period in which she worked is a testimony to her genius and her faith.

As black women and as artists, we are prepared, I think, to keep that faith. There are other choices, but they are despicable.

Zora Neale Hurston, who went forth into the world with one dress to her name, and who was permitted, at other times in her life, only a single pair of shoes, rescued and recreated a world which she labored to hand us whole, never underestimating the value of her gift, if at times doubting the good sense of its recipients. She appreciated us, in any case, *as we fashioned ourselves*. That is something. And of all the people in the world to be, she chose to be herself, *and more and more herself*. That, too, is something.

ALICE WALKER

Looking for Zora

"On January 16, 1959, Zora Neale Hurston, suffering from the
effects of a stroke and writing painfully in longhand, composed a letter to the
'editorial department' of Harper & Brothers inquiring if they would be
interested in seeing 'the book I am laboring upon at present—a life of Herod
the Great.' One year and twelve days later, Zora Neale Hurston died
without funds to provide for her burial, a resident of the St. Lucie County,
Florida, Welfare Home. She lies today in an unmarked grave in a
segregated cemetery in Fort Pierce, Florida, a resting place generally symbolic
of the black writer's fate in America.

"Zora Neale Hurston is one of the most significant unread authors in
America, the author of two minor classics and four other major books."

—ROBERT HEMENWAY; "Zora Hurston and the Eatonville
    Anthropology," from *The Harlem Renaissance Remembered*, edited by
    Arna Bontemps (Dodd, 1972)

On August 15, 1973, I wake up just as the plane is lowering over Sanford,
Florida, which means I am also looking down on Eatonville, Zora Neale
Hurston's birthplace. I recognize it from Zora's description in *Mules and
Men*: "the city of five lakes, three croquet courts, three hundred brown skins,
three hundred good swimmers, plenty guavas, two schools, and no jail-
house." Of course I cannot see the guavas, but the five lakes are still there,
and it is the lakes I count as the plane prepares to land in Orlando.

From the air, Florida looks completely flat, and as we near the ground
this impression does not change. This is the first time I have seen the interior

From *I Love Myself When I Am Laughing . . . And Then Again When I Am Looking Mean and
Impressive: A Zora Neale Hurston Reader*. © 1979 by Alice Walker. The Feminist Press, 1979.
Originally entitled "Afterword: Looking for Zora."

of the state, which Zora wrote about so well, but there are the acres of orange groves, the sand, mangrove trees, and scrub pine that I know from her books. Getting off the plane I walk through the hot moist air of midday into the tacky but air-conditioned airport. I search for Charlotte Hunt, my companion on the Zora Hurston expedition. She lives in Winter Park, Florida, very near Eatonville, and is writing her graduate dissertation on Zora. I see her waving—a large pleasant-faced white woman in dark glasses. We have written to each other for several weeks, swapping our latest finds (mostly hers) on Zora, and trying to make sense out of the mass of information obtained (often erroneous or simply confusing) from Zora herself—through her stories and autobiography—and from people who wrote about her.

Eatonville has lived for such a long time in my imagination that I can hardly believe it will be found existing in its own right. But after twenty minutes on the expressway, Charlotte turns off and I see a small settlement of houses and stores set with no particular pattern in the sandy soil off the road. We stop in front of a neat gray building that has two fascinating signs: EATONVILLE POST OFFICE and EATONVILLE CITY HALL.

Inside the Eatonville City Hall half of the building, a slender, dark brown-skin woman sits looking through letters on a desk. When she hears we are searching for anyone who might have known Zora Neale Hurston, she leans back in thought. Because I don't wish to inspire foot-dragging in people who might know something about Zora they're not sure they should tell, I have decided on a simple, but I feel profoundly *useful*, lie.

"I am Miss Hurston's niece," I prompt the young woman, who brings her head down with a smile.

"I think Mrs. Moseley is about the only one still living who might remember her," she says.

"Do you mean *Mathilda* Moseley, the woman who tells those 'woman-is-smarter-than-man' lies in Zora's book?"

"Yes," says the young woman. "Mrs. Moseley is real old now, of course. But this time of day, she should be at home."

I stand at the counter looking down on her, the first Eatonville resident I have spoken to. Because of Zora's books, I feel I know something about her; at least I know what the town she grew up in was like years before she was born.

"Tell me something," I say, "do the schools teach Zora's books here?"

"No," she says, "they don't. I don't think most people know anything about Zora Neale Hurston, or know about any of the great things she did. She was a fine lady. I've read all of her books myself, but I don't think many other folks in Eatonville have."

"Many of the church people around here, as I understand it," says Charlotte in a murmured aside, "thought Zora was pretty loose. I don't think they appreciated her writing about them."

"Well," I say to the young woman, "thank you for your help." She clarifies her directions to Mrs. Moseley's house and smiles as Charlotte and I turn to go.

"The letter to Harper's does not expose a publisher's rejection of an unknown masterpiece, but it does reveal how the bright promise of the Harlem Renaissance deteriorated for many of the writers who shared in its exuberance. It also indicates the personal tragedy of Zora Neale Hurston: Barnard graduate, author of four novels, two books of folklore, one volume of autobiography, the most important collector of Afro-American folklore in America, reduced by poverty and circumstance to seek a publisher by unsolicited mail."—Robert Hemenway

"Zora Hurston was born in 1901, 1902, or 1903—depending on how old she felt herself to be at the time someone asked."—Librarian, Beinecke Library, Yale University

The Moseley house is small and white and snug, its tiny yard nearly swallowed up by oleanders and hibiscus bushes. Charlotte and I knock on the door. I call out. But there is no answer. This strikes us as peculiar. We have had time to figure out an age for Mrs. Moseley—not dates or a number, just old. I am thinking of a quivery, bedridden invalid when we hear the car. We look behind us to see an old black-and-white Buick—paint peeling and grillwork rusty—pulling into the drive. A neat old lady in a purple dress and white hair is straining at the wheel. She is frowning because Charlotte's car is in the way.

Mrs. Moseley looks at us suspiciously. "Yes, I knew Zora Neale," she says, unsmilingly and with a rather cold stare at Charlotte (who I imagine feels very *white* at that moment), "but that was a long time ago, and I don't want to talk about it."

"Yes ma'am," I murmur, bringing all my sympathy to bear on the situation.

"Not only that," Mrs. Moseley continues, "I've been sick. Been in the hospital for an operation. Ruptured artery. The doctors didn't believe I was going to live, but you see me alive, don't you?"

"Looking well, too," I comment.

Mrs. Moseley is out of her car. A thin, sprightly woman with nice gold-studded false teeth, uppers and lowers. I like her because she stands *straight* beside her car, with a hand on her hip and her straw pocketbook on her arm. She wears white T-strap shoes with heels that show off her well-shaped legs.

"I'm eighty-two years old, you know," she says. "And I just can't remember things the way I used to. Anyhow, Zora Neale left here to go to school and she never really came back to live. She'd come here for material for her books, but that was all. She spent most of her time down in South Florida."

"You know, Mrs. Moseley, I saw your name in one of Zora's books."

"You did?" she looks at me with only slightly more interest. "I read some of her books a long time ago, but then people got to borrowing and borrowing and they borrowed them all away."

"I could send you a copy of everything that's been reprinted," I offer. "Would you like me to do that?"

"No," says Mrs. Moseley promptly. "I don't read much any more. Besides, all of that was *so* long ago . . ."

Charlotte and I settle back against the car in the sun. Mrs. Moseley tells us at length and with exact recall every step in her recent operation, ending with: "What those doctors didn't know—when they were expecting me to die (and they didn't even think I'd live long enough for them to have to take out my stitches!)—is that Jesus is the best doctor, and if *He* says for you to get well, that's all that counts."

With this philosophy, Charlotte and I murmur quick assent: being Southerners and church bred, we have heard that belief before. But what we learn from Mrs. Moseley is that she does not remember much beyond the year 1938. She shows us a picture of her father and mother and says that her father was Joe Clarke's brother. Joe Clarke, as every Zora Hurston reader knows, was the first mayor of Eatonville; his fictional counterpart is Jody Starks of *Their Eyes Were Watching God*. We also get directions to where Joe Clarke's store *was*—where Club Eaton is now. Club Eton, a long orange-beige nightspot we had seen on the main road, is apparently famous for the good times in it regularly had by all. It is, perhaps, the modern equivalent of the store porch, where all the men of Zora's childhood came to tell "lies," that is, black folktales, that were "made and used on the spot," to take a line from Zora. As for Zora's exact birthplace, Mrs. Moseley has no idea.

After I have commented on the healthy growth of her hibiscus bushes, she becomes more talkative. She mentions how much she *loved* to dance, when she was a young woman, and talks about how good her husband was. When he was alive, she says, she was completely happy because he allowed her to be completely free. "I was so free I had to pinch myself sometimes to tell if I was a married woman."

Relaxed now, she tells us about going to school with Zora. "Zora and I went to the same school. It's called Hungerford High now. It *was* only to the eighth grade. But our teachers were so good that by the time you left you knew college subjects. When I went to Morris Brown in Atlanta, the teachers there were just teaching me the same things I had already learned right in Eatonville. I wrote Mama and told her I was going to come home and help her with her babies. I wasn't learning anything new."

"Tell me something, Mrs. Moseley," I ask, "why do you suppose Zora was against integration? I read somewhere that she was against school de-segregation because she felt it was an insult to black teachers."

"Oh, one of them [white people] came around asking me about inte-gration. One day I was doing my shopping. I heard 'em over there talking about it in the store, about the schools. And I got on out of the way because I knew if they asked me, they wouldn't like what I was going to tell 'em. But they came up and asked me anyhow. 'What do you think about this integration?' one of them said. I acted like I thought I had heard wrong. 'You're asking *me* what *I* think about integration?' I said. 'Well, as you can see I'm just an old colored woman'—I was seventy-five or seventy-six then— 'and this is the first time anybody ever asked me about integration. And nobody asked my grandmother what she thought, either, but her daddy was one of you all.' " Mrs. Moseley seems satisfied with this memory of her rejoinder. She looks at Charlotte. "I have the blood of three races in my veins," she says belligerently, "white, black, and Indian, and nobody asked me *anything* before."

"Do you think living in Eatonville made integration less appealing to you?"

"Well, I can tell you this: I have lived in Eatonville all my life, and I've been in the governing of this town. I've been everything but Mayor and I've been *assistant* Mayor. Eatonville was and is an all-black town. We have our own police department, post office, and town hall. Our own school and good teachers. Do I need integration?

"They took over Goldsboro, because the black people who lived there never incorporated, like we did. And now I don't even know if any black folks live there. They built big houses up there around the lakes. But we didn't let that happen in Eatonville, and we don't sell land to just anybody. And you see, we're still here."

When we leave, Mrs. Moseley is standing by her car, waving. I think of the letter Roy Wilkins wrote to a black newspaper blasting Zora Neale for her lack of enthusiasm about the integration of schools. I wonder if he knew the experience of Eatonville she was coming from. Not many black people in America have come from a self-contained, all-black community where loyalty and unity are taken for granted. A place where black pride is nothing new.

There is, however, one thing Mrs. Moseley said that bothered me.

"Tell me, Mrs. Moseley," I had asked, "why is it that thirteen years after Zora's death, no marker has been put on her grave?"

And Mrs. Moseley answered: "The reason she doesn't have a stone is because she wasn't buried here. She was buried down in South Florida somewhere. I don't think anybody really knew where she was."

> *"Only to reach a wider audience, need she ever write books—because she is a perfect book of entertainment in herself. In her youth she was always getting scholarships and things from wealthy white people, some of whom simply paid her just to sit around and represent the Negro race for them, she did it in such a racy fashion. She was full of sidesplitting anecdotes, humorous tales, and tragicomic stories, remembered out of her life in the South as a daughter of a traveling minister of God. She could make you laugh one minute and cry the next. To many of her white friends, no doubt, she was a perfect 'darkie,' in the nice meaning they give the term—that is, a naïve, childlike, sweet, humorous, and highly colored Negro.*
>
> *"But Miss Hurston was clever, too—a student who didn't let college give her a broad 'a' and who had great scorn for all pretensions, academic or otherwise. That is why she was such a fine folklore collector, able to go among the people and never act as if she had been to school at all. Almost nobody else could stop the average Harlemite on Lenox Avenue and measure his head with a strange-looking, anthropological device and not get bawled out for the attempt, except Zora, who used to stop anyone whose head looked interesting, and measure it."*—Langston
> Hughes, *The Big Sea* (Knopf)
>
> *"What does it matter what white folks must have thought about her?"*—Student, "Black Women Writers" class, Wellesley
> College

Mrs. Sarah Peek Patterson is a handsome, red-haired woman in her late forties, wearing orange slacks and gold earrings. She is the director of Lee-Peek Mortuary in Fort Pierce, the establishment that handled Zora's burial. Unlike most black funeral homes in Southern towns that sit like palaces among the general poverty, Lee-Peek has a run-down, *small* look. Perhaps this is because it is painted purple and white, as are its Cadillac chariots. These colors do not age well. The rooms are cluttered and grimy, and the bathroom is a tiny, stale-smelling prison, with a bottle of black hair dye (apparently used to touch up the hair of the corpses) dripping into the face bowl. Two pine burial boxes are resting in the bathtub.

Mrs. Patterson herself is pleasant and helpful.

"As I told you over the phone, Mrs. Patterson," I begin, shaking her hand and looking into her penny-brown eyes, "I am Zora Neale Hurston's niece, and I would like to have a marker put on her grave. You said, when I called you last week, that you could tell me where the grave is."

By this time I am, of course, completely into being Zora's niece, and the lie comes with perfect naturalness to my lips. Besides, as far as I'm concerned, she *is* my aunt—and that of all black people as well.

"She was buried in 1960," exlaims Mrs. Patterson. "That was when my father was running this funeral home. He's sick now or I'd let you talk to him. But I know where she's buried. She's in the old cemetery, the Garden of the Heavenly Rest, on Seventeenth Street. Just when you go in the gate there's a circle and she's buried right in the middle of it. Hers is the only grave in that circle—because people don't bury in that cemetery any more."

She turns to a stocky, black-skinned woman in her thirties, wearing a green polo shirt and white jeans cut off at the knee. "This lady will show you where it is," she says.

"I can't tell you how much I appreciate this," I say to Mrs. Patterson, as I rise to go. "And could you tell me something else? You see, I never met my aunt. When she died, I was still a junior in high school. But could you tell me what she died of, and what kind of funeral she had?"

"I don't know exactly what she died of," Mrs. Patterson says. "I know she didn't have any money. Folks took up a collection to bury her. . . . I believe she died of malnutrition."

"*Malnutrition?*"

Outside, in the blistering sun, I lean my head against Charlotte's even more blistering cartop. The sting of the hot metal only intensifies my anger.

"*Malnutrition,*" I manage to mutter. "Hell, our condition hasn't changed *any* since Phillis Wheatley's time. *She* died of malnutrition!"

"Really?" says Charlotte, "I didn't know that."

> "*One cannot overemphasize the extent of her commitment. It was so great that her marriage in the spring of 1927 to Herbert Sheen was short-lived. Although divorce did not come officially until 1931, the two separated amicably after only a few months, Hurston to continue her collecting, Sheen to attend Medical School.*"—Robert Hemenway

"What is your name?" I ask the woman who has climbed into the back seat.

"Rosalee," she says. She has a rough, pleasant voice, as if she is a singer who also smokes a lot. She is homely, and has an air of ready indifference.

"Another woman came by here wanting to see the grave," she says, lighting up a cigarette. "She was a little short, dumpty white lady from one of these Florida schools. Orlando or Daytona. But let me tell you something before we gets started. All I know is where the cemetery is. I don't know one thing about that grave. You better go back in and ask her to draw you a map."

A few moments later, with Mrs. Patterson's diagram of where the grave is, we head for the cemetery.

We drive past blocks of small, pastel-colored houses and turn right onto 17th Street. At the very end, we reach a tall curving gate, with the words "Garden of the Heavenly Rest" fading into the stone. I expected, from Mrs. Patterson's small drawing, to find a small circle—which would have placed Zora's grave five or ten paces from the road. But the "circle" is over an acre large and looks more like an abandoned field. Tall weeds choke the dirt road and scrape against the sides of the car. It doesn't help either that I step out into an active anthill.

"I don't know about y'all," I say, "but I don't even believe this." I am used to the haphazard cemetery-keeping that is traditional in most Southern black communities, but this neglect is staggering. As far as I can see there is nothing but bushes and weeds, some as tall as my waist. One grave is near the road, and Charlotte elects to investigate it. It is fairly clean, and belongs to someone who died in 1963.

Rosalee and I plunge into the weeds; I pull my long dress up to my hips. The weeds scratch my knees, and the insects have a feast. Looking back, I see Charlotte standing resolutely near the road.

"Aren't you coming?" I call.

"No," she calls back. "I'm from these parts and I know what's out there." She means snakes.

"Shit," I say, my whole life and the people I love flashing melodramatically before my eyes. Rosalee is a few yards to my right.

"How're you going to find anything out here?" she asks. And I stand still a few seconds, looking at the weeds. Some of them are quite pretty, with tiny yellow flowers. They are thick and healthy, but dead weeds under them have formed a thick gray carpet on the ground. A snake could be lying six inches from my big toe and I wouldn't see it. We move slowly, very slowly, our eyes alert, our legs trembly. It is hard to tell where the center of the circle is since the circle is not really round, but more like half of something round. There are things crackling and hissing in the grass. Sandspurs are sticking to the inside of my skirt. Sand and ants cover my feet. I look toward the road and notice that there are, indeed, *two* large curving stones, making an entrance and exit to the cemetery. I take my bearings from them and try to navigate to exact center. But the center of anything can be very large, and a grave is not a pinpoint. Finding the grave seems positively hopeless. There is only one thing to do:

"Zora!" I yell, as loud as I can (causing Rosalee to jump), "are you out here?"

"If she is, I sho hope she don't answer you. If she do, I'm gone."

"Zora!" I call again. "I'm here. Are you?"

"If she is," grumbles Rosalee, "I hope she'll keep it to herself."

"Zora!" Then I start fussing with her. "I hope you don't think I'm going to stand out here all day, with these snakes watching me and these ants having a field day. In fact, I'm going to call you just one or two more times." On a clump of dried grass, near a small bushy tree, my eye falls on one of the largest bugs I have ever seen. It is on its back, and is as large as three of my fingers. I walk toward it, and yell "Zo-ra!" and my foot sinks into a hole. I look down. I am standing in a sunken rectangle that is about six feet long and about three or four feet wide. I look up to see where the two gates are.

"Well," I say, "this is the center, or approximately anyhow. It's also the only sunken spot we've found. Doesn't this look like a grave to you?"

"For the sake of not going no farther through these bushes," Rosalee growls, "yes, it do."

"Wait a minute," I say, "I have to look around some more to be sure this is the only spot that resembles a grave. But you don't have to come."

Rosalee smiles—a grin, really—beautiful and tough.

"Naw," she says, "I feels sorry for you. If one of these snakes got ahold of you out here by yourself I'd feel *real* bad." She laughs. "I done come this far, I'll go on with you."

"Thank you, Rosalee," I say. "Zora thanks you too."

"Just as long as she don't try to tell me in person," she says, and together we walk down the field.

"The gusto and flavor of Zora Neal{e} Hurston's storytelling, for example, long before the yarns were published in "Mules and Men" and other books, became a local legend which might . . . have spread further under different conditions. A tiny shift in the center of gravity could have made them bestsellers."—Arna Bontemps, *Personals* (Paul Bremen, Ltd., London, 1963)

"Bitter over the rejection of her folklore's value, especially in the black community, frustrated by what she felt was her failure to convert the Afro-American world view into forms of prose fiction, Hurston finally gave up."—Robert Hemenway

When Charlotte and I drive up to the Merritt Monument Company, I immediately see the headstone I want.

"How much is this one?" I ask the young woman in charge, pointing to a tall black stone. It looks as majestic as Zora herself must have been when she was learning voodoo from those root doctors down in New Orleans.

"Oh, *that* one," she says, "that's our finest. That's Ebony Mist,"

"Well, how much is it?"

"I don't know. But wait," she says, looking around in relief, "here comes somebody who'll know."

A small, sunburned man with squinty green eyes comes up. He must be the engraver, I think, because his eyes are contracted into slits, as if he has been keeping stone dust out of them for years.

"That's Ebony Mist," he says. "That's our best."

"How much is it?" I ask, beginning to realize I probably *can't* afford it.

He gives me a price that would feed a dozen Sahelian drought victims for three years. I realize I must honor the dead, but between the dead great and the living starving, there is no choice.

"I have a lot of letters to be engraved," I say, standing by the plain gray marker I have chosen. It is pale and ordinary, not at all like Zora, and makes me momentarily angry that I am not rich.

We go into his office and I hand him a sheet of paper that has:

ZORA NEALE HURSTON
"A GENIUS OF THE SOUTH"
NOVELIST   FOLKLORIST
ANTHROPOLOGIST
1901   1960

"A genius of the South" is from one of Jean Toomer's poems.

"Where is this grave?" the monument man asks. "If it's in a new cemetery, the stone has to be flat."

"Well, it's not a new cemetery and Zora—my aunt—doesn't need anything flat because with the weeds out there, you'd never be able to see it. You'll have to go out there with me."

He grunts.

"And take a long pole and 'sound' the spot," I add. "Because there's now way of telling it's a grave, except that it's sunken."

"Well," he says, after taking my money and writing up a receipt, in the full awareness that he's the only monument dealer for miles, "you take this flag" (he hands me a four-foot-long pole with a red-metal marker on top) "and take it out to the cemetery and put it where you think the grave is. It'll take us about three weeks to get the stone out there."

I wonder if he knows he is sending me to another confrontation with the snakes. He probably does. Charlotte has told me she will cut my leg and suck out the blood, if I am bit.

"At least send me a photograph when it's done, won't you?"

He says he will.

"Hurston's return to her folklore-collecting in December of 1927 was made possible by Mrs. R. Osgood Mason, an elderly white patron of the arts, who at various times also helped Langston Hughes, Alain Locke, Richmond Barthe, and Miguel Covarrubias. Hurston apparently came to her attention through the intercession of Locke, who frequently served as a kind of liaison between the young black talent and Mrs. Mason. The entire relationship between this woman and the Harlem Renaissance deserves extended study, for it represents much of the ambiguity involved in white patronage of black artists. All her artists were instructed to call her 'Godmother'; there was a decided emphasis on the 'primitive' aspects of black culture, apparently a holdover from Mrs. Mason's interest in the Plains Indians. In Hurston's case there were special restrictions imposed by her patron: although she was to be paid a handsome salary for her folklore collecting, she was to limit her correspondence and publish nothing of her research without prior approval."—Robert Hemenway

"You have to read the chapters Zora left out of her autobiography."—Student, Special Collections Room, Beinecke Library, Yale University

Dr. Benton, a friend of Zora's and a practicing M.D. in Fort Pierce, is one of those old, good-looking men whom I always have trouble not liking. (It no longer bothers me that I may be constantly searching for father figures; by this time I have found several and dearly enjoyed knowing them all.) He is shrewd, with steady brown eyes under hair that is almost white. He is probably in his seventies, but doesn't look it. He carries himself with dignity, and has cause to be proud of the new clinic where he now practices medicine.

His nurse looks at us with suspicion, but Dr. Benton's eyes have the penetration of a scalpel cutting through skin. I guess right away that if he knows anything at all about Zora Hurston, he will not believe I am her niece. "Eatonville?" Dr. Benton says, leaning forward in his chair, looking first at me, then at Charlotte. "Yes, I know Eatonville, I grew up not far from there. I knew the whole bunch of Zora's family." (He looks at the shape of my cheekbones, the size of my eyes, and the nappiness of my hair.) "I knew her daddy. The old man. He was a hardworking, Christian man. Did the best he could for his family. He was the mayor of Eatonville for a while, you know.

"My father was the mayor of Goldsboro. You probably never heard of it. It never incorporated like Eatonville did, and has just about disappeared. But Eatonville is still all-black."

He pauses and looks at me. "And you're Zora's niece," he says wonderingly.

"Well," I say with shy dignity, yet with some tinge, I hope, of a 19th-century blush, "I'm illegitimate. That's why I never knew Aunt Zora."

I love him for the way he comes to my rescue. "You're *not* illegitimate!" he cries, his eyes resting on me fondly. "All of us are God's children! Don't you even *think* such a thing!"

And I hate myself for lying to him. Still, I ask myself, would I have gotten this far toward getting the headstone and finding out about Zora Hurston's last days without telling my lie? Actually, I probably would have. But I don't like taking chances that could get me stranded in Central Florida.

"Zora didn't get along with her family. I don't know why. Did you read her autobiography, *Dust Tracks on a Road?*"

"Yes, I did," I say. "It pained me to see Zora pretending to be naive and grateful about the old white 'Godmother' who helped finance her research, but I loved the part where she ran off from home after falling out with her brother's wife."

Dr. Benton nodded. "When she got sick, I tried to get her to go back to her family, but she refused. There wasn't any real hatred; they just never had gotten along and Zora wouldn't go to them. She didn't want to go to the county home, either, but she had to, because she couldn't do a thing for herself."

"I was surprised to learn she died of malnutrition."

Dr. Benton seems startled. "Zora *didn't* die of malnutrition," he says indignantly. "Where did you get that story from? She had a stroke and she died in the welfare home." He seems peculiarly upset, distressed, but sits back reflectively in his chair: "She was an incredible woman," he muses.

"Sometimes when I closed my office, I'd go by her house and just talk to her for an hour or two. She was a well-read, well-traveled woman and always had her own ideas about what was going on . . ."

"I never knew her, you know. Only some of Carl Van Vechten's photographs and some newspaper photographs. . . . What did she look like?"

"When I knew her, in the fifties, she was a big woman, *erect*. Not quite as light as I am [Dr. Benton is dark beige], and about five foot, seven inches, and she weighed about two hundred pounds. Probably more. She . . ."

"What! Zora was *fat*! She wasn't, in Van Vechten's pictures!"

"Zora loved to eat," Dr. Benton says complacently. "She could sit down with a mound of ice cream and just eat and talk till it was all gone."

While Dr. Benton is talking, I recall that the Van Vechten pictures were taken when Zora was still a young woman. In them she appears tall, tan, and healthy. In later newspaper photographs—when she was in her forties—I remembered that she seemed heavier and several shades lighter. I reasoned that the earlier photographs were taken while she was busy collecting folklore materials in the hot Florida sun.

"She had high blood pressure. Her health wasn't good. . . . She used to live in one of my houses—on School Court Street. It's a block house . . . I don't recall the number. But my wife and I used to invite her over to the house for dinner. *She always ate well*," he says emphatically.

"That's comforting to know," I say, wondering where Zora ate when she wasn't with the Bentons.

"Sometimes she would run out of groceries—after she got sick—and she'd call me. 'Come over here and see 'bout me,' she'd say. And I'd take her shopping and buy her groceries.

"She was always studying. Her mind—before the stroke—just worked all the time. She was always going somewhere, too. She once went to Honduras to study something. And when she died, she was working on that book about Herod the Great. She was so intelligent! And really had perfect expressions. Her English was beautiful." (I suspect this is a clever way to let me know Zora herself didn't speak in the "black English" her characters used.)

"I used to read all of her books," Dr. Benton continues, "but it was a long time ago. I remember one about . . . it was called, I think, 'The Children of God' [*Their Eyes Were Watching God*], and I remember Janie and Teapot [Tea Cake] and the mad dog riding on the cow in that hurricane and bit old Teapot on the cheek . . ."

I am delighted that he remembers even this much of the story, even if the names are wrong, but seeing his affection for Zora I feel I must ask him about her burial. "Did she *really* have a pauper's funeral?"

"She *didn't* have a pauper's funeral!" he says with great heat. "Everybody around here *loved* Zora."

"We just came back from ordering a headstone," I say quietly, because he *is* an old man and the color is coming and going on his face, "but to tell the truth, I can't be positive what I found is the grave. All I know is the spot I found was the only grave-size hole in the area."

"I remember it wasn't near the road," says Dr. Benton, more calmly. "Some other lady came by here and we went out looking for the grave and I took a long iron stick and poked all over that part of the cemetery but we didn't find anything. She took some pictures of the general area. Do the weeds still come up to your knees?"

"And beyond," I murmur. This time there isn't any doubt. Dr. Benton feels ashamed.

As he walks us to our car, he continues to talk about Zora. "She couldn't really write much near the end. She had the stroke and it left her weak; her mind was affected. She couldn't think about anything for long.

"She came here from Daytona, I think. She owned a houseboat over there. When she came here, she sold it. She lived on that money, then she worked as a maid—for an article on maids she was writing—and she worked for the *Chronicle* writing the horoscope column.

"I think black people here in Florida got mad at her because she was for some politician they were against. She said this politician *built* schools for blacks while the one they wanted just talked about it. And although Zora wasn't egotistical, what she thought, she thought; and generally what she thought, she said."

When we leave Dr. Benton's office, I realize I have missed my plane back home to Jackson, Mississippi. That being so, Charlotte and I decide to find the house Zora lived in before she was taken to the county welfare home to die. From among her many notes, Charlotte locates a letter of Zora's she has copied that carries the address: 1734 School Court Street. We ask several people for directions. Finally, two old gentlemen in a dusty gray Plymouth offer to lead us there. School Court Street is not paved, and the road is full of mud puddles. It is dismal and squalid, redeemed only by the brightness of the late afternoon sun. Now I can understand what a "block" house is. It is a house shaped like a block, for one thing, surrounded by others just like it. Some houses are blue and some are green or yellow. Zora's is light green. They are tiny—about fifty by fifty feet, squatty with flat roofs. The house Zora lived in looks worse than the others, but that is its only distinction. It also has three ragged and dirty children sitting on the steps.

"Is this where y'all live?" I ask, aiming my camera.

"No, ma'am," they say in unison, looking at me earnestly. "We live over yonder. This Miss So-and-So's house; but she in the horspital."

We chatter inconsequentially while I take more pictures. A car drives up with a young black couple in it. They scowl fiercely at Charlotte and don't look at me with friendliness, either. They get out and stand in their doorway across the street. I go up to them to explain. "Did you know Zora Hurston used to live right across from you?" I ask.

"Who?" They stare at me blankly, then become curiously attentive, as if they think I made the name up. They are both Afro-ed and he is somberly dashiki-ed.

I suddenly feel frail and exhausted. "It's too long a story," I say, "but tell me something, is there anybody on this street who's lived here for more than thirteen years?"

"That old man down there," the young man says, pointing. Sure enough, there is a man sitting on his steps three houses down. He has graying hair and is very neat, but there is a weakness about him. He reminds me of Mrs. Turner's husband in *Their Eyes Were Watching God*. He's rather "vanishing"-looking, as if his features have been sanded down. In the old days, before black was beautiful, he was probably considered attractive, because he has wavy hair and light-brown skin; but now, well, light skin has ceased to be its own reward.

After the preliminaries, there is only one thing I want to know: "Tell me something," I begin, looking down at Zora's house, "did Zora like flowers?"

He looks at me queerly. "As a matter of fact," he says, looking regretfully at the bare, rough yard that surrounds her former house, "she was crazy about them. And she was a great gardener. She loved azaleas, and that running and blooming vine [morning glories], and she really loved that night-smelling flower [gardenia]. She kept a vegetable garden year-round, too. She raised collards and tomatoes and things like that.

"Everyone in this community thought well of Miss Hurston. When she died, people all up and down this street took up a collection for her burial. We put her away nice."

"Why didn't somebody put up a headstone?"

"Well, you know, one was never requested. Her and her family didn't get along. They didn't even come to the funeral."

"And did she live down there by herself?"

"Yes, until they took her away. She lived with—just her and her companion, Sport,"

My ears perk up. "Who?"

"Sport, you know, her dog. He was her only companion. He was a big brown-and-white dog."

When I walk back to the car, Charlotte is talking to the young couple on their porch. They are relaxed and smiling.

"I told them about the famous lady who used to live across the street from them," says Charlotte as we drive off. "Of course they had no idea Zora ever lived, let alone that she lived across the street. I think I'll send some of her books to them."

"That's real kind of you," I say.

> *"I am not tragically colored. There is no great sorrow damned up in my soul, nor lurking behind my eyes. I do not mind at all. I do not belong to the sobbing school of Negrohood who hold that nature somehow has given them a lowdown dirty deal and whose feelings are all hurt about it. . . . No, I do not weep at the world—I am too busy sharpening my oyster knife."*—Zora Neale Hurston, "How It Feels to Be Colored Me," World Tomorrow, 1928

There are times—and finding Zora Hurston's grave was one of them—when normal responses of grief, horror, and so on, do not make sense because they bear no real relation to the depth of the emotion one feels. It was impossible for me to cry when I saw the field full of weeds where Zora is. Partly this is because I have come to know Zora through her books and she was not a teary sort of person herself; but partly, too, it is because there is a point at which even grief feels absurd. And at this point, laughter gushes up to retrieve sanity.

It is only later, when the pain is not so direct a threat to one's own existence that what was learned in that moment of comical lunacy is understood. Such moments rob us of both youth and vanity. But perhaps they are also times when greater disciplines are born.

MARY HELEN WASHINGTON

A Woman Half in Shadow

*"She walked into my study one day by telephone appointment; carelessly, a
big-boned, good-boned young woman, handsome and light yellow."*
—FANNIE HURST, Zora Hurston's employer; novelist

"Zora was rather short and squat and black as coal."
—THEODORE PRATT, writer for the Florida
Historical Society

"She was reddish light brown."
—MRS. ALZEDA HACKER, a
friend of Zora Hurston

Whether Zora Neale Hurston was black as coal, light yellow, or light
brown seems to have depended a great deal on the imagination and mind
set of the observer. These three divergent descriptions of her color serve as
a paradigm for the way Zora Hurston, the personality, and Zora Hurston,
the writer, have been looked upon by the world which judged her. Outstanding novelist, skilled folklorist, journalist, and critic, Zora Hurston was
for thirty years the most prolific black woman writer in America. And yet,
from what has been written about her, it would be difficult to judge the
quality of her work or even to know what color she was.

In all of the various personality sketches, full-length literary studies,

From *I Love Myself When I Am Laughing . . . And Then Again When I Am Looking Mean and
Impressive: A Zora Neale Hurston Reader.* © 1979 by Alice Walker. The Feminist Press, 1979.
Originally entitled "Introduction: Zora Neale Hurston: A Woman Half in Shadow."

forewords, and afterwords inspired by Hurston, there is a broad range of contradictory reactions. There were those who saw her as a highly reserved and serious writer, so private that few people ever knew her correct age or that she had been married several times; she was also described as loud and coarse, playing the happy darky role to entertain whites. Some critics put her writing in the same category as minstrel shows; others praised her as the most significant "unread" author in America. One critic wrote that her work reveals an unconscious desire to be white. But a student who heard Hurston speak at Bennett College in 1941 said that what the students were most impressed with was this woman's deep sense of racial pride.

Certainly nothing ever written about her or her work is lukewarm. Partly, this is attributable to her own unique personality. From the anecdotes and apocryphal tales told about Hurston, one must conclude that she was nothing if not controversial, highly outspoken, arrogant, independent, and eccentric. She was also a black woman determined, in the period between 1920 and 1950, to have a career as a writer, which in itself was eccentric. Though she lived in controversy, died penniless, and was out of print for thirty years, Zora Neale Hurston did indeed establish herself as a writer and folklorist. In her thirty-year career, she published four novels, two books of folklore, an autobiography, numerous stories, articles, and plays.

To a large extent, the attention focused on Zora Hurston's controversial personality and lifestyle has inhibited any objective critical analysis of her work. Few male critics have been able to resist sly innuendoes and outright attacks on Hurston's personal life, even when the work in question was not affected by her disposition or her private affairs. But these controversies have loomed so large in the reviews of her work that once again the task of confronting them must precede any reappraisal or reevaluation of her highly neglected work. Jumping up and down in the same foot-tracks, as Zora would call it.

Three recent literary events signaled the end of the inadequate, some-times venomous, often highly inaccurate, assessment of Hurston's life and work: the appearance of Robert Hemenway's excellent and thoroughly re-searched book, *Zora Neale Hurston: A Literary Biography;* the reissue of Hur-ston's finest novel, *Their Eyes Were Watching God;* and the publication of [the anthology], *I Love Myself When I Am Laughing . . .* These are three important steps in bringing Hurston to the place her mother meant for her to occupy when she urged Zora to "jump at de sun."

Questions and controversies have surrounded Hurston and her career since she stepped into New York City in 1925 to join the Harlem Renais-sance. Like the "lyin' tales" Hurston collected in her folklore research, some have become as familiar as legend and have the same degree of veracity. But still the questions must be posed and answered if one is to understand the richly complicated Zora Hurston. How did this poor, unschooled girl from a peasant background in the all-black town of Eatonville, Florida, manage, in the early 1900s, to get to Howard University, Barnard College, and Columbia University, and eventually become one of the shapers of the important black literary and cultural movement of the twenties, the Harlem Renaissance? Is there any truth to the often-made accusation that Hurston played the obsequious role of the swinging, happy darkie in order to sustain the financial support of wealthy white patrons? Did Hurston deliberately avoid any condemnation of racism in order not to offend white friends? What is the truth behind the 1948 morals charge that she sexually abused a ten-year-old boy? How did this celebrant of black folk culture become, in later years, a right-wing Republican, publicly supporting a staunch segregationist and opposing the 1954 Supreme Court desegregation decision? Why, in the last decade of her life, did she remove herself from all her acquaintances and contacts and die in poverty in a Florida county welfare home?

Any probing of the life and times of Zora Neale Hurston must begin in the town of Eatonville, Florida, where she was born, *probably* around 1901. Incorporated in 1886 as an all-black town, Eatonville, Florida, five miles from Orlando, was, according to Hurston's autobiography, a "pure Negro town—charter, mayor, council, town marhsal and all." It was neither ghetto, nor slum, nor black bottom, but a rich source of black cultural traditions where Zora would be nourished on black folktales and tropical fruits and sheltered from the early contacts with racial prejudice that have so indelibly marked almost all other Afro-American writers. It was a sheltering for which Hurston paid dearly, as it caused her to develop attitudes that were out of the mainstream, particularly in the protest years of the forties.

The most critical fact of Zora Neale Hurston's childhood was that her mother, Lucy Hurston, who encouraged her daughter's indomitable and creative spirit, died when Zora was nine. In the years that followed, Zora went from one relative to another and was eventually rejected by her father and his new wife. She hired herself out as a domestic in several homes, and, around the age of fourteen, she joined a Gilbert and Sullivan traveling dramatic troupe as a wardrobe girl and maid, ending up, after eighteen months, in Baltimore. There she enrolled in Morgan Academy (now Morgan State University), with one dress, a change of underwear, a pair of oxfords, and the intelligence and drive that were her hallmarks. After graduation in June 1918, she went on to Howard University in Washington, D.C. She received an associate degree in 1920, though she studied intermittently at Howard until 1924, getting A's in courses she liked, and F's in those she didn't.

During her years in school, Zora Hurston was frequently in debt, though she worked at all sorts of jobs from a manicurist in a Washington barber shop to a maid for distinguished black families. Throughout her life, Hurston would not be a stranger to either debt or hard work. In 1950, when she was a noted American writer, she was discovered "masquerading" as a maid for a wealthy white woman in a fashionable section of Miami. Though she claimed she was temporarily "written out" and wanted the experience for an article about domestics, the truth was she was living in a shabby studio, had received a number of rejection slips for stories, was hustling speaking dates and borrowing from friends, and was flat broke. These were some of the most critical facts of her adult life. On the other hand, during her earlier writing period, Zora Hurston was extremely adept at finding people to give her money to further her career, a talent which sparked the accusation that she pumped whites for money, compromising her own dignity in the process. Fellow artist Langston Hughes, who for years was supported by the same white woman as Hurston, said that "In her youth she was always getting scholarships and things from wealthy white people, some of whom simply paid her just to sit around and represent the Negro race for them, she did it in such a racy fashion. . . . To many of her white friends, no doubt, she was a perfect 'darkie'. . . ."

Behind that spurious comment was an old feud between these one-time good friends over their collaboration in writing the play *Mule Bone*. Each accused the other of stealing a part of the play. Robert Hemenway concludes, in his biography of Hurston, that while most of the play was Hurston's work, she reneged on the partnership when Hughes tried to include a third party, a woman, in the deal. Hughes's self-serving, chauvinistic remark about the incident, "Girls are funny creatures," was designed to make Hurston look childish and fickle, rather than like a colleague who felt betrayed, however mistaken she might have been.

Critic Nathan Huggins gives Hurston the same kind of going over in his book, *Harlem Renaissance*. Huggins says Hurston thrived on her dependent relationship to an elderly white patron, Mrs. R. Osgood Mason, and deliberately played the role of the simple, childlike primitive. In his critical evaluation of Hurston, Huggins devotes an entire page to Wallace Thurman's satire of Hurston in his book, *Infants of the Spring*, in which Thurman caricatures Hurston as Sweetie Mae Carr, a Negro opportunist cutting the fool for white folks in order to get her tuition paid and her stories sold.

Nearly every word of the four and one-half pages on Zora Hurston is taken up with whether or not Hurston's "darky act" was real or put-on, and there is little effort by Huggins to examine her literary contributions to the period.

There are other invasions of Hurston's personality under the guise of critical commentary. Theodore Pratt of the Florida Historical Society says she was pampered and spoiled, having been given too many scholarships, fellowships, and grants. And Darwin Turner's lengthy critique of Hurston in his book, *In a Minor Chord,* makes clear that, like previous critics, he intends to evaluate Hurston's work on the basis of her personality. Turner describes her as a "quick-tempered woman, arrogant toward her peers, obsequious toward her supposed superiors, desperate for recognition and reassurance to assuage her feelings of inferiority. . . ." Then he concludes: "It is in reference to this image that one must examine her novels, her folklore, and her view of the Southern scene." It is ironic and telling that in his critique of Renaissance writer Jean Toomer in the very same book, Turner does not evaluate Toomer's work on the basis of his marriage to a white woman or his refusal to be identified with blacks after the publication of *Cane.* On the contrary, Turner delicately tiptoes around that controversy and declares that Toomer's vehement insistence that he was neither "Negro" nor Caucasian—but a member of the "American" race—is "philosophically viable and utterly sincere." Few critics ever considered Hurston's idiosyncratic views "philosophically viable," and even fewer excused her because she was sincere. Although Darwin Turner blames Zora Hurston's obscurity on the fact that she got sandwiched in between the exotic primitivism of the Harlem Renaissance and the protest mood of the forties, another possibility suggests itself: she was a black woman whose entire career output was subjected to the judgment of critics, both white and black, who were all men.

Much of the criticism of Zora Hurston that was commonplace from the twenties on seems to have stemmed from her early relationship with a white patron. Just what did go on between Zora Hurston and Mrs. R. Osgood Mason of Park Avenue, New York, and why did it inspire such severe and, in some cases, venomous attacks on Hurston? According to the letters she wrote to the wealthy Mrs. Mason, Zora Hurston signed a contract on December 8, 1928, granting her a monthly allowance of two hundred dollars so that she could collect folklore in the South, gathering materials for her first book. The contract stipulated that Hurston's folklore collections would become Mrs. Mason's exclusive property, and that she would exercise full control over Hurston's work because she felt Hurston could not be trusted to know best what to do with it. Over a period of five years, Mrs. Mason gave Hurston approximately fifteen thousand dollars for her work and self-support. Although the entire collection, except for the contract, is a one-way correspondence—all of the letters between them are from Hurston to Mrs. Mason—there is a great deal about Mrs. Mason that can be read between the lines. She must have been an extremely controlling woman because Zora Hurston was kept walking a tightrope so as not to offend her. Hurston wrote an article in which she said that "white people could not be trusted to collect the lore of others," and "Godmother" Mason was so upset that Hurston had to hastily explain that "Godmother" was not included in that remark. "Godmother" encouraged a childlike dependency from those under her patronage and demanded obedience and loyalty in return for the monthly checks. Hurston felt that she could not make a move in her career without this woman's permission, and, according to the terms of the contract, she was absolutely correct.

The letters reveal some unpleasant things about Hurston too. She was capable not only of surviving the terrible constrictures of this arrangement, but of dredging up some pretty self-serving flattery for the woman she addressed variously as "Dearest Godmother," "little mother of the primitive world," "the immaculate conception," and "a glimpse of the holy grail." Some letters sound almost mystical, as though Hurston is petitioning favors from a high priestess. This poetic tribute to Mrs. Mason, dated Sunday morning, 1931, would be humorous in its excessiveness if it were not also so hopelessly servile:

> Out of the essence of my Godmother
> Out of the True one
> Out of the Wise one I am made to be
> From her breath I am born
> Yes, as the world is made new by the breath of Spring
> And is strengthened by the winds of Summer
> The Sea is stirred by its passion
> Thus, I have taken from the breath of your mouth
> From the vapor of your soul I am made to be
> By the warmth of your love I am made to stand erect
> You are the Spring and Summer of my existence.

The next letter, dated August 14, 1932, begins:

> Now about the money, Godmother.

Beneath all the subterfuge and posturing in these letters is one cold, inescapable fact: Zora was hard-pressed for the money for her career. She needed to travel to the South to spend time with people who knew the folk stories and would tell them only to trusted friends. Few black scholars had the kind of money to finance such an expedition. But even the contract with Mrs. Mason did not relieve Hurston of money worries. At one time she had to itemize her expenses for Mrs. Mason to show her how she was handling the money. She had to account for such obvious necessities as shoe repair, car fare, and medicine; even a box of Kotex is listed. Once or twice she mentions the intestinal problem that was beginning to trouble her, in order to justify buying medication for treatment. In a letter dated April 27, 1932, Hurston was reduced to begging "Godmother darling" for a pair of shoes;

> I really need a pair of shoes. You remember that we discussed the matter in the fall and agreed that I should own only one pair at a time. I bought a pair in mid-December and they have held up until now. My big toe is about to burst out of my right shoe and so I must do something about it.

There are many letters from this period documenting Hurston's efforts to become self-supporting. She staged concerts and plays in order to make money on her own, and at one point proposed utilizing her culinary skills by becoming a "chicken specialist," making chicken soup, salad, à la king, and supplying hot chicken at a moment's notice to fifty to one hundred customers—"an exclusive mouth to mouth service" to New York's finer hostesses. In her efforts to economize, she washed her face with laundry soap and ignored a growing and painful stomach ailment.

If one thinks of the arrogant, individualistic woman who once went after her domineering stepmother with a hatchet, then these letters are strangely un-Hurston-like. But Zora Hurston was fiercely determined to have a career, no matter what or who had to be sacrificed. In consideration of that determined will, perhaps the most Hurston-like statement in the whole passel of letters is one which is unintentionally revealing of the use to which Mrs. Mason had been put: "I shall wrassle me up a future or die trying."

Zora Hurston had been able to "wrassle up" a scholarship to Barnard College, where she studied under the noted anthropologist, Dr. Franz Boas. Later she continued to work under him at Columbia University. Her association with "Papa" Franz, as she called him, was partly responsible for sending Hurston back to her hometown of Eatonville in 1927 to do formal folklore research. There was a gold mine for a folklorist, a rich storehouse of authentic tales, songs, and folkways of black people—unresearched by any black scholar until Hurston. Thus began the unique effort of Zora Neale

Hurston to tell the tales, sing the songs, do the dances, and repeat the raucous sayings and doings of the Negro farthest down. It was out of this material that Hurston would fashion her career as folklorist and novelist.

The decade of the thirties was the meridian of Hurston's career. In 1935, she published her first book of folklore, *Mules and Men*, based on material she collected in Florida and Louisiana. A classic in form and style, *Mules and Men* goes far beyond the mere reproduction of the tales; it introduces the reader to the whole world of jook joints, lying contests, and tall-tale sessions that make up the drama of the folk life of black people in the rural South. The tales are set in the framework of a story in which Hurston herself is a character. The other characters, who in conventional folklore collections are merely informants, are real personalities in *Mules and Men*, exposing their prejudices, love affairs, jealousies, while they tell the old stories about how black people got black or how John outwitted Ole Massa during slavery. In her first novel, *Jonah's Gourd Vine*, also published in the thirties, Zora Hurston continued to use the folk life of Eatonville as the essential experience. Loosely based on the lives of her parents, *Jonah's Gourd Vine* presents one of Hurston's many powerful women characters—Lucy Pearson, wife of the town's philandering preacher, John Pearson. On her deathbed, Lucy Pearson is such a strong-willed woman that John is afraid to be in the same room with her, and with the advice she gives Isis (probably Zora), she bequeaths the spirit to her daugher: "You always strain tuh be de bell-cow, never be de tail uh nothin'." With these publications and the ones that were to follow in the thirties, Zora Hurston had begun to take her work in directions that would earn her both high praise and severe censure. In an era when many educated and cultured blacks prided themselves on removing all traces of their rural black origins, when a high-class "Negro" virtue was not to "act one's color," Zora not only celebrated the distinctiveness of black culture, but saw those traditional black folkways as marked improvements over the "imaginative wasteland of white society."

Then, in 1937, came the novel in which Hurston triumphed in the art of taking the imagery, imagination, and experiences of black folk and making literature—*Their Eyes Were Watching God*. Hurston says in her autobiography that she wrote the novel in seven straight weeks in the Caribbean after a love affair ended, and, though the circumstances were difficult, she tried to "embalm" the novel with all of her tenderness for this man.

Perhaps because the novel's main character, Janie Woods, has a succession of husbands and finally finds joy and fulfillment in her third marriage, the novel has generally been thought of as a love story about love. On a much deeper and more important level, however, its theme is Janie's search for identity, an identity which finally begins to take shape as she throws off the false images which have been thrust upon her because she is both black and woman in a society where neither is allowed to exist naturally and freely. Hurston uses two images from nature to symbolize Janie's quest: the horizon and the blossoming pear tree. One, the horizon, suggests that the search is an individual quest; the other, the pear tree in blossom, suggests a fulfillment in union with another. Janie describes her journey to find herself in a language that takes us deep into black folk traditions:

> Ah been a delegate to de big 'ssociation of life. Yessuh! De Grand Lodge, de big convention of livin' is just where Ah been dis year and a half y'all ain't seen me.

Folk language, folkways, and folk stories work symbolically in the novel as a measure of a character's integrity and freedom. Those characters whose self-esteem and identity are based on illusion and false values are alienated from the black folk community, and, conversely, those, like Janie herself, who struggle against those self-alienating values toward a deeper sense of community, experience wholeness. Janie is both humiliated and angered by the attempts of her first two husbands to win her with materialistic gifts and to make her subservient to them. Thus the dramatic tension of the novel takes place on two levels: Janie has to resist both male domination and the empty materialism of white culture in order to get to the horizon.

Janie (née Crawford) Killicks Starks Woods is one of the few—and certainly the earliest—heroic black women in the Afro-American literary tradition. Critic Robert Stepto says that the primary voice in a literary tradition is "the personal, heroic voice, delineating the dimensions of heroism by aspiring to a heroic posture . . . or expressing an awareness of that which they ought to be." Janie assumes this heroic stature by her struggles for self-definition, for autonomy, for liberation from the illusions that others have tried to make her live by or that she herself has submitted to. Moreover, she is always the aware voice, consciously undergoing the most severe tests of that autonomy.

In *Their Eyes Were Watching God,* Hurston the creative artist and Hurston the folklorist were perfectly united. Zora Neale Hurston went on to publish two more books in the next two years—*Tell My Horse* (1938), a book of folklore from her experiences in Haiti, and another novel, *Moses, Man of the Mountain* (1939), a re-creation of the Moses myth with black folk characters. By the end of the thirties, she deserved her title: the best and most prolific black woman writer in America.

If the thirties were Hurston's meridian, they were also the beginning of a ground swell of criticism that would become the intellectual lynching of Zora Neale Hurston. The 1936 review of *Mules and Men* written by educator and critic Sterling Brown praised *Mules* for its dramatic appeal but was extremely critical of the book's failure to reveal the exploitation and terrorism in southern black life. This was criticism of Hurston that became commonplace, though undeserved. Brown felt that southern black life was rendered "pastorally" in *Mules,* the characters made to appear easygoing and carefree in a land "shadowed by squalor, poverty, disease, violence, enforced ignorance, and exploitation." It was not a bitter enough book for Brown, especially considering that 1935, the year of the Scottsboro trial, was a very bitter time for blacks. Brown was expressing an honest concern; Hurston's point of view *is* open to misinterpretation because her views on race, true to her personality, were unpredictable, ambivalent, sometimes contradictory, but certainly never conventional.

In the twenties, thirties, and forties, there were tremendous pressures on black writers. Militant organizations, like the National Association for the Advancement of Colored People, expected them to be "race" people, defending black people, protesting against racism and oppression; while the advocates of the genteel school of literature wanted black writers to create respectable characters that would be "a credit to the race." Many black writers chafed under these restrictions, including Hurston, who chose to write about the positive side of the black experience and to ignore the brutal side. She saw black lives as psychologically integral—not mutilated half-lives, stunted by the effects of racism and poverty. She simply could not depict blacks as defeated, humiliated, degraded, or victimized, because she did not experience black people or herself that way. In her now famous and somewhat controversial essay, "How It Feels to Be Colored Me," she boldly asserts:

> But I am not tragically colored. There is no great sorrow dammed up in my soul, nor lurking behind my eyes. I do not mind at all. I do not belong to the sobbing school of Negrohood who hold that nature somehow has given them a lowdown dirty deal and whose feelings are hurt about it. . . . No, I do not weep at the world—I am too busy sharpening my oyster knife.

Sadly for Zora Hurston's career, "tragically colored" was in vogue in the forties. Richard Wright's bestsellers, *Uncle Tom's Children* (1937); *Native Son* (1940); and *Black Boy* (1945), were clearly in the mode of radical racial protest literature. Wright's black characters, in contrast to Hurston's, are victimized, hunted people who, in Hurston's view, created the impression that black lives were nothing more than the sum total of their oppression. They were "a problem," economically deprived and psychologically crippled. Hurston was determined to write about black life as it existed apart from racism, injustice, Jim Crow—where black people laughed, celebrated, loved, sorrowed, struggled—unconcerned about white people and completely unaware of being "a problem." Wright said Hurston's characters were nothing but minstrels. In a niggling review of *Their Eyes Were Watching God,* in 1937, he says the novel "carries no theme, no message, no thought"; it is just a "minstrel technique" to make white folks laugh. Richard Wright, it must be noted, brooded aloud in *Black Boy* about "the strange absence of real kindness in Negroes, how unstable was our tenderness, how lacking in genuine passion we were, how void of great hope, how timid our joy, how bare our traditions. . . ."

The great power of Wright lay in his ability to depict the violence and brutality of oppression and the resulting tensions in black life; but these preoccupations were also restrictions. Being black was such grimly serious business to Wright that he was incapable of judging Hurston's characters, who laugh and tease as well as suffer and who do not hate themselves or their blackness. But Wright was one of the big names of the forties. He set the model for the period, while Zora Hurston "suffered through devastating critical and popular neglect, inspired no imitators [her work being out of print] and finally died with not even a marker to identify her grave."

The controversy over Hurston's work and her political views, which surfaced after the publication of *Mules and Men* in 1935, mushroomed and spread in the forties and fifties as Hurston, typically erratic, continued to make unorthodox and paradoxical assertions on racial issues. She was quoted in one newspaper interview as saying that the Jim Crow system worked, and that blacks were better off in the South because, although there was no social intermingling, blacks had the "equivalent" of everything whites had. Roy Wilkins of the NAACP wrote a scathing rebuke of Hurston in New York's black newspaper, *The Amsterdam News,* accusing her of being a publicity hound and selling out her people in order to promote her books. Wilkins obviously did not question the accuracy of the quote, and Hurston insisted she had been misquoted, which was probably true, given that she had few illusions about Jim Crow or the South. She hated, however, the hypocritical notion that intolerance was located in the South, and that, by comparison, the North was a haven of equality.

> They [northern whites] use the Negro vote up there to get power,
> and then bar us from jobs and decent living quarters, and if there

is any protests, [they] riot, and terrify Negro workers away from town and jobs, and then laugh up their sleeves while they brush it off with folk-lore about the south the Sout [sic] is certainly doing its bit toward discrimination down here, but they are not pulling off that up there. That is a monstrous insult to our intelligence, or is it?

In another news article, entitled "Author Plans to Upbraid Own Race," Hurston was quoted as saying she was planning a book "that would give her own people 'an awful going over,' particularly the ones who talk about the tragedy of being Negroes." In typical Hurston fashion, she emphasized that what she deplored even more than prejudice was the "appalling waste of young genius" while prosperous Negroes, who could help these young black boys and girls, complain that they "can't go to tea at the Ritz."

Hurston's most highly controversial stand was her opposition to the 1954 Supreme Court desegregation decision, which she criticized because she thought it implied the inferiority of black teachers, black students, and black schools in the South. She resented any suggestion that whites were superior and that blacks could learn better if they went to school with them. This was consistent with her cultural philosophy that blacks had adorned a rather pallid American culture with colorful, dramatic, and dynamic contributions. In every art form, she saw truly original expression rooted in black culture. In language, for example, Hurston claimed that

> whatever the Negro does of his own volition he embellishes. His religious service is for the greater part excellent prose poetry. Both prayers and sermons are tooled and polished until they are true works of art. . . . The prayer of the white man is considered humorous in its bleakness. The beauty of the Old Testament does not exceed that of a Negro prayer.

Little wonder, then, that she, as well as many other southern blacks, feared that they would be the losers in the integration plan. It is both ironic and sad to realize that Hurston would not have been denounced for any of these views in the sixties or seventies. She might even have been considered militant.

For Zora Hurston, the forties were "Hell's Basement." In his biography of Hurston, Hemenway calls this chapter in her life, "The Pots in Sorrow's Kitchen," after the old Gulla proverb, "Ah done been in sorrow's kitchen and ah licked de pots clean." Almost like an augur of what the coming years held in store for her, Zora began the decade with a bitter divorce from her second husband, a twenty-three-year-old man named Albert Price III, who claimed in his counter suit that Zora was practicing hoodoo on him. In 1942, her autobiography, *Dust Tracks on a Road*, was published—a strangely disoriented book which Alice Walker calls "oddly false-sounding." Zora used all sorts of manipulative and diversionary tactics in the autobiography to avoid any real self-disclosure. The sections on her adult life are a study in the art of subterfuge. The chapter on "Love" begins,

> What do I really know about love? I have had some experiences and feel fluent enough for my own satisfaction. Love, I find is like singing. Everybody can do enough to satisfy themselves, though it may not impress the neighbors as being very much. That is the way it is with me, but whether I know anything unusual, I couldn't say. Don't look for me to call a string of names and point out chapter and verse. Ladies do not kiss and tell any more than gentlemen do. . . .
>
> But pay no attention to what I say about love. . . . Just because my mouth opens like a prayer book, it does not have to flap like a Bible. And then again, anybody whose mouth is cut cross-ways is given to lying, unconsciously as well as knowingly.

The autobiography provides a fairly clear view of Hurston as a child, and it is especially useful for detailing her relationships with her mother, father, and Eatonville, but the rest of it rambles on from one pose to another, sometimes boasting about her achievements and at all times deftly avoiding self-revelation. She was later to admit that she did not want to write the book at all because "it is too hard to reveal one's inner self." The mask Hurston assumed in *Dust Tracks* was a sign of the growing evisceration of her work. After *Dust Tracks,* which was a commercial success, [Hemenway notes,] "her mission to celebrate black folkways lost its public intensity." Although she still collected folklore for her own use, she did not write about it after 1942.

The 1940s continued their spiraling trend downward for Zora Hurston. In 1945, she was stricken with a gall bladder and colon infection, a condition which became chronic and seriously impaired her ability to support herself. That same year, her publisher, Lippincott, rejected her proposal for a book on the lives of upper-class blacks. In the essay "What White Publishers Won't Print," written in 1950 for *Negro Digest,* Hurston indicated her belief that the racist American publishing industry was uninterested in the "average struggling non-morbid Negro," because there was more money to be made exploiting the race problem with stereotyped stories of simple, oppressed sharecroppers. Zora spent part of 1947 and 1948 in British Honduras, where she wrote the major portion of her worst novel, *Seraph on the Suwanee* (1948). All of the main characters in *Seraph* are white, and, apparently, Zora wrote this strange book to prove that she was capable of writing about white people. The intent may have been admirable, but all the white characters in *Seraph* sound exactly like the Eatonville folks sitting on Joe Clarke's front porch. The result is an awkward and contrived novel, as vacuous as a soap opera. It was as though, in abandoning the source of her unique esthetic—the black cultural tradition—she also submerged her power and creativity.

Hurston sailed home from Honduras to take her turn in sorrow's kitchen. On September 13, 1948, she was arrested in New York and charged, along with two other adults she had never met, with sodomizing a young boy, the son of a woman who had rented her a room during the winter of 1946–47. The evidence presented was so flimsy and so contradictory—Hurston was out of the country during the time of the alleged crime, and the boy was found to be psychologically disturbed—that the district attorney, convinced of Zora's innocence, ordered the case dismissed. A court employee leaked the story to a national black newspaper. The October 23, 1948, issue of the *New York Age* featured these headlines: "NOTED NOVELIST DENIES SHE 'ABUSED' 10-YEAR-OLD BOY: ZORA NEALE HURSTON RELEASED ON BAIL." *The Afro-American,* a black Baltimore newspaper, released an even more sensationalized account, using this quote from the novel *The Seraph on the Suwanee:* "I'm just as hungry as a dog for a knowing and doing love," intimating that this quote might represent the author's own desperate need for love. The papers accurately described Hurston as "hysterical and almost prostrate." She was terribly demoralized and even contemplated suicide: "I care nothing for anything anymore. My country has failed me utterly. My race has seen fit to destroy me without reason, and with the vilest tools conceived of by man so far. . . . I have resolved to die."

This tragedy did not kill Zora. Nor, as it has been popularly recounted, did she retire immediately to obscurity, eccentricity, and penury. But the last decade of her life—the fifties—was a difficult time, mainly because she had very little money and few means of self-support other than her writing, which was not going well. She did a few journalistic pieces for the *Saturday Evening Post* and an anti-Communist article for the *American Legion Magazine* which documents a developing political conservatism. She supported the Republican Taft in the 1952 presidential primary and denounced communism during the rabid McCarthy era. This growing conservatism, which was interpreted as antiblack, is difficult to explain. Hurston always saw herself as a self-made success, and she had the kind of individualism and egoism that generally accompanies that belief. Moreover, her very positive experiences in Eatonville encouraged her to believe that brilliance and talent will out, regardless of political conditions. Thus, she was able to dismiss slavery as an anachronism, which no longer concerned her, since all the slaveholders were long since dead and she was too busy getting on with the future to care. It was a naïve and dangerous viewpoint, and one that led directly to her right-wing politics.

With the one thousand dollars she received from the *Saturday Evening Post* article, Hurston moved to a one-room cabin in Eau Gallie, Florida, where she lived quite peacefully for five years,

> digging in my garden, painting my house, planting seeds . . .
> I have planted pink verbena, and around the palms and the park-
> like ground west of the stones, I have scattered bright colored
> poppies. Going to let them run wild . . .
>
> Living the kind of life for which I was made, strenuous and
> close to the soil, I am happier than I have been for at least ten
> years.

Still, there was the problem of money and the recurring stomach ailment. Scribner's rejected a manuscript in 1955, and she was forced to work as a librarian at Patrick Air Force Base in Florida in 1956 for $1.88 per hour, hating every minute of it. In 1956, her landlord sold the little cabin where she had lived modestly but happily for five years. She moved to Fort Pierce and worked briefly as a substitute teacher. In 1959, weighing over two hundred pounds and having suffered a stroke, Zora Neale Hurston, penniless, entered the Saint Lucie county welfare home, and, three months later, on January 28, 1960, she died. Contrary to rumor, Hurston did not die in total obscurity. More than a hundred people attended the funeral services, testament to the fact that she was well known and loved by the people who perhaps knew her best.

Robert Hemenway has a term for the genius of Zora Hurston. He calls it her "autonomous imagination." Partly that just means that Hurston did as she pleased. More importantly, it means that she insisted on a medium, however unorthodox, that would satisfy her need to be both folklorist and creative artist. She succeeded magnificently in *Their Eyes Were Watching God*. When Langston Hughes urged the young black writers of the Harlem Renaissance to create a truly racial art based on the rich cultural heritage of black people and to stop trying to ape white writers and artists, in all probability, he did not realize how prophetically he spoke of Hurston:

> [The common folks] furnish a wealth of colorful, distinctive material for any artist because they still hold their own individuality in the face of American standardizations. *And perhaps these common people will give to the world its truly great Negro artist, the one who is not afraid to be himself* [emphasis mine].

Change *himself* to read *herself,* and this is a perfect description of Hurston. She believed wholeheartedly in the beauty of black expression and traditions and in the psychological wholeness of black life. With little to guide her, except fidelity to her own experience, she documented the survival of love, loyalty, joy, humor, and affirmation, as well as tragedy, in black life.

Who can help wondering what would have been the difference in Zora Hurston's life and career if there had been a large black reading public, and if she had been able to earn enough money to be self-supporting? Behind those deceptively simple "ifs," and the conditions they allude to, are the very severe complications in Zora's career that would have destroyed a weaker person—that did, in fact, diminish her powers so that we will never know the full potential of this pioneer artist.

"What did it mean for a black woman to be an artist in our grandmother's time? It is a question with an answer cruel enough to stop the blood." The answer is shown in the life of Zora Neale Hurston. It meant that the black woman who chose to work as artist, as creator, would be subjected to the same kind of violence that a black domestic worker had to face. It meant the kind of economic oppression that reduced Hurston to beg her publishers to look at her work—even after she was an established writer. It meant that, besides the struggle every writer faces to find her own voice, to combat loneliness, she would have to work with little hope of triumph.

And yet, she did work. In poverty and ill health, dogged by an undeserved scandal, and without the support of any academic or intellectual community, Zora Neale Hurston worked as writer and scholar for thirty years. She worked without the freedom and peace, without the time to contemplate, that Virginia Woolf insisted were essential for any woman to write. She worked consistently without the necessary five hundred pounds a year, without a room of her own with lock and key. Indeed, she worked most of the time without a door of her own on which to put a lock. What she left us is only a fraction of what she might have accomplished. We should be grateful for the work she did.

We should be grateful for her survival.

MICHAEL G. COOKE

The Beginnings of Self-Realization

If man's life goes
Beyond the bone
Man must go lonely
And alone
Unhelped, unhindered,
On his own
—STERLING BROWN

And find sweet grace alone.
—LEROI JONES

Zora Neale Hurston has been regarded as a daughter or heir of the Harlem Renaissance. It is truer to think of her as a fully grounded and amply evolved post-Depression figure, and to think of the Harlem Renaissance as an explosive but foiled striving in the fissure between the First World War and the Depression. In the main, characters of the 1920s—whether McKay's or Larsen's or Toomer's (or for that matter the proto-Renaissance J. W. Johnson's)—have about them a sort of self-exhausting mobility, a rootlessness in time or space. Langston Hughes's *Not Without Laughter* may be said to resist this tendency, but at the ironic cost of merely breeding up a black bourgeois. They are as it were unwittingly *in transition*. Hurston's Janie is as subject to circumstances, as much in motion as they, but bears with her a brooding power of inevitable development. The more she is threatened, the more

From *Afro-American Literature in the Twentieth Century*. © 1984 by Michael G. Cooke. Yale University Press, 1984. Originally entitled "Solitude: The Beginnings of Self-Realization in Zora Neale Hurston, Richard Wright, and Ralph Ellison."

resourceful she becomes. The more she is deprived, the more self-sufficient she becomes. That inner stability and outer indomitability mark her off from anything that has gone before; these traits will not appear again before Alice Walker's *Meridian* in the 1970s. The confinement of this phenomenon to women's hands is perhaps telling itself, showing the capacity to bear not just children, or the continuance of life, but to bear life itself. It is a rare phenomenon, even among women.

The story of Janie Crawford in *Their Eyes Were Watching God* (1937) is the record of black development from materialism and passivity (her grandmother's belief that money and/or white patronage are the essence of a good life) to self-respect, self-reliance, and (qualified) self-realization. Janie is said to be "full of that oldest human longing—self-revelation." The difficulty of getting a bead on that self is severe enough. Hurston renders the stock scene of racial discovery with rare delicacy, complexity, and resonance. Not social prejudice or personal meanness but *affection* leads to Janie's discovery that she is black. Without distinction, along with the white children of the family her grandmother works for, she has lived and played and been naughty and gotten "a good lickin' "; and in that spirit she is included in a photograph of the group. She looks for herself in the picture and where she is supposed to be sees only "a real dark little girl with long hair," whom she does not recognize. "Where is me? Ah don't see me," she complains. She has taken the image, perhaps the imprint, of her white companions.

It is a poignant rather than a wrenching or crushing scene; "everybody laughed" at her failure to tell herself. Her reaction to instruction ("Aw, aw! Ah'm colored") evokes further laughter. In this unusual rendition there is little of the trauma of repudiation, and a good dash of humor and consolation. But Hurston reinforces the "discovery" scene with what we may term the *nemo* syndrome: the little girl who doesn't know her own face also doesn't know her own name. "Dey all useter call me Alphabet," Janie recalls, " 'cause so many people had done named me different names." As a nickname Alphabet implies something both extravagant and defective, the elements of any name or all names without the shape or strength of one. Janie's grandmother sets forth her ambition for the child: "Ah wanted you to look upon yo'self. Ah don't want yo' feathers always crumpled by folks throwin' up things in yo'face." But Janie, as the photograph proves, can't look upon herself with recognition or confidence. In the burgeoning tradition of Afro-American literature, her grandmother's desire to see her "safe in life" resounds ominously. The desire to be "safe" has undermined every value and underscored every disaster for Irene Redfield, in Nella Larsen's *Passing*.

The source of confidence and safety her grandmother contrives harks back to the materialism we have identified in black literature, here in the form of marriage to the old farmer Logan Killicks. The deadliness of that age-old materialism, though, is intuitively grasped by Janie, who sees Killicks as "some ole skullhead in de grave yard." It is not clear whether Killicks, destroying Janie's sense of sunup and blossoming pear trees, is destroying Janie's spirit or her sexuality. The two perhaps intertwine for her. Some naturalistic romance of beginning summons her; and Killicks, who "don't take nothin' to count but sow-belly and corn-bread," can only detain and thwart her with his sixty acres of "seed p'taters" and "manure." Johnson's millionaire has shown us abstract materialism, his money detached from work or any particular source; Logan Killicks brings materialism down to earth, and shows it is not only deadly but dreary and foul.

At first blush Janie's resistance to Logan Killicks's needs and ways must seem like the old May–January pattern, and more so as she quits her kitchen to run off (bigamously) with dapper Joe Starks. But much more is afoot. Not only does Janie Crawford-Killicks not cancel herself in the interest of materialism, but she puts materialism on the defensive. Logan Killicks is made to feel that he has no leg to stand on, and soon to feel ugly and impotent. He reacts by redoubling rather than revising his materialism, trying to make Janie into a surrogate mule on the grounds that the farm requires more and more work. When she refuses, he makes a gesture that embodies the philosophical weakness and functional despotism of the materialistic way: Logan Killicks threatens to take an ax to Janie and kill her.

With Joe Starks, Janie enters the terra incognita beyond materialism. Two pieces of data furnish preliminary clues to this world. First, Joe Starks appeals to Janie's yearning for the "far horizon," without touching her feeling for "sun-up and pollen and blooming trees," which is to say that he probably won't be able to satisfy her deepest, primary needs. And second, Joe Starks takes overnight, where Logan Killicks took at least a few weeks, to stop "making speeches with rhymes" to Janie, which is to say he probably won't be out to satisfy those needs. As things develop, Joe publicly prevents Janie from speaking in public ("her place is in de home"), and has so much to do as "Mayor-postmaster-landlord-storekeeper" of the "colored town" of Eatonville (incidentally the name of Hurston's birthplace in Florida) that he has neither time nor thought for her. "You oughta be glad," he intones, " 'cause dat makes uh big woman outa you." In short, Janie finds herself in a world of paradox, where to be neglected and belittled is to become "big."

Materialism, which in its own terms means access to possessions and comfort and luxury, has yielded to political power as a goal. (This is a notable turning point; as late as 1933, Jessie Fauset's *There Is Confusion* and *Comedy, American Style* had shown materialism's tenacity.) Joe Starks's profits prove secondary to his control over other people. He will not let Janie, or anyone else, near that power, but what he is offering to Janie alone is the opportunity to be the beneficiary rather than a victim of materialism (as the other people of Eatonville are victims, disliking and even mistrusting Joe Starks but putting up with him and admiring him in return for creature comforts like street lights and a provisioned store).

Though in terms of social history what Joe Starks is doing may look necessary and desirable, the way he does it changes from bold to coercive and cold before our eyes. (William Melvin Kelley in *A Different Drummer* brings Tucker Caliban, like a Moses, to the stage where one would expect the founding of a black township, but does not delineate any way in which Eatonville's pitfalls might be avoided.) An ominous quality clings to Joe Starks's work both publicly and domestically, and Janie has neither instinct nor argument—as with Logan Killicks—to protect herself against him. Nothing brings out more sharply the harmful development of Starks's town than the images of metamorphosis that grow up around him.

The first metamorphosis is cumulative and has to do with Joe Starks's appurtenances. The townspeople see him turning into a white man, or a cento of white men, with a "promenading white" house like that of "Bishop Whipple, W. B. Jackson and the Vanderpool's," a desk "like Mr. Hill or Mr. Galloway over in Maitland," and a "gold-looking" spittoon like "his used-to-be bossman used to have in his bank . . . in Atlanta." We recall in fact that when Joe Starks first appears "he acts like [white] Mr. Washburn . . . to Janie." She intuits at once what the townsfolk will only slowly and obliquely recognize. But she is not bred to act on her intuitions. The second metamorphosis goes beyond trappings into the basic makeup of the character: "It was like seeing your sister turn into a 'gator." Strictly, this is analogy rather than metamorphosis, but the townspeople are representing a moral and social passage in Joe Starks from one state of being to another, and representing equally—such is the consciousness of analogy—a change in their own attitude.

What they do defensively and passively to Joe Starks, to keep some perspective and self-esteem, he eventually does to Janie in a forthright and hostile way. He metamorphoses her into a barnyard animal, again not lit-erally, but as a way of expressing a social judgment: "Somebody got to think for women and chillun and chickens and cows." In point of fact, Janie has been reduced to a projection of Joe Starks's ambition, without substance or activity of her own. It is striking how little of the Eatonville section of the novel deals with her, as her existence falls into a pattern of seeing others as real, and seeming rather than being an individual.

If Janie has escaped materialism, or being "run off down a back road after *things,*" she has not advanced very far. She has attached herself to a believer in images, and it seems truer to say that she has herself become, than that she has developed, an image. Her lack of self-image in the photograph scene entailed at least a poignant humor. Her capitulation to the Killicks order of images has a grim, stifling air. Thus it is important that when Joe Starks slaps her around for presenting him a "tasteless mess" of a meal, "her image of [him] tumbled down and shattered." This clears the way for a further stage of development. She has seen mere substance in Killicks, illusory substance in Starks. Now Hurston alerts us to another level of experience in Janie by reinvoking, and exorcising, Janie's naturalistic romance:

> She had no more blossomy openings dusting pollen over her man,
> neither any glistening young fruit where the petals used to be.
> She found that she had a host of thoughts she had never expressed
> to him, and numerous emotions she had never let Jody know
> about.

The change that occurs in Janie is at first internal, secret; she bears her new realization a long time before she is driven, by Joe's carping insults, to retort it against him: "You big-bellies round here and put out a lot of brag, but 'tain't nothin' to it but yo' big voice. . . . Talkin' about *me* lookin' old! When you pull down yo' britches, you look lak de change uh life." As she says this in the presence of townsfolk, the whole world of illusion evaporates. In that moment, the text draws a distinction between power and possessions on the one hand and personhood on the other. Joe Starks feels that Janie has "cast down his empty armor before men. . . . They'd look with envy at *the things* and pity *the man*" (italics added). We may note the blunt assault on Joe Starks here, as opposed to the metaphorical distancing in the townsfolk's judgment. They refer to their "sister" as a " 'gator" and only thus convey their shock and distress at Joe Starks's transformation. Attention is called to the transformation more strictly than to Joe himself, and they retain at least a baffled sympathy: "You keep seeing your sister in the 'gator and the 'gator in your sister, and you'd rather not." But Janie holds Joe directly before us, not so much transformed as *exposed,* and exposed as an unmanned being in a state of decay; the "change of life" pertains to a woman whose fertility is past. She not only unmans but feminizes Joe Starks. (Janie, in fact, makes her first husband feel impotent, tells her second publicly that

he is so, and kills the third. It is an arresting, anthropophobic pattern which
the text does not allow us to search to its foundation.)

If the townsfolk were addressing Joe, they might be said to be signifying. Janie has all but lost the patience or style to signify. She puts her
husband down, and out, sexually and socially. Indeed, she does not even
address Joe Starks, she *categorizes* him in the merciless synecdoche of the
verb "big-bellies." The townspeople might have set the example in un-
manning Joe Starks, but they use the term "big-belly" *of* rather than *to* him,
and at least retain enough of a sense of human relationship to adopt the
indirection of signifying and think of him as a metamorphosed sister. They
say Janie is "really playin' de dozens"; in fact there is little verbal play on
Joe's part, and on Janie's a deadly bluntness that seems to crash through
signifying and into denunciation. She is rectifying an imbalance of power,
as signifying fundamentally sets itself to do. But she is working head on,
whereas signifying leads the mind to an awareness of entities and forces and
values not explicit in the actual words used. The signifying gesture instigates
a conclusion that it does not itself reach. To illustrate, the word *abraxas* is
significant of the supreme power, yet still observes the law that the supreme
power must go unnamed. The monkey never goes up into the lion's face,
but signifies at a distance, from the trees.

Joe Starks experiences her action as a deliberate attempt to kill, though
she only means him to live in another light. It takes him a good second to
realize what her retort amounts to, and that is an omen of his unwillingness
or inability to change. In imputing to her a desire to kill, he is indicating
that he will die to hold on to his position. Change would be tantamount
to death. He is wholly accustomed to putting her down with impunity; she
takes him, and herself, by surprise when she rises up to keep from being
psychically *put away*. For all her long-suffering, for all her willingness to
present herself in his image, Janie will not be cancelled. Her attitude here
poignantly anticipates her confrontation with the maddened, deadly, beloved
Tea Cake.

It gives proof of *her* mind's going beyond images, beyond credulity,
that when Joe Starks calls in a conjure man she can withstand that worthy's
manipulation of the townspeople's minds. Both materialism and image-
bearing are past for Janie. Before she announces Joe Starks's death to the
waiting townspeople (the conjurer can neither harm Janie nor help her
husband, unlike the Chesnutt pattern of a scant four decades earlier), Janie
looks at herself in the mirror, and recognizes herself, though changed, and
approves of herself. For the first time in her life, from the childhood photograph through the dreaminess under the pear tree to the coercive facade

of life as Joe Starks's mate, image and substance fuse, so that image as such loses its force. When she lets down her rich hair that Joe had jealously obliged her to bind up, she is asserting not only the rightness of her beauty and her confidence in it, but also the rightness of her self. Janie takes a place in the long tradition, from the Bible to *La Femme du Boulanger,* of expressing inner freedom by freeing the confined hair. To evaluate this freedom, let us look at what Janie has been through.

Despite the marked differences in manner and purpose among them, the three principal persons in Janie's life to this point, her grandmother, her aged-farmer husband and then her entrepreneur-politician husband, all make the same demand on her: to cancel herself. She appears to yield to her grandmother's devotion and emotion, and again to Joe Starks's presence and rhetoric, but at bottom she holds fast to something as unknown as indomitable.

That "something" is her freedom, or her ability as a forty-year-old widow who has been largely silenced and set aside to move with eloquence and direction into the town and beyond it into the future. Let us note that she is not bursting out afresh and full of vigor from a comatose state, like the sleeping beauty. Rather she has been tacitly prepared to cope by her entire experience since puberty, in that her experience with her grandmother and both her husbands has been one of essential *solitude.* She has not joined or shared with anyone. Her life has been an unconscious preparation for being by herself. Only now she is aware of it, and herself links freedom and solitude: "She liked being lonesome for a change. This freedom feeling was fine."

At this stage Janie's solitude is simple, that is, uncomplicated by desire or deficiency, and her freedom is rudimentary—it is freedom from falsehood or obstacles, but without any positive expression or form. Her relationship with Vergible Woods, "Tea Cake," first gives Janie to herself by confirming and eliciting her powers, physical and social and moral. There is a dash of sentimentality or hyperbole in the treatment ("He was a glance from God"), but Janie and Tea Cake share something with all the propriety of what is genuine and all the unorthodoxy (in relative age, wealth, position) of what is original. The upshot of the relationship is to give form to Janie's freedom while paradoxically also giving depth and force to her solitude.

Janie and Tea Cake occupy a world of applied pastoral, with a dash of the Wife of Bath—that is, their feelings are elevated and lovely, but their setting is a rather realistic environment of gambling and railroad workers and "money and fun and foolishness." In this situation Janie, who has withstood two husbands and considerable social pressure, submits herself wholly to Tea Cake, the way Chaucer's Wife gives "maistrie" to her devoted, young, fifth husband. Like the Wife of Bath, Janie fulfills herself by surrendering herself, in that surrendering to one who surrenders to her causes the fiction of domination to disappear: "Janie . . . felt a soul-crushing love. *So* her soul crawled out from its hiding place" (italics added). If on the face of it the phrase "soul-crushing love" does not quite have the favorable ring the context suggests it is meant to, perhaps the best response would be to take the soul as nutmeg or oregano, its flavor and aroma elicited by crushing.

The violence and unpredictability that from the outset dwell on the edge of the relationship between Janie and Tea Cake slowly close in, culminating in the hurricane and Tea Cake's being bitten by a rabid dog from which he is trying to save Janie. They learn too late that he has been infected. It is a cruel irony that he, who had a pattern of abrupt disappearances and who has taught Janie a legitimate faith in him absent, cannot stand to have her out of his sight. The symptom of his illness is the symptom of his love gone mad. A sense of irony becomes almost overwhelming when Tea Cake, paranoid in illness, comes at Janie with a gun and is shot in horrified self-defense by the woman he has lovingly taught to shoot. And yet the final air of the novel is neither tragic nor melodramatic.

Beginning in accidental solitude with her grandmother, and passing to accepted solitude with Logan Killicks and Joe Starks, Janie ends in what may best be called accomplished solitude. Tea Cake, part bean-planter and part happy-go-lucky gambler, has shown her not only the far horizon Joe Starks promised but also sunup and pear trees in bloom, which her instinctive mind had desired: "he could be a bee to a . . . pear-tree blossom in the spring." Life has shown her the rest, including the need to kill even the beloved for the sake of life. Above all, Tea Cake and life together have shown her herself, *Janie* (Crawford and Killicks and Starks and Woods are inadequate surnames, appendages). And Janie is a woman with (1) the strength to survive and to even forgive the slanderers (first Tea Cake's friends in "De Muck" and then her own friends back in Eatonville) who would belie and befoul her time with Tea Cake; and (2) the command and lucidity before experience to see that "Love is lak de sea. It's uh movin' thing, but still and all, it takes its shape from de shore it meets, and it's different with every shore."

Finally, Janie is a woman with power enough to transcend her two greatest ambitions: to have a man like Tea Cake and to have the gift of ready speech. Perhaps she has the first transcendence forced upon her, but that takes little away from the merit of being able to sit, grieving over killing and being nearly killed by Tea Cake, and thanking him "for giving her the chance for loving service." She is, as Arnold enjoins, seeing things steadily and seeing them whole. The second transcendence, of silence, is again bathed in paradox: even as she resorts to words to tell her story, Janie can say of the word-mongers:

> Talkin' don't amount tuh uh hill uh beans when yuh can't do nothin' else. And listenin' tuh dat kind uh talk [the slanderers] is jus' lak openin' yo' mouth and lettin' de moon shine down yo' throat.

The problem of finding a voice haunts black literature. Even in 1981 David Bradley harks back to it in *The Chaneysville Incident:* Moses Washington (the name explains itself) carefully marks the passage in Jeremiah that says "I cannot speak; for I am a child," thus giving Biblical authority to the difficulty of finding a voice. The passage contains God's promise that "thou shalt speak," which represents a positive breakthrough. But it is to be noted that the central character, who tells the story, encounters resistance to the black world and people of the story from his wife. And she is white and named Judith (who undid the foreign Holofernes). One hesitates to extrapolate any special intimation on Bradley's part.

Needless to say, difficulty in finding a voice is hardly an exclusive burden of the black writer. Gibbon experienced it, and so did Coleridge. Repeatedly rewriting the first chapter of *The Decline and Fall of the Roman Empire* constituted an attempt on Gibbon's part to sound right before he spoke out; as soon as the voice came right, the work swept on to its grand conclusion. And Gibbon had the same sort of experience when he came to pen his autobiography. For that, he got up to six versions, none of them even close to complete. Coleridge, in turn, not only wrestled with an assortment of poems left fragmentary, but largely gave over the will to express his poetic inspiration. The final section of "Kubla Khan" dramatizes his psychic conviction, in the thick of a drug- and dream-induced access of inspiration, that he could not find an effective voice, could not keep alive the desired "symphony and song." We may note with interest here that in his *Preface to a Twenty-Volume Suicide Note,* Jones makes an analogous protestation: "I am thinking / of a dance One I could / invent, if there / were music" ("The Death of Nick Charles").

What gives singularity to the black writer's burden in searching for a voice is the twofold factor of frequency and context. Either directly or in projection through a central character, black writer after black writer, generation upon generation, from Frederick Douglass to Alice Walker, evinces the problem of voice. And it is appropriate to regard the most outspoken black writers of the protest movement as bearers of the burden in another guise. Theirs is not so much a free voice as the forced voice of reaction and resentment.

The matter of context gives a special poignancy to the black writer's problem of voice. Let us recall the obliquity of blues and of signifying, and set that beside comments made by Jonathan Edwards in Puritan America and William Faulkner in modern secular America. In his Nobel Prize speech, which we tend to remember mostly for the comment on surviving and prevailing, Faulkner in fact explains *how* man will prevail. Man alone, he says, "has an *inexhaustible voice*" (italics added). Edwards's comment is personal, whereas Faulkner's is generic, but it assumes the same freedom and the same global import as Faulkner's:

> I spent most of my time in thinking of divine things, year after
> year[,] often walking alone in the woods . . . ; and it was always
> my manner, at such times, to sing forth my contemplations.

Wordsworth, we may recall in passing, composed poetry in a similar way. In other words, the woods in which black people hid and counted on silence were fields of stimulation and expression for others.

Freedom of voice was not only limited in practice but was positively curtailed for black people. Frances Anne Kemble, in her *Journal of a Residence on a Georgia Plantation, 1838–1839,* records that she has "heard that many of the masters and overseers prohibit melancholy tunes or words, and encourage nothing but cheerful music and senseless words." To encourage "senseless words" goes beyond denying an authentic voice; it insures that there will be no voice at all. As we find in Dorothy Porter's important edition of *Early Negro Writing,* another form of the same insurance was recorded by a black man, James Forten, Sr.: slaveowners, Forten wrote, simply could be expected to send off to a proposed colony "those among their bondmen who feel they should be free" and who are thus "dangerous to [their] quiet," while "the tame and submissive will be retained and subjected to increased rigor."

Other sources of the problem of voice also come readily to mind. The separation of family and friends and the denial to black people of the right of assembly were decidedly inhibiting to communication. As even the uncomplaining slave Equiano complained, in *The Interesting Narrative of the Life of Olaudah Equiano, or Gustavus Vassa, the African* (1789), "I had no person to speak to that I could understand."

But one of the most poignant and arresting cases of the problem of voice occurs with Frederick Douglass, who reports that at the deathbed of the aged and debilitated Captain Auld, his former master, he was "speechless." Douglass was by then a noted figure in his own right, and came in a position of strength. What made him "speechless"? Unexpected nostalgic grief, which it would have been unseemly to express? Unexpected living resentment and vindictiveness, which decency obliged him to contain? A spontaneous upsurge of feelings of subjection and inferiority? A century later Ralph Ellison will speak of "the barriers of [the] stifling, provincial world," but indicate that he somehow collaborated: "my struggle became a desperate battle which was usually fought . . . in silence; a guerrilla action in a larger war in which I found some of the most treacherous assaults against me committed by those who regarded themselves either as neutrals, as sympathizers, or as disinterested military advisers" (*Shadow and Act*).

Janie Crawford inherits or rather embodies such quandaries in *Their Eyes Were Watching God*. To say that Janie has reached a state of accomplished solitude is to recognize both the progress she has made in personal development and the denial she encounters in the social sphere. Her home is a symbol of her condition, free and proud and yet radically unshared. She is not disposed to come out to the community, and the townsfolk are in one sense afraid and in another unfit to come in to her. Phoeby (whose name, as a variant of Phoebus, may be meant to convey light) comes in, but she does not carry word, or light, back out. The reverence she comes to feel for Janie will if anything baffle the community, since her very reverence will prevent her from profanely broadcasting the story. Phoeby confirms rather than offsets Janie's solitude. Hers has become an inner world, where all light concentrates on Janie: "The light in her hand was like a spark of sun-stuff washing her face in fire."

Janie's transcendence of Joe Starks's image-world is tacitly reaffirmed in the closing scenes of *Their Eyes*. She remains wholly unconcerned about the image the townsfolk have of her. She neither courts nor defies their opinion. Her life is beyond that. Phoeby will not be a sunrise for the new Janie, for that Janie, while unable to express herself at large, cannot be reduced to a superficial image.

BLYDEN JACKSON

Moses, Man of the Mountain:
A *Study of Power*

Hurston wrote *Moses, Man of the Mountain* during the years when her own life, both personal and professional, seems to have been most vibrant and her powers as a creative artist at their peak. It was her Illyrian spring. It was also the time when she was as responsive as she ever would be to the wonders and the wealth of black American folklore. With justifiable pride she could preen herself upon her role among anthropologists as the agent provocateur of an outstanding revelation. In her reports on her folklore findings she tended both to enlighten and correct many other observers of the southern Negro. She distanced herself not only from blackface minstrelsy and the fanatic band of followers of Thomas Nelson Page, to whom no rose could blow so red as that which symbolized their consecrated image of the antebellum South, but also from white so-called savants like Mississippian Newbell Niles Puckett, whose book, *Folk Beliefs of the Southern Negro,* published in 1926, acquired validity only if its perception of the Negro as a creature hardly more civilized than the hunter-gatherers of the late Stone Age is accepted as truth.

Hurston's folklore did not idealize common Negroes into noble savages. But neither did it turn them into Rastuses and Sambos nor deprive their behavior of logical and respectable roots in the conditions of a regional culture whose impact had been distilled into Negro spirituals or the blues. Without her folklore her comprehension of the art she invoked in her best fiction, long and short, would have been far weaker and poorer than it was. The protagonist of *Jonah's Gourd Vine* was more than merely a replica of her

From *Moses, Man of the Mountain* (by Zora Neale Hurston). © 1984 by the Board of Trustees of the University of Illinois. University of Illinois Press, 1984. Originally entitled "Introduction."

preacher-father. He was a folk figure representing hundreds of semiliterate pastors and evangelists across the black South whose lack of formal training had not diminished their sense of poetry and whose piety had not blinded their eye for a pretty ankle. In his very special and very important way, Tea Cake of *Their Eyes Were Watching God* was a folk figure, too, as was Jim Boy of Langston Hughes's *Not Without Laughter* and Simple of Hughes's Simple Stories. Poignantly he appears in the portrait of Big Boy Davis in Sterling Brown's "When De Saints go Ma'ching Home." In all of Hurston's major fiction, in both its content and its rhetoric, Hurston's experience with black folklore affects commendably what she does. In none of that fiction is her experience with black folklore more of a positive force than in *Moses*. For in *Moses* Hurston's folklore goes beyond a mere contribution to the atmosphere of a tale—where, indeed, it does work no less advantageously than it does in either *Jonah's Gourd Vine* or *Their Eyes Were Watching God*. In *Moses* Hurston's folklore enters crucially into Hurston's whole conception of her novel as well as its execution at every point. Here, in this novel, Hurston is writing an allegory, telling the story, at one level of her narration, of some Hebrews caught in Egypt and their march to a promised land. And her story at this level is repetitive. It does not deviate by one essential whit from the same story as it is told in the Bible. Yet, from beginning to end, her novel is also, on a second level of narration, a story about black America, not because Hurston anywhere says that it is, but because Hurston's folklore everywhere happily transports Hurston's readers to a position from which every Jew in Goshen is converted into an American Negro and every Egyptian in Old Pharaoh's Egypt into a white in the America where Hurston's folk Negroes live.

Moses, then, is Hurston's most ambitious work. It requires from her a bold essay into a demanding display of superlative virtuosity. And it cannot be called a failure. Rather, it is possible to read it simply for the excellence with which it preserves its allegory and find it a genuinely astounding success. Yet, Hurston also conducts, simultaneously, an absorbing investigation of a theme. Hardly less than Machiavelli in *The Prince,* she discusses power—the kind of power, political in its nature, which is the prime object of concern for the Florentine in his famous treatise on statesmanship. Magic accounts for much of the power released by Moses in his contest with the Pharaoh. The plagues Moses brings to bear against the Pharaoh and his people cannot be credited to some particular skill or wisdom Moses has acquired in the difficult business of managing people. They are at best, when most charitably interpreted as an element in Hurston's allegory, a linking of the *Exodus* with voodoo and thus a splendid opportunity, which

Hurston does not miss, for Hurston to live again some of her intense, unforgettable moments of sharing hallowed practices of the occult in New Orleans and the Caribbean. But magic does not obtrude in the picture Hurston presents of Moses's relations with the Hebrews, whom he must move from their subjugation in Egypt to a control of their own destinies in some place where Hebrew word is law. It could not obtrude in the thought of anyone contemplating the Negro minority in America and a program of leadership that might suffice to solve the problem of bringing this minority into a new and better relation with the white majority all too literally over them in a caste-bound social order sustained by a status quo apparently as impervious to change as the seasons and the hills. Faith healers, conjurors, medicine men, sorcerers of whatever kind obviously could not produce such a program. Not that Hurston's Moses is solely explicable in terms of factors such as training and experience that can be divorced from chance and other influences beyond human ken. Such influences exist. They always have. Conceivably they always will. Thus, Hurston's Moses is a leader partly because he was born to be a leader, with a capacity in his mighty hands for controlling people and natural phenomena that is indubitably a gift from God. Moreover, Moses talks with God and speaks for God, so that the elements of the given and the chosen in his leadership are inescapable. Yet he is also guided in the steps he takes as a leader by his reflections on what has happened to him or seemed worthy of his attention when it happened to other men. He dislikes war because he has seen so much of it as the commanding general of Pharaoh's army. He has grown sick of intrigue at the top of a social pyramid because he has lived in the Pharaoh's palace. And he has grown to love common humanity because of such developments in his own life as his affection for his servant, Mentu. A blend of the human and the extra-human make him what he is. Molded by that blend he shapes anew the history of the Hebrews.

If there was meant to be a lesson for the black leadership of Hurston's day in *Moses,* it is difficult to say of what that lesson was intended to consist. Hurston was no social visionary. She was neither another Percy Shelley nor another Karl Marx hypothesizing terms, loose or precise, for an earthly paradise. It was much more of the guild of Aristophanes and Gilbert and Sullivan—all, like her, conservatives—to which she belonged. Consequently, allegory though it is, *Moses* is also satire. Both witty and profound are Hurston's observations about black America with its, as it seemed to her, regrettably wide and deep division in loyalties among its upper class, its black bourgeoisie, and the Negro masses from whom her folklore came. The prominence of mulattos in the black bourgeoisie had not escaped Hur-

ston's sardonic eye. And she appears to make her Moses a mulatto, although
his non-Egyptian blood is Assyrian rather than Hebrew. But it is not Moses,
after all, of whom she is as critical as a representative of Negro leadership
as it is Miriam and Aaron. These two, it appears, are black bourgeoisie who
have made their way up into the leadership class from the ranks of the Negro
masses. Of Miriam and Aaron she has many unkind things to say. Nor is
she always kind to the ordinary Hebrews who must be, in her allegory, the
rank and file of the Negro folk. Pettiness and ingratitude, especially, she
notes in them. Yet she is more balanced than biased in what she says in
Moses of both her leaders and those whom her leaders too often do not lead.
If she is not a prophet, a seer, using her fiction to prescribe, more or less
in specific detail, the hopeful pilgrim's path to a new and finer social order,
she is, at least, a historian sufficiently nondogmatic and nonideological to
present her panorama of a human scene in a truly engaging way. Let others
hymn, she seems to say, utopian tracts. Her *Moses* is, as it was meant to
be, only life, actual, imperfect, sometimes difficult, and always true.

One thing more, however, must be said of *Moses,* especially, perhaps,
since it was written by a Negro, and Negro writers, certainly by the 1930s,
even if they were "New Negroes of the Harlem Renaissance," had become
addicted (quite understandably) to the writing of racial protest. It may well
be possible to interpret *Moses* as such a protest. Indeed, it can be argued
that in the context of black culture Moses himself is inseparable from
protest—as, for instance, "Go Down, Moses" eloquently attests—so that
merely to write a novel about Moses is to initiate a double train of thought
and emotion associated with the Negro's struggles in America to be free.
What appears, nevertheless, of greater remarkability about *Moses* is that it
lacks virtually all of the characteristics endemic to the Negro protest novel.
For intensity, bitterness, truculence, and stridency of tone, it substitutes
humor and, on the strength of that substitution alone, confers upon itself
something of a distinction among all the poetry and the prose ever written
by American blacks.

And incidentally, *Moses* is neither monotonous nor drab. It rings many
changes on the feelings it inspires because it inspires feeling of various kinds
and is far from flatulent in its prose or devoid of drama and color in the
incidents it depicts. But its *vade mecum* throughout its entire length is
laughter. Its constant solvent for any of its possible hypertension is comedy.
Even at a moment as tender as that in which a Hebrew family consigns, in
effect, to the great unknown the baby in a basket with whom Moses will
eventually—and mistakenly—be identified by the Hebrews, underneath the
catch in the throat there is an amusing turn to the prayer, "Nile, youse

such a great, big river and he is such a little bitty thing. Show him some mercy, please." Never, in *Moses,* does Hurston lose the capacity of detachment from her material which permits her the aesthetic distance in her stance as an artist that she must have to employ comedy. Never does her sense of humor fail to invest her account of Moses with the accomplished ease of manner and the universality (whatever that is) so often said to be absent from protest literature. In *Moses* Hurston rises to an occasion decidedly rare in Afro-American literature and even rarer in the national literature of which Afro-American literature is an integral part. If *Moses* is not Hurston's most acclaimed novel, it certainly should not be overlooked. It is protest that is, beautifully, all the better protest for the protest it is not.

BARBARA JOHNSON

Metaphor, Metonymy and Voice in
Their Eyes Were Watching God

Not so very long ago, metaphor and metonymy burst into prominence as the salt and pepper, the Laurel and Hardy, the Yin and Yang, and often the Scylla and Charybdis of literary theory. Then, just as quickly, this cosmic couple passed out of fashion again. How did it happen that such an arcane rhetorical opposition was able to acquire the brief but powerful privilege of dividing and naming the whole of human reality, from Mommy and Daddy or Symptom and Desire all the way to God and Country or Beautiful Lie and Sober Lucidity?

The contemporary sense of the opposition between metaphor and metonymy was first formulated by Roman Jakobson in an article entitled "Two Aspects of Language and Two Types of Aphasic Disturbances." That article, first published in English in 1956, derives much of its celebrity from the central place accorded by the French structuralists to the 1963 translation of a selection of Jakobson's work, entitled *Essais linguistiques,* which included the aphasia study. The words "metaphor" and "metonymy" are not, of course, of twentieth-century coinage: they are classical tropes traditionally defined as the substitution of a figurative expression for a literal or proper one. In metaphor, the substitution is based on resemblance or analogy; in metonymy, it is based on a relation or association other than that of similarity (cause and effect, container and contained, proper name and qualities or works associated with it, place and event or institution, instrument and user, etc.). The use of the name "Camelot" to refer to John Kennedy's Washington is thus an example of metaphor, since it implies an analogy

From *Black Literature and Literary Theory.* © 1984 by Methuen & Company, Ltd.

between Kennedy's world and King Arthur's, while the use of the word "Watergate" to refer to the scandal that ended Richard Nixon's presidency is a metonymy, since it transfers the name of an arbitrary place of origin onto a whole sequence of subsequent events.

Jakobson's use of the two terms is an extension and polarization of their classical definitions. In studying patterns of aphasia (speech dysfunction), Jakobson found that they fell into two main categories: similarity disorders and contiguity disorders. In the former, grammatical contexture and lateral associations remain while synonymity drops out; in the latter, heaps of word substitutes are kept while grammar and connectedness vanish. Jakobson concludes:

> The development of a discourse may take place along two different semantic lines: one topic may lead to another either through their similarity or through their contiguity. The metaphoric way would be the most appropriate term for the first case and the metonymic way for the second, since they find their most condensed expression in metaphor and metonymy respectively. In aphasia one or the other of these two processes is restricted or totally blocked— an effect which makes the study of aphasia particularly illuminating for the linguist. In normal verbal behavior both processes are continually operative, but careful observation will reveal that under the influence of a cultural pattern, personality, and verbal style, preference is given to one of the two processes over the other.
>
> In a well-known psychological test, children are confronted with some noun and told to utter the first verbal response that comes into their heads. In this experiment two opposite linguistic predilections are invariably exhibited: the response is intended either as a substitute for, or as a complement to the stimulus. In the latter case the stimulus and the response together form a proper syntactic construction, most usually a sentence. These two types of reaction have been labeled substitutive and predicative.
>
> To the stimulus *hut* one response was *burnt out;* another, *is a poor little house.* Both reactions are predicative; but the first creates a purely narrative context, while in the second there is a double connection with the subject *hut:* on the one hand, a positional (namely, syntactic) contiguity, and on the other a semantic similarity.
>
> The same stimulus produced the following substitutive reac-

tions: the tautology *hut;* the synonyms *cabin* and *hovel;* the ant-
onym *palace,* and the metaphors *den* and *burrow.* The capacity of
two words to replace one another is an instance of positional
similarity, and, in addition, all these responses are linked to the
stimulus by semantic similarity (or contrast). Metonymical responses to the same stimulus, such as *thatch, litter,* or *poverty,*
combine and contrast the positional similarity with semantic
contiguity.

In manipulating these two kinds of connection (similarity and
contiguity) in both their aspects (positional and semantic)—se-
lecting, combining, and ranking them—an individual exhibits
his personal style, his verbal predilections and preferences.

Two problems immediately arise that render the opposition between
metaphor and metonymy at once more interesting and more problematic
than at first appears. The first is that there are not two poles here but four:
similarity, contiguity, semantic connection and syntactic connection. A more
adequate representation of these oppositions can be schematized as in Figure
1. Jakobson's contention that poetry is a syntactic extension of metaphor
("The poetic function projects the principle of equivalence from the axis of
selection into the axis of combination"), while realist narrative is an extension
of metonymy, can be added to the graph as in Figure 2.

The second problem that arises in any attempt to apply the metaphor/
metonymy distinction is that it is often very hard to tell the two apart. In
Ronsard's poem "Mignonne, allons voir si la rose . . .," the speaker invites
the lady to go for a walk with him (the walk being an example of contiguity)
to see a rose which, once beautiful (like the lady), is now withered (as the
lady will eventually be): the day must therefore be seized. The metonymic
proximity to the flower is designed solely to reveal the metaphoric point of
the poem: enjoy life while you still bloom. The tendency of contiguity to
become overlaid by similarity and vice versa may be summed up in the

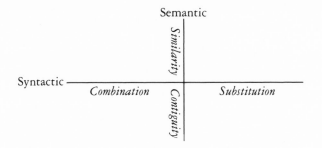

Figure 1

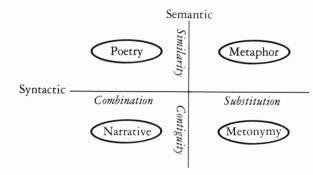

Figure 2

proverb, "Birds of a feather flock together"—"Qui se ressemble s'assemble."
One has only to think of the applicability of this proverb to the composition
of neighborhoods in America to realize that the question of the separability
of similarity from contiguity may have considerable political implications.
The controversy surrounding the expression "legionnaires' disease" provides
a more comical example: while the name of the disease derives solely from
the contingent fact that its first victims were at an American Legion Convention, and is thus a metonymy, the fear that it will take on a metaphoric
color—that a belief in some natural connection or similarity may thereby
be propagated between legionnaires and the disease—has led spokesmen for
the legionnaires to attempt to have the malady renamed. And finally, in
the sentence "The White House denied the charges," one might ask whether
the place name is a purely contiguous metonymy for the presidency, or
whether the whiteness of the house isn't somehow metaphorically connected
to the whiteness of its inhabitant.

One final prefatory remark about the metaphor/metonymy distinction:
far from being a neutral opposition between equals, these two tropes have
always stood in hierarchical relation to each other. From Aristotle to George
Lakoff, metaphor has always, in the Western tradition, had the privilege of
revealing unexpected truth. As Aristotle puts it: "Midway between the
unintelligible and the commonplace, it is a metaphor which most produces
knowledge." Paul de Man summarizes the preference for metaphor over
metonymy by aligning analogy with necessity and contiguity with chance:
"The inference of identity and totality that is constitutive of metaphor is
lacking in the purely relational metonymic contact: an element of truth is
involved in taking Achilles for a lion but none in taking Mr Ford for a motor
car." De Man then goes on to reveal this "element of truth" as the product
of a purely rhetorical—and ultimately metonymical—sleight of hand, thus

overturning the traditional hierarchy and deconstructing the very basis for the seductiveness and privilege of metaphor.

I should like now to turn to the work of an author acutely conscious of, and superbly skilled in, the seductiveness and complexity of metaphor as privileged trope and trope of privilege. Zora Neale Hurston, novelist, folklorist, essayist, anthropologist and Harlem Renaissance personality, cut her teeth on figurative language during the tale-telling or "lying" sessions that took place on a store porch in the all-black town of Eatonville, Florida, where she was born around 1901. She devoted her life to the task of recording, preserving, novelizing and analyzing the patterns of speech and thought of the rural black south and related cultures. At the same time, she deplored the appropriation, dilution and commodification of black culture (through spirituals, jazz, etc.) by the pre-Depression white world, and she constantly tried to explain the difference between a reified "art" and a living culture in which the distinctions between spectator and spectacle, rehearsal and performance, experience and representation, are not fixed. "Folklore," she wrote, "is the arts of the people before they find out that there is such a thing as art."

> Folklore does not belong to any special area, time, nor people. It is a world and an ageless thing, so let us look at it from that viewpoint. It is the boiled down juice of human living and when one phase of it passes another begins which shall in turn give way before a successor.
>
> Culture is a forced march on the near and the obvious. . . . The intelligent mind uses up a great part of its lifespan trying to awaken its consciousness sufficiently to comprehend that which is plainly there before it. Every generation or so some individual with extra keen perception grasps something of the obvious about us and hitches the human race forward slightly by a new "law." Millions of things had been falling on men for thousands of years before the falling apple hit Newton on the head and he saw the law of gravity.

Through this strategic description of the folkloric heart of scientific law, Hurston dramatizes the predicament not only of the anthropologist but also of the novelist: both are caught between the (metaphorical) urge to universalize or totalize and the knowledge that it is precisely "the near and the obvious" that will never be grasped once and for all but will only be (metonymically) named and renamed, as different things successively strike different heads. I shall return to this problem of universality at the end of this essay, but first I should like to take a close look at some of the figurative operations at work in Hurston's best-known novel, *Their Eyes Were Watching God*.

The novel presents, in a combination of first- and third-person narration, the story of Janie Crawford and her three successive husbands. The first, Logan Killicks, is chosen by Janie's grandmother for his sixty acres and as a socially secure harbor for Janie's awakening sexuality. When Janie realizes that love does not automatically follow upon marriage and that Killicks completely lacks imagination, she decides to run off with ambitious, smart-talking, stylishly dressed Joe Starks, who is headed for a new all-black town where he hopes to become what he calls a "big voice." Later, as mayor and store owner of the town, he proudly raises Janie to a pedestal of property and propriety. Because this involves her submission to his idea of what a mayor's wife should be, Janie soon finds her pedestal to be a straitjacket, particularly when it involves her exclusion—both as speaker and as listener—from the tale-telling sessions on the store porch and at the mock funeral of a mule. Little by little, Janie begins to talk back to Joe, finally insulting him so profoundly that, in a sense, he dies of it. Some time later, into Janie's life walks Tea Cake Woods, whose first act is to teach Janie how to play checkers. "Somebody wanted her to play," says the text in free indirect discourse; "Somebody thought it natural for her to play." Thus begins a joyous liberation from the rigidities of status, image and property—one of the most beautiful and convincing love stories in any literature. In a series of courtship dances, appearances and disappearances, Tea Cake succeeds in fulfilling Janie's dream of "a bee for her blossom." Tea Cake, unlike Joe and Logan, regards money and work as worth only the amount of play and enjoyment they make possible. He gains and loses money unpredictably until he and Janie begin working side by side picking beans on "the muck" in the Florida everglades. This idyll of pleasure, work and equality ends dramatically with a hurricane during which Tea Cake, while saving Janie's life, is bitten by a rabid dog. When Tea Cake's subsequent hydrophobia transforms him into a wild and violent animal, Janie is forced to shoot him in self-defense. Acquitted of murder by an all-white jury, Janie returns to Eatonville, where she tells her story to her friend Phoeby Watson.

The passage on which I should like to concentrate both describes and dramatizes, in its figurative structure, a crucial turning point in Janie's relation to Joe and to herself. The passage follows an argument over what Janie has done with a bill of lading, during which Janie shouts, "You sho loves to tell me whut to do, but Ah can't tell you nothin' Ah see!"

"Dat's 'cause you need tellin'," he rejoined hotly. "It would be pitiful if Ah didn't. Somebody got to think for women and chillun and chickens and cows. I god, they sho don't think none theirselves."

"Ah knows uh few things, and womenfolks thinks sometimes too!"

"Aw naw they don't. They just think they's thinkin'. When Ah see one thing Ah understands ten. You see ten things and don't understand one."

Times and scenes like that put Janie to thinking about the inside state of her marriage. Time came when she fought back with her tongue as best she could, but it didn't do her any good. It just made Joe do more. He wanted her submission and he'd keep on fighting until he felt he had it.

So gradually, she pressed her teeth together and learned how to hush. The spirit of the marriage left the bedroom and took to living in the parlor. It was there to shake hands whenever company came to visit, but it never went back inside the bedroom again. So she put something in there to represent the spirit like a Virgin Mary image in a church. The bed was no longer a daisy-field for her and Joe to play in. It was a place where she went and laid down when she was sleepy and tired.

She wasn't petal-open anymore with him. She was twenty-four and seven years married when she knew. She found that out one day when he slapped her face in the kitchen. It happened over one of those dinners that chasten all women sometimes. They plan and they fix and they do, and then some kitchen-dwelling fiend slips a scrochy, soggy, tasteless mess into their pots and pans. Janie was a good cook, and Joe had looked forward to his dinner as a refuge from other things. So when the bread didn't rise and the fish wasn't quite done at the bone, and the rice was scorched, he slapped Janie until she had a ringing sound in her ears and told her about her brains before he stalked on back to the store.

Janie stood where he left her for unmeasured time and thought. She stood there until something fell off the shelf inside her. Then she went inside there to see what it was. It was her image of Jody tumbled down and shattered. But looking at it she saw that it never was the flesh and blood figure of her dreams. Just something she had grabbed up to drape her dreams over. In a way she turned her back upon the image where it lay and looked further. She had no more blossomy openings dusting pollen over her man, neither any glistening young fruit where the petals used to be. She found that she had a host of thoughts she had never expressed to him, and numerous emotions she had never let Jody know about. Things packed up and put away in parts of her heart where he could never find them. She was saving up feelings for some man she had never seen. She had an inside and an outside now and suddenly she knew how not to mix them.

This opposition between an inside and an outside is a standard way of describing the nature of a rhetorical figure. The vehicle, or surface meaning, is seen as enclosing an inner tenor, or figurative meaning. This relation can be pictured somewhat facetiously as a gilded carriage—the vehicle—containing Luciano Pavarotti, the tenor. Within the passage cited from *Their Eyes Were Watching God,* I should like to concentrate on the two paragraphs that begin respectively "So gradually . . ." and "Janie stood where he left her . . ." In these two paragraphs Hurston plays a number of interesting variations on the inside/outside opposition.

In both paragraphs, a relation is set up between an inner "image" and outward, domestic space. The parlor, bedroom and store full of shelves already exist in the narrative space of the novel: they are figures drawn metonymically from the familiar contiguous surroundings. Each of these paragraphs recounts a little narrative of, and within, its own figurative terms. In the first, the inner spirit of the marriage moves outward from the bedroom to the parlor, cutting itself off from its proper place, and replacing itself with an image of virginity, the antithesis of marriage. Although Joe is constantly exclaiming, "I god, Janie," he will not be as successful as his namesake in uniting with the Virgin Mary. Indeed, it is his godlike self-image that forces Janie to retreat to virginity. The entire paragraph is an externalization of Janie's feelings onto the outer surroundings in the form of a narrative of movement from private to public space. While the whole of the figure relates metaphorically, analogically, to the marital situation it is designed to express, it reveals the marriage space to be metonymical, a movement through a series of contiguous rooms. It is a narrative not of union but of separation centered on an image not of conjugality but of virginity.

In the second passage, just after the slap, Janie is standing, thinking, until something "fell off the shelf inside her." Janie's "inside" is here represented as a store that she then goes in to inspect. While the former paragraph was an externalization of the inner, here we find an internalization of the outer: Janie's inner self resembles a store. The material for this metaphor is drawn from the narrative world of contiguity: the store is the place where Joe has set himself up as lord, master and proprietor. But here Jody's image is broken, and reveals itself never to have been a metaphor but only a metonymy of Janie's dream: "looking at it she saw that it never was the flesh and blood figure of her dreams. Just something she had grabbed up to drape her dreams over."

What we find in juxtaposing these two figural mini-narratives is a kind of chiasmus, or cross-over, in which the first paragraph presents an externalization of the inner, a metaphorically grounded metonymy, while the second paragraph presents an internalization of the outer, or a metonymically grounded metaphor. In both cases, the quotient of the operation is the revelation of a false or discordant "image." Janie's image, as Virgin Mary, acquires a new intactness, while Joe's lies shattered on the floor. The reversals operated by the chiasmus map out a reversal of the power relations between Janie and Joe. Henceforth, Janie will grow in power and resistance, while Joe deteriorates both in his body and in his public image.

The moral of these two figural tales is rich with implications: "She had an inside and an outside now and suddenly she knew how not to mix them." On the one hand, this means that she knew how to keep the inside and the outside separate without trying to blend or merge them into one unified identity. On the other hand it means that she has stepped irrevocably into the necessity of figurative language, where inside and outside are never the same. It is from this point on in the novel that Janie, paradoxically, begins to speak. And it is by means of a devastating figure—"You look like the change of life"—that she wounds Jody to the quick. Janie's acquisition of the power of voice thus grows not out of her identity but out of her division into inside and outside. Knowing how not to mix them is knowing that articulate language requires the co-presence of two distinct poles, not their collapse into oneness.

This, of course, is what Jakobson concludes in his discussion of metaphor and metonymy. For it must be remembered that what is at stake in the maintenance of both sides—metaphor and metonymy, inside and outside—is the very possibility of speaking at all. The reduction of a discourse to oneness, identity—in Janie's case, the reduction of woman to mayor's wife—has as its necessary consequence aphasia, silence, the loss of the ability to speak: "she pressed her teeth together and learned how to hush."

What has gone unnoticed in theoretical discussions of Jakobson's article is that behind the metaphor/metonymy distinction lies the much more serious distinction between speech and aphasia, between silence and the capacity to articulate one's own voice. To privilege *either* metaphor *or* metonymy is thus to run the risk of producing an increasingly aphasic *critical* discourse. If both, or all four, poles must be operative in order for speech to function fully, then the very notion of an "authentic voice" must be redefined. Far from being an expression of Janie's new wholeness or identity as a character, Janie's increasing ability to speak grows out of her ability not to mix inside with outside, not to pretend that there is no difference, but to assume and articulate the incompatible forces involved in her own division. The sign of an authentic voice is thus not self-identity but self-difference.

The search for wholeness, oneness, universality and totalization can nevertheless never be put to rest. However rich, healthy or lucid fragmentation and division may be, narrative seems to have trouble resting content with it, as though a story could not recognize its own end as anything other than a moment of totalization—even when what is totalized is loss. The ending of *Their Eyes Were Watching God* is no exception:

> Of course [Tea Cake] wasn't dead. He could never be dead until she herself had finished feeling and thinking. The kiss of his memory made pictures of love and light against the wall. Here was peace. She pulled in her horizon like a great fish-net. Pulled it from around the waist of the world and draped it over her shoulder. So much of life in its meshes! She called in her soul to come and see.

The horizon, with all of life caught in its meshes, is here pulled into the self as a gesture of total recuperation and peace. It is as though self-division could be healed over at last, but only at the cost of a radical loss of the other.

This hope for some ultimate unity and peace seems to structure the very sense of an ending as such, whether that of a novel or that of a work of literary criticism. At the opposite end of the "canonical" scale, one finds it, for example, in the last chapter of Erich Auerbach's *Mimesis,* perhaps the greatest of modern monuments to the European literary canon. That final chapter, entitled "The Brown Stocking" after the stocking that Virginia Woolf's Mrs Ramsay is knitting in *To the Lighthouse,* is a description of certain narrative tendencies in the modern novel: "multipersonal representation of consciousness, time strata, disintegration of the continuity of exterior events, shifting of narrative viewpoint," etc.

> Let us begin with a tendency which is particularly striking in our text from Virginia Woolf. She holds to minor, unimpressive,

random events: measuring the stocking, a fragment of a conversation with the maid, a telephone call. Great changes, exterior turning points, let alone catastrophes, do not occur.

Auerbach concludes his discussion of the modernists' preoccupation with the minor, the trivial and the marginal by saying:

> It is precisely the random moment which is comparatively independent of the controversial and unstable orders over which men fight and despair. . . . The more numerous, varied, and simple the people are who appear as subjects of such random moments, the more effectively must what they have in common shine forth. . . . So the complicated process of dissolution which led to fragmentation of the exterior action, to reflection of consciousness, and to stratification of time seems to be tending toward a very simple solution. Perhaps it will be too simple to please those who, despite all its dangers and catastrophes, admire and love our epoch for the sake of its abundance of life and the incomparable historical vantage point which it affords. But they are few in number, and probably they will not live to see much more than the first forewarnings of the approaching unification and simplication.

Never has the desire to transform fragmentation into unity been expressed so succinctly and authoritatively—indeed, almost prophetically. One cannot help but wonder, though, whether the force of this desire has not been provoked by the fact that the primary text it wishes to unify and simplify was written by a woman. What Auerbach calls "minor, unimpressive, random events"—measuring a stocking, conversing with the maid, answering the phone—can all be identified as conventional *women*'s activities. "Great changes," "exterior turning points" and "catastrophes" have been the stuff of heroic *male* literature. Even plot itself—up until *Madame Bovary*, at least—has been conceived as the doings of those who do *not* stay at home, i.e. men. Auerbach's urge to unify and simplify is an urge to re-subsume female difference under the category of the universal, which has always been unavowedly male. The random, the trivial and the marginal will simply be added to the list of things all *men* have in common.

If "unification and simplification" is the privilege and province of the male, it is also, in America, the privilege and province of the white. If the woman's voice, to be authentic, must incorporate and articulate division and self-difference, so, too, has Afro-American literature always had to assume its double-voicedness. As Henry Louis Gates, Jr., puts it in "Criticism in the Jungle":

> In the instance of the writer of African descent, her or his texts
> occupy spaces in at least two traditions—the individual's Eu-
> ropean or American literary tradition, and one of the three related
> but distinct black traditions. The "heritage" of each black text
> written in a Western language, then, is a double heritage, two-
> toned, as it were. . . . Each utterance, then, is double-voiced.

This is a reformulation of W. E. B. DuBois's famous image of the "veil"
that divides the black American in two:

> The Negro is a sort of seventh son, born with a veil, and gifted
> with second sight in this American world,—a world which yields
> him no true self-consciousness, but only lets him see himself
> through the revelation of the other world. It is a peculiar sen-
> sation, this double-consciousness, this sense of always looking at
> one's self through the eyes of others, of measuring one's soul by
> the tape of a world that looks on in amused contempt and pity.
> One ever feels his twoness—an American, a Negro; two souls,
> two thoughts, two unreconciled strivings; two warring ideals in
> one dark body, whose dogged strength alone keeps it from being
> torn asunder.
>
> The history of the American Negro is the history of this
> strife,—this longing to attain self-conscious manhood, to merge
> his double self into a better and truer self.

James Weldon Johnson, in his *Autobiography of an Ex-Colored Man,* puts it
this way:

> This is the dwarfing, warping, distorting influence which operates
> upon each and every colored man in the United States. He is
> forced to take his outlook on all things, not from the view-point
> of a citizen, or a man, or even a human being, but from the
> view-point of a *colored* man. . . . This gives to every colored man,
> in proportion to his intellectuality, a sort of dual personality.

What is striking about the above two quotations is that they both assume
without question that the black subject is male. The black woman is totally
invisible in these descriptions of the black dilemma. Richard Wright, in
his review of *Their Eyes Were Watching God,* makes it plain that for him,
too, the black female experience is nonexistent. The novel, says Wright,
lacks

a basic idea or theme that lends itself to significant interpretation.
. . . [Hurston's] dialogue manages to catch the psychological
movements of the Negro folk-mind in their pure simplicity, but
that's as far as it goes. . . . The sensory sweep of her novel carries
no theme, no message, no thought.

No message, no theme, no thought: the full range of questions and
experiences of Janie's life are as invisible to a mind steeped in maleness as
Ellison's Invisible Man is to minds steeped in whiteness. If the black *man*'s
soul is divided in two, what can be said of the black woman's? Here again,
what is constantly seen exclusively in terms of a binary opposition—black
versus white, man versus woman—must be redrawn at least as a tetrapolar
structure (see Figure 3). What happens in the case of a black woman is that
the four quadrants are constantly being collapsed into two. Hurston's work
is often called non-political simply because readers of Afro-American literature tend to look for confrontational *racial* politics, not sexual politics. If
the black woman voices opposition to male domination, she is often seen as
a traitor to the cause of racial justice. But, if she sides with black men
against white oppression, she often winds up having to accept her position
within the Black Power movement as, in Stokely Carmichael's words,
"prone." This impossible position between two oppositions is what I think
Hurston intends when, at the end of the novel, she represents Janie as
acquitted of the murder of Tea Cake by an all-white jury but condemned
by her fellow blacks. This is not out of a "lack of bitterness toward whites,"
as one reader would have it, but rather out of a knowledge of the standards
of male dominance that pervade both the black and the white worlds. The
black crowd at the trial murmurs, "Tea Cake was a good boy. He had been
good to that woman. No nigger woman ain't never been treated no better."
As Janie's grandmother puts it early in the novel:

> "Honey, de white man is de ruler of everything as fur as Ah been
> able tuh find out. Maybe it's some place way off in de ocean

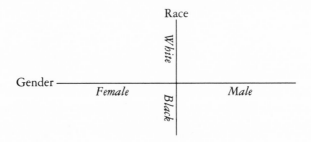

Figure 3

where de black man is in power, but we don't know nothin' but
what we see. So de white man throw down de load and tell de
nigger man tuh pick it up. He pick it up because he have to,
but he don't tote it. He hand it to his womenfolks. De nigger
woman is de mule uh de world so fur as Ah can see."

In a very persuasive book on black women and feminism entitled *Ain't
I a Woman,* Bell Hooks (Gloria Watkins) discusses the ways in which black
women suffer from both sexism and racism within the very movements whose
ostensible purpose is to set them free. Watkins argues that "black woman"
has never been considered a separate, distinct category with a history and
complexity of its own. When a president appoints a black woman to a
cabinet post, for example, he does not feel he is appointing a person belonging
to the category "black woman"; he is appointing a person who belongs *both*
to the category "black" *and* to the category "woman," and is thus killing
two birds with one stone. Watkins says of the analogy often drawn—particularly by white feminists—between blacks and women:

> Since analogies derive their power, their appeal, and their very
> reason for being from the sense of two disparate phenomena
> having been brought closer together, for white women to ac-
> knowledge the overlap between the terms "blacks" and "women"
> (that is, the existence of black women) would render this analogy
> unnecessary. By continuously making this analogy, they unwit-
> tingly suggest that to them the term "women" is synonymous
> with "white women" and the term "blacks" synonymous with
> "black men."

The very existence of black women thus disappears from an analogical discourse designed to express the types of oppression from which black women
have the most to suffer.

In the current hierarchical view of things, this tetrapolar graph can be
filled in as in Figure 4. The black woman is both invisible and ubiquitous:
never seen in her own right but forever appropriated by the others for their
own ends.

Ultimately, though, this mapping of tetrapolar differences is itself a
fantasy of universality. Are all the members of each quadrant the same?
Where are the nations, the regions, the religions, the classes, the professions?
Where are the other races, the interracial subdivisions? How can the human
world be totalized, even as a field of divisions? In the following quotation
from Zora Neale Hurston's autobiography, we see that even the *same* black
woman can express self-division in two completely different ways:

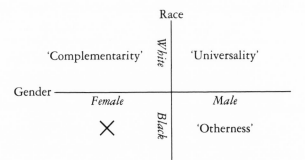

Figure 4

Work was to be all of me, so I said. . . . I had finished that
phase of research and was considering writing my first book,
when I met the man who was really to lay me by the heels. . . .

He was tall, dark brown, magnificently built, with a beautifully modeled back head. His profile was strong and good. The
nose and lips were especially good front and side. But his looks
only drew my eyes in the beginning. I did not fall in love with
him just for that. He had a fine mind and that intrigued me.
When a man keeps beating me to the draw mentally, he begins
to get glamorous. . . . His intellect got me first for I am the
kind of woman that likes to move on mentally from point to
point, and I like for my man to be there way ahead of me. . . .

His great desire was to do for me. *Please* let him be a
man! . . .

That very manliness, sweet as it was, made us both suffer. My
career balked the completeness of his ideal. I really wanted to
conform, but it was impossible. To me there was no conflict.
My work was one thing, and he was all the rest. But I could not
make him see that. Nothing must be in my life but himself.
. . . We could not leave each other alone, and we could not
shield each other from hurt. . . . In the midst of this, I received
my Guggenheim Fellowship. This was my chance to release him,
and fight myself free from my obsession. He would get over me
in a few months and go on to be a very big man. So I sailed off
to Jamaica [and] pitched in to work hard on my research to
smother my feelings. But the thing would not down. The plot
was far from the circumstances, but I tried to embalm all the
tenderness of my passion for him in *Their Eyes Were Watching
God.*

The plot is indeed far from the circumstances, and, what is even more striking, it is lived by what seems to be a completely different woman. While Janie struggles to attain equal respect *within* a relation to a man, Zora readily submits to the pleasures of submission yet struggles to establish the legitimacy of a professional life *outside* the love relation. The female voice may be universally described as divided, but it must be recognized as divided in a multitude of ways.

There is no point of view from which the universal characteristics of the human, or of the woman, or of the black woman, or even of Zora Neale Hurston, can be selected and totalized. Unification and simplification are fantasies of domination, not understanding.

The task of the writer, then, would seem to be to narrate both the appeal and the injustice of universalization, in a voice that assumes and articulates its own, ever differing self-difference. In the opening pages of *Their Eyes Were Watching God* we find, indeed, a brilliant and subtle transition from the seduction of a universal language through a progressive de-universalization that ends in the exclusion of the very protagonist herself. The book begins:

> Ships at a distance have every man's wish on board. For some they come in with the tide. For others they sail forever on the horizon, never out of sight, never landing until the Watcher turns his eyes away in resignation, his dreams mocked to death by Time. That is the life of men.
>
> Now, women forget all those things they don't want to remember, and remember everything they don't want to forget. The dream is the truth. Then they act and do things accordingly.
>
> So the beginning of this was a woman, and she had come back from burying the dead. Not the dead of sick and ailing with friends at the pillow and the feet. She had come back from the sodden and the bloated; the sudden dead, their eyes flung wide open in judgment.
>
> The people all saw her come because it was sundown . . .

At this point Janie crosses center stage and goes out, while the people, the "bander log," pass judgment on her. The viewpoint has moved from "every man" to "men" to "women" to "a woman" to an absence commented on by "words without masters," the gossip of the front porch. When Janie begins to speak, even the universalizing category of "standard English" gives way to the careful representation of dialect. The narrative voice in this novel expresses its own self-division by shifts between first and third person, standard English and dialect. This self-division culminates in the frequent use of free indirect discourse, in which, as Henry Louis Gates, Jr., points out, the inside/outside boundaries between narrator and character, between standard and individual, are both transgressed and preserved, making it impossible to identify and totalize either the subject or the nature of discourse.

Narrative, it seems, is an endless fishing expedition with the horizon as both the net and the fish, the big one that always gets away. The meshes continually enclose and let escape, tear open and mend up again. Mrs Ramsay never finishes the brown stocking. A woman's work is never done. Penelope's weaving is nightly re-unraveled. The porch never stops passing the world through its mouth. The process of de-universalization can never, universally, be completed.

Chronology

who urge that all creative work emphasize the problems between races. Depicting blacks only in relation to white
oppression is itself exploitative, Hurston, Hughes, and Thurman say; their first responsibility is to their art.

1927   Hurston undertakes first anthropological field research, going
          to Alabama for Carter G. Woodson and the Association for
          the Study of Negro Life and History to interview Cudjo
          Lewis, an ex-slave. Results published as "Cudjo's Own Story
          of the Last African Slaves" in the *Journal of Negro History*. (A
          low point in Hurston's career: though the article includes
          material of her own, it has since been revealed that it also
          draws heavily on, perhaps plagiarizes Emma Langdon
          Roache's *Historic Sketches of the Old South,* published in 1914.)
          Great Day, a play, published. Contract signed with the patron
          Mrs. Rufus Osgood Mason (whom Hurston calls "God-
          mother"). Mrs. Mason supports Hurston in anthropological
          field work in Eatonville, Fla., Alabama, Louisiana, and the
          West Indies from 1927 to 1932; she insists on owning all
          of Hurston's material and on approving all uses of it, as she
          feels Hurston cannot be trusted to manage it properly. Mar-
          riage to Herbert Sheen for four months, after a relationship
          of six years.

1928   Receives B.A. from Barnard College.

1930   "Dance Songs and Tales from the Bahamas" published.
          Works with Langston Hughes on a play, *Mule Bone,* of which
          only the third act is published. They quarrel over who is to
          receive credit for the body of the work, a conflict which is
          never clearly resolved.

1931   "Hoodoo in America" published. Returns to interview Cudjo
          Lewis and writes a full-length (unpublished) work based on
          his life.

1933   "The Gilded Six-Bits" published.

1934   Receives a Rosenwald Fellowship. *Jonah's Gourd Vine,* Hur-
          ston's first novel, published. It is praised for its use of folklore
          and criticized for its lack of a statement on the effects of
          racism on Southern blacks.

1935   *Mules and Men* published, an anthropological study of the folklore of American blacks. It is the result of intensive participatory research into ceremonies and rituals, and is the first such study written by a black woman. It, too, is praised for its contribution to the knowledge of folklore, but criticized for its lack of political statement.

1936   Receives a Guggenheim Fellowship. Uses it to study folklore in the West Indies.

1937   "Fannie Hurst" published. *Their Eyes Were Watching God* published, perhaps Hurston's most artistically successful work, which was written in seven weeks after a devastating love affair.

1938   *Tell My Horse* published, the first major work on Caribbean folklore.

1939   *Moses, Man of the Mountain* published. Marriage to and separation from Albert Price III, a man several years Hurston's junior. She wrote that her romantic affairs failed at the point when she was expected to give up her work and assume a more traditional role as a wife.

1942   "Story in Harlem Slang" published. *Dust Tracks on a Road*, Hurston's autobiography, published. It is her most commercially successful publication thus far (though perhaps not a factually accurate representation of her life).

1943   "The Pet Negro System," "High John de Conquer," and "Negroes Without Self-Pity" published.

1943–46 In this period, Hurston has trouble obtaining funding for her prospective research, a study of blacks in Central America.

1944   "Black Ivory Finale" and "My Most Humiliating Jim Crow Experience" published.

1945   "Beware the Begging Joints" and "Crazy for this Democracy" published. Stricken with a gall bladder and colon infection, a condition which becomes chronic and affects her ability to support herself.

1947   Sails for British Honduras, partially financed by an advance for the novel *Seraph on the Suwanee*.

1948   *Seraph on the Suwanee* published, her first and only novel depicting the lives of whites. Arrested on a morals charge involving a young boy. She was out of the country at the time of the supposed offense and the boy turns out to be psychologically disturbed. The unsubstantiated charges are dropped and she is cleared; but the press, especially the black press, sensationalizes the case. Overwhelmed, she returns to the South, working for a short time as a drama instructor at North Carolina College and as a scriptwriter for Paramount Pictures.

1950   "The Conscience of the Land" and "What White Publishers Won't Print" published. Discovered by a newspaper reporter working as a maid for a wealthy white woman in a fashionable section of Miami. She claims that she is researching an article on domestics, but she is living in squalor.

1950–60   Occasional publications during this period, contributions to such journals as *American Legion Magazine,* seem to indicate a growing political conservatism; or an attitude formed growing up in a secure, all-black community. She opposes the 1954 Supreme Court desegregation decision *Brown v. Board of Education,* saying that desegregation implies a degradation of black teachers, students, and schools.

1951   "I Saw Negro Votes Peddled" published. Moves to Eau Gallie, Florida, where she begins to write *Mules and Men.*

1955   Scribner's rejects a manuscript.

1959   Writes and asks Harper and Brothers if they would be interested in publishing a book she is working on, "A Life of Herod the Great." Enters the St. Lucie County Welfare Home in Florida.

1960   Dies without funds to provide for her burial, a resident of the St. Lucie County Welfare Home. She is buried in an unmarked grave in a segregated cemetery in Fort Pierce, Florida.

1973   Alice Walker places a gravestone in the cemetery where Hurston is buried, unable to pinpoint the exact location of the grave.

Contributors

HAROLD BLOOM, Sterling Professor of the Humanities at Yale University, is the author of *The Anxiety of Influence, Poetry and Repression,* and many other volumes of literary criticism. His forthcoming study, *Freud: Transference and Authority,* attempts a full-scale reading of all of Freud's major writings. A MacArthur Prize Fellow, he is general editor of five series of literary criticism published by Chelsea House.

FRANZ BOAS was one of the most distinguished anthropologists of this century. His most influential works include *Race, Language, and Culture, Handbook of the American Indian Languages, Primitive Art,* and several studies of the Kwakiutl Indians.

NICK AARON FORD is the author of *The Contemporary Negro Novel: A Study in Race Relations.*

BENJAMIN BRAWLEY was a professor and dean at Howard University. He is the author of *A Social History of the American Negro* and *The Negro Genius.*

LANGSTON HUGHES was a poet, columnist, songwriter, and an innovator in jazz music. He is the author of *The Weary Blues, Shakespeare in Harlem,* and *The Big Sea.* He and Zora Neale Hurston were friends and collaborators during the Harlem Renaissance.

ROBERT BONE is a professor of English at Columbia University and the author of *The Negro Novel in America.*

FANNIE HURST wrote short stories, novels, plays, and motion picture scenarios during her forty-year career. Her best-known works include the short story collections *Gaslight Sonatas* and *Humoresque,* and the novels *Star-Dust, Backstreet,* and *Imitation of Life.*

179

LARRY NEAL is the editor of *Black Fire: An Anthology of Afro-American Writing.*

ROGER ROSENBLATT is the author of *Black Fiction.*

ADDISON GAYLE, JR. is a professor of English at Baruch College in New York and is the author of *The Way of the New World: The Black Novel in America, Richard Wright: Ordeal of a Native Son,* and *Claude McKay: The Black Poet at War.*

THERESA R. LOVE is a professor of English at Southern Illinois University and the author of *The Morphological Study of Black Dialect.*

ALICE WALKER is an editor of *Ms.* magazine and the author of *The Color Purple* and *Meridian.* She has edited a collection of the works of Zora Neale Hurston, *I Love Myself When I Am Laughing . . . And Then Again When I Am Looking Mean And Impressive.*

ROBERT E. HEMENWAY is a professor of English at the University of Kentucky and the author of *Zora Neale Hurston: A Literary Biography.*

SHERLEY ANNE WILLIAMS is a professor of literature at the University of California, San Diego, and the author of *Give Birth to Brightness: A Thematic Study in Neo-Black Literature.*

MARY HELEN WASHINGTON is the Director of the Center for Black Studies at the University of Detroit and the editor of two collections of stories by black women, *Black-Eyed Susans* and *Midnight Birds.*

MICHAEL G. COOKE is a professor of English at Yale University and the author of *Afro-American Literature in the Twentieth Century.*

BLYDEN JACKSON is a professor of English at the University of North Carolina and the author of *Black Poetry in America* and *The Waiting Years: Essays on American Negro Literature.*

BARBARA JOHNSON is a professor of comparative literature and French at Harvard University and the author of *The Critical Difference: Essays in the Contemporary Rhetoric of Reading.*

Bibliography

Bone, Robert. *The Negro Novel in America.* New Haven: Yale University Press, 1958.

Bontemps, Arna. *The Harlem Renaissance Remembered.* New York: Dodd, Mead, and Company, 1972.

Brawley, Benjamin. *The Negro Genius.* New York: Dodd, Mead, and Company, 1937.

Byrd, James W. "Zora Neale Hurston: A Novel Folklorist." *Tennessee Folklore Society Bulletin* 21 (1955): 37–41.

Christian, Barbara. *Black Women Novelists.* Westport, Conn.: Greenwood Press, 1980.

Cooke, Michael G. *Afro-American Literature in the Twentieth Century.* New Haven: Yale University Press, 1984.

Davis, Arthur P. *From the Dark Tower: Afro-American Writers, 1900–1960.* Washington, D. C.: Howard University Press, 1974.

Ford, Nick Aaron. *The Contemporary Negro Novel: A Study in Race Relations.* College Park, Md.: McGrath Publishing, 1936.

Gates, Henry Louis, Jr. *Black Literature and Literary Theory.* New York: Methuen, 1984.

Gayle, Addison, Jr. *The Way of the New World: The Black Novel in America.* Garden City, N.Y.: Anchor Press, 1975.

Giles, James R. "The Significance of Time in Zora Neale Hurston's *Their Eyes Were Watching God.*" *Negro American Literature Forum* (Summer 1972): 52–60.

Gloster, Hugh M. "Zora Neale Hurston: Novelist and Folklorist." *Phylon* 4 (1943): 153–59.

Hemenway, Robert E. *Zora Neale Hurston: A Literary Biography.* Chicago: University of Illinois Press, 1977.

———. "Folklore Field Notes from Zora Neale Hurston." *The Black Scholar* 7 (1975–76): 30–46.

Huggins, Nathan. *Harlem Renaissance*. New York: Oxford University Press, 1971.

Hughes, Carl Milton. *The Negro Novelist*. New York: The Citadel Press, 1953.

Hughes, Langston. *The Big Sea*. New York: Hill and Wang, 1963.

Jordan, June. "On Richard Wright and Zora Neale Hurston: Notes Toward Balancing Love and Hatred." *Black World* 23 (August 1974): 5.

Kilson, Marion. "The Transformation of Eatonville's Ethnographer." *Phylon* 33 (1972): 112–19.

Kunitz, Stanley, and Howard Haycraft. *Twentieth-Century Authors*. New York: H. W. Wilson, 1972.

Neal, Larry. "A Profile: Zora Neale Hurston," *Southern Exposure* 1 (Winter 1974): 160–68.

Perry, Margaret. *Silence to the Drums: A Survey of the Literature of the Harlem Renaissance*. Westport, Conn.: Greenwood Press, 1976.

Pratt, Theodore. "A Memoire: Zora Neale Hurston: Florida's First Distinguished Author." *Negro Digest* (February 1962): 54.

Rambeau, James. "The Fiction of Zora Neale Hurston." *The Markham Review* 5 (Summer 1976): 61–64.

Rayson, Ann. "The Novels of Zora Neale Hurston." *Studies in Black Literature* 5 (Winter 1974): 1–11.

Rosenblatt, Roger. *Black Fiction*. Cambridge: Harvard University Press, 1974.

Schraufnagel, Noel. *From Apology to Protest: The Black American Novel*. Deland, Fl.: Everett, Edwards, Inc., 1973.

Southerland, Ellease. "Zora Neale Hurston." *Black World* 23 (August 1974): 20–30.

Starke, Catherine Juanita. *Black Portraiture in American Fiction*. New York: Basic Books, 1971.

Thurman, Wallace. *Infants of the Spring*. New York: MacCauley Company, 1932.

Tischler, Nancy M. *Black Masks: Negro Characters in Modern Southern Fiction*. University Park, Penn.: The Pennsylvania State University Press, 1969.

Turner, Darwin. *In a Minor Chord*. Carbondale: Southern Illinois University Press, 1971.

Walker, S. Jay. "Zora Neale Hurston's *Their Eyes Were Watching God:* Black Novel of Sexism." *Modern Fiction Studies* 20 (1974–75): 519–27.

Washington, Mary Helen. "The Black Woman's Search for Identity." *Black World* 21 (August 1972): 69–75.

Acknowledgments

"Preface to *Mules and Men*" (originally entitled "Preface") by Franz Boas from *Mules and Men* by Zora Neale Hurston, © 1935 by Zora Neale Hurston, renewed 1963 by John C. Hurston and Joel Hurston. Reprinted by permission.

"A Study in Race Relations—A Meeting with Zora Neale Hurston" (originally entitled "Postscript") by Nick Aaron Ford from *The Contemporary Negro Novel: A Study in Race Relations* by Nick Aaron Ford, © 1936 by Edward K. Meador. Reprinted by permission of McGrath Publishing Company.

"One of the New Realists" (originally entitled "The New Realists") by Benjamin Brawley from *The Negro Genius* by Benjamin Brawley, © 1937 by Dodd, Mead and Company, Inc. Reprinted by permission of the publisher.

"A Perfect Book of Entertainment in Herself" (originally entitled "Harlem Literati") by Langston Hughes from *The Big Sea* by Langston Hughes, © 1940 by Langston Hughes, copyright renewed © 1968 by Arna Bontemps and George Houston Bass. Reprinted by permission of Farrar, Straus & Giroux, Inc.

"Ships at a Distance: The Meaning of *Their Eyes Were Watching God*" (originally entitled "Aspects of the Racial Past") by Robert Bone from *The Negro Novel in America*, © 1958 by Yale University Press, Inc., revised edition © 1965 by Yale University. Reprinted by permission of Yale University Press of Brandeis University and Washington University.

"A Personality Sketch" (originally entitled "Zora Hurston: A Personality Sketch") by Fannie Hurst from *The Yale University Library Gazette* 35, no. 1 (July 1960), © 1960 by Brandeis University and Washington

University. Reprinted by permission of Brandeis University and Washington University.

"The Spirituality of *Jonah's Gourd Vine*" (originally entitled "Introduction") by Larry Neal from *Jonah's Gourd Vine* by Zora Neale Hurston, © 1971 by Larry Neal. Reprinted by permission.

"*Their Eyes Were Watching God*" (originally entitled "Eccentricities") by Roger Rosenblatt from *Black Fiction,* © 1974 by the President and Fellows of Harvard College. Reprinted by permission of Harvard University Press.

"The Outsider" by Addison Gayle, Jr. from *The Way of the New World: The Black Novel in America,* © 1975 by Addison Gayle, Jr. Reprinted by permission.

"Zora Neale Hurston's America" by Theresa R. Love from *Papers on Language and Literature* 12, no. 4 (Fall 1976), © 1976 by the Board of Trustees of Southern Illinois University. Reprinted by permission.

"A Cautionary Tale and a Partisan View" (originally entitled "Foreword: Zora Neale Hurston—A Cautionary Tale and a Partisan View") by Alice Walker from *Zora Neale Hurston: A Literary Biography* by Robert Hemenway, © 1977 by the Board of Trustees of the University of Illinois. Reprinted by permission of the University of Illinois Press.

"Crayon Enlargements of Life" by Robert E. Hemenway from *Zora Neale Hurston: A Literary Biography,* © 1977 by the Board of Trustees of the University of Illinois. Reprinted by permission of the University of Illinois Press.

"That Which the Soul Lives By" (originally entitled "Introduction") by Robert E. Hemenway from *Mules and Men* by Zora Neale Hurston, © 1978 by Robert E. Hemenway. Reprinted by permission.

"Janie's Burden" (originally entitled "Foreword") by Sherley Anne Williams from *Their Eyes Were Watching God* by Zora Neale Hurston, © 1978 by the Board of Trustees of the University of Illinois. Reprinted by permission of the University of Illinois Press.

"On Refusing to Be Humbled by Second Place in a Contest You Did Not Design" (originally entitled "Dedication: On Refusing to Be Humbled by Second Place in a Contest You Did Not Design: A Tradition by Now") by Alice Walker from *I Love Myself When I Am Laughing . . .*

And Then Again When I Am Looking Mean and Impressive: A Zora Neale Hurston Reader edited by Alice Walker, © 1979 by Alice Walker. Reprinted by permission.

"Looking for Zora" (originally entitled "Afterword: Looking for Zora") by Alice Walker from *I Love Myself When I Am Laughing . . . And Then Again When I Am Looking Mean and Impressive: A Zora Neale Hurston Reader* by Alice Walker, © 1979 by Alice Walker. Reprinted by permission.

"A Woman Half in Shadow" (originally entitled "Introduction: Zora Neale Hurston: A Woman Half in Shadow") by Mary Helen Washington from *I Love Myself When I Am Laughing . . . And Then Again When I Am Looking Mean and Impressive: A Zora Neale Hurston Reader* by Alice Walker, © 1979 by Alice Walker. Reprinted by permission.

"The Beginnings of Self-Realization" (originally entitled "Solitude: The Beginnings of Self-Realization in Zora Neale Hurston, Richard Wright, and Ralph Ellison") by Michael G. Cooke from *Afro-American Literature in the Twentieth Century*, © 1984 by Michael G. Cooke. Reprinted by permission.

"*Moses, Man of the Mountain:* A Study of Power" (originally entitled "Introduction") by Blyden Jackson from *Moses, Man of the Mountain* by Zora Neale Hurston, © 1984 by the Board of Trustees of the University of Illinois. Reprinted by permission of the University of Illinois Press.

"Metaphor, Metonymy, and Voice in *Their Eyes Were Watching God*" by Barbara Johnson from *Black Literature and Literary Theory* edited by Henry Louis Gates, Jr., © 1984 by Methuen & Company, Ltd. Reprinted by permission.

Index